SAGE was founded in 1965 by Sara Miller McCune to support the dissemination of usable knowledge by publishing innovative and high-quality research and teaching content. Today, we publish over 900 journals, including those of more than 400 learned societies, more than 800 new books per year, and a growing range of library products including archives, data, case studies, reports, and video. SAGE remains majority-owned by our founder, and after Sara's lifetime will become owned by a charitable trust that secures our continued independence.

Los Angeles | London | New Delhi | Singapore | Washington DC | Melbourne

AGAINST ALL ODDS

Thank you for choosing a SAGE product!
If you have any comment, observation or feedback,
I would like to personally hear from you.

Please write to me at **contactceo@sagepub.in**

Vivek Mehra, Managing Director and CEO, SAGE India.

Bulk Sales

SAGE India offers special discounts
for purchase of books in bulk.
We also make available special imprints
and excerpts from our books on demand.

For orders and enquiries, write to us at

Marketing Department
SAGE Publications India Pvt Ltd
B1/I-1, Mohan Cooperative Industrial Area
Mathura Road, Post Bag 7
New Delhi 110044, India

E-mail us at **marketing@sagepub.in**

Subscribe to our mailing list
Write to **marketing@sagepub.in**

This book is also available as an e-book.

AGAINST ALL ODDS

Psychosocial Distress and Healing among Women

MAHIMA NAYAR

Los Angeles | London | New Delhi
Singapore | Washington DC | Melbourne

Copyright © Mahima Nayar, 2019

All rights reserved. No part of this book may be reproduced or utilised in any form or by any means, electronic or mechanical, including photocopying, recording, or by any information storage or retrieval system, without permission in writing from the publisher.

First published in 2019 by

SAGE Publications India Pvt Ltd
B1/I-1 Mohan Cooperative Industrial Area
Mathura Road, New Delhi 110 044, India
www.sagepub.in

YODA Press
79 Gulmohar Enclave
New Delhi 110049
www.yodapress.co.in

SAGE Publications Inc
2455 Teller Road
Thousand Oaks, California 91320, USA

SAGE Publications Ltd
1 Oliver's Yard, 55 City Road
London EC1Y 1SP, United Kingdom

SAGE Publications Asia-Pacific Pte Ltd
18 Cross Street #10-10/11/12
China Square Central
Singapore 048423

Published by Vivek Mehra for SAGE Publications India Pvt Ltd, typeset in 10.5/13 pts Berkeley by Zaza Eunice, Hosur, Tamil Nadu, India and printed at Chaman Enterprises, New Delhi.

Library of Congress Cataloging-in-Publication Data Available

ISBN: 978-93-532-8191-5 (HB)

SAGE Yoda Team: Amrita Dutta, Guneet Kaur, Arpita Das, Ishita Gupta and Tanya Singh

CONTENTS

List of Illustrations vii
Preface ix
Acknowledgements xv

Chapter 1   Introduction: So What is Abnormal?   1
Chapter 2   Culture, Context and Distress   34
Chapter 3   Finding a Way through the Labyrinth   60
Chapter 4   Deconstructing Madness: Possession and Pains   85
Chapter 5   Women, Social Structure and Distress   130
Chapter 6   Learning to Live Alone: *Paisa, Bimari aur Jinn*   189
Chapter 7   Conclusion: Pathways to Health and Healing   214

Bibliography   230
Index   254
About the Author   257

LIST OF ILLUSTRATIONS

TABLES

2.1	Committees and Recommendations (in relation to Mental Health)	55
3.1	Occupational Details of the Women	76
3.2	Number of Children	79
4.1	Sources of Help within the Household	111
5.1	Descriptions of Financial Difficulties	177

FIGURES

4.1	Explanations of Madness	87
4.2	Factors Responsible for Everyday Distress	99
4.3	Sources of Help Available in the Communities	110
5.1	Factors Affecting Psychosocial Distress	131
5.2	Aspects of Gender Regime	146
5.3	Households and Psychosocial Distress	156
5.4	Factors Leading to Financial Constraints	174

PREFACE

'It is the presence of an essential thing in a very small detail which one must catch to expose larger things.'

—*Satyajit Ray*

Madness, insanity and mental disorders have been subjects of discussion for a long time. The manner of viewing and understanding them has changed according to the historical period and the developmental stage that a particular society finds itself in. In most eras, it is the voice of the professionals and not the voices of the people who are living through the experience which has dominated the discourse. There is a silence around how everyday routines/patterns and life-circumstances lead to madness or mental disorders. The aspect of distress often goes unrecognized in the larger imagery of 'mad' people. In the twenty-first century where change is occurring at an unprecedented pace, the everyday lives of women are often considered a 'small detail' in the larger historical landscape. However, the distress that they face in their everyday lives reveals the link between macro changes and their impact on the day-to-day lives of people. This book attempts to explore the everyday meaning of distress in order to understand these larger changes.

Distress is an unpleasant subjective feeling characterized by feelings of sadness, restlessness, nervousness and hopelessness (Ross and Van Willigen, 1997). Mental health discourse categorizes the feelings of psychosocial distress as mental health problems or mental disorders.

Mental health problems are said to constitute about 8 per cent of the global burden of disease, and more than 15 per cent of adults in developing societies are estimated to suffer from 'mental illness' (Desjarlais, Eisenberg, Good, and Kleinman, 1995). The burden of mental disorders affects different segments of population in different ways. Groups with adverse circumstances and the least resources face the highest burden of vulnerability to such disorders. These groups include women; migrants, especially refugees and displaced persons; people living in extreme poverty such as slum dwellers; people traumatized by conflicts and wars; children and adolescents with disrupted nurturing; and indigenous populations (WHO, 2001). The poor experience environmental and psychological adversity that increases their vulnerability to mental disorders (Patel, 2001).

Being female is reported to be a risk factor for common mental disorders. Studies from India have shown that poverty and deprivation are independently associated with the risk for common mental disorder in women and that they add to the sources of stress associated with woman (Patel, Kirkwood, Pednekar, Weiss, 2006). This study was designed to explore the extent of psychosocial distress faced by women living in a low-income neighbourhood in Delhi. Drawing on the data gathered by epidemiological studies conducted in our country since the 1960s, Davar (1999) in her critique of these studies pointed out that despite their methodological shortcomings and politically misleading inferences, the data converged qualitatively on some significant dimensions of being a woman with mental distress in India. While no marked gender difference has been seen in the case of severe mental disorders that have a biological basis, women were found to be at least twice as frequently ill as men in the case of common mental disorders which have a psychosocial aetiology. In cases where 'mental illness' has a biological aetiology, as in severe mental disorders, frequency of illness is the same across gender. On the other hand, where mental illness has a psychosocial basis, more women have been found to be 'mentally ill' than men. Therefore, a bio-medical approach to women's mental health is inadequate. A larger part of mental disorder epidemiology in women is constituted by common mental disorders whose causes are located in psychosocial factors. This underscores the necessity of adopting a different and exclusive approach to women's mental health concerns.

In our country we do not have research that specifically addresses the question of depression in women(men) in lower socio-economic classes although there is some evidence of psychiatric morbidity being high in the most deprived sections and unclassified categories of the workforce such as among beggars, prostitutes and domestic maids (Davar, 1995) and low-income, slum dwelling and uneducated women (Blue et al., 1995). The socio-demographic profile of 'mentally ill' women indicated that women in their reproductive years, those who were married, those employed as agricultural labourers, housewives and those with least education were the most affected groups (Vindhya, 2001). Another area which needs to be explored further is the duality characterized in the social domains of marriage, family and kinship. These play an important role in determining the kind of difficulties women face as they carry elements of security, support and care even as they entail elements of control—even oppression—limiting people's options to realize their own welfare and interests or of those for whom they take particular responsibility (Palriwala and Risseeuw, 1996: 39).

The social roles and spaces assigned to women are related to the high stress that they face and thereby the greater prevalence of common mental disorders amongst women. Glimpses of this relationship were evident in the outpatient clinic of a psychiatric hospital where I worked. While working there I met many women whose distress was not high enough for admission but they frequently visited the clinics for medication. None of the medications really seemed to help them. In the short meetings they described several difficulties in their family life ranging from issues related to poverty, to those of health issues and violence. Questions related to social structures and their impact on the individual were emerging in this clinical set-up and there was a need to explore this further. This research explores the linkages between the sociocultural, political and economic conditions of a community and their impact on the level of psychosocial distress faced by women. To establish a relationship between social structures, women and psychosocial distress, it was important to understand the manner in which psychosocial distress, madness and mental health were defined in the community. Did the class, caste, region of the women have an impact on the understanding of distress? This understanding would remain partial without knowing what the women themselves thought about it. Therefore, exploring the ways in which women perceived and defined psychosocial distress was important. A related objective of the research was to explore whether women considered their distress important enough to seek help and if they did, then what kind of help did they seek. Help-seeking by women also depends on the avenues of help available to the women and therefore it was important to explore the healthcare systems in the community which cater to the health needs of women and the modes of healing present within the community.

This book begins with an introduction to the different ways of understanding 'psychosocial distress' which has often been understood as madness, neurosis or hysteria among women. It establishes the linkages between health and the social location of the individuals, epidemiology of mental disorders, and the movement from an illness to a disability model to explain 'madness' and psychosocial distress. The different theoretical approaches—sociological, cultural and anthropological, feminist, psychological, biological and bio-psychosocial—are also discussed to understand the different ways in which 'abnormal' has been understood and defined. The 'Introduction' also looks at perspectives from India about mental illness, mental health and distress.

The book then moves on to examine what it means to live in a low-income and urban environment.

The second chapter thus explores psychosocial distress in the context of prevailing social, cultural, economic and political conditions.

Social and cultural space, the concomitant gender regime, urbanization, globalization and their impact on mental health are discussed in order to establish linkages between the individual situations and structures present within the community. For a comprehensive structural understanding of mental health and illness, this chapter also presents a brief overview of the state's initiative to promote mental health.

Chapter 3 provides a picture of our location of research, Jahangirpuri, and provides details of the people who were interviewed for this research. It explains the methodology used and the changes that were required in the 'methods'. It also presents the reflexive journey of the researcher in conducting the research.

'Deconstructing Madness: Possession and Pains' (Chapter 4) goes on to explore the connotations of 'madness' or mental illness that exist in the community. These include supernatural as well as human and social explanations. Illness narratives of women illustrate the ways in which women articulate their distress and the people they approach for help. Some of the healers/health providers whom the women approached were also interviewed during the research process, and their narratives are presented here as well. The narratives of the women and the healers/health providers complement each other and help us in understanding the meanings of 'madness' and 'distress' in the community. This chapter thus attempts to deconstruct the ideas of madness through the lived experiences of people.

Chapter 5 looks at the physical and social structures that exert influence on the everyday lives of people. These structures either contribute to or protect the individual from the development of psychosocial distress. There are times that they do both. The linkages between them and psychosocial distress are explained further through the use of Bourdieu's concepts of habitus and social space. The intersections between physical and social space, household organization and psychosocial distress are brought out in the chapter.

'Learning to Live Alone: *Paisa, Bimari aur Jinn*' (Chapter 6) looks at the concept of psychosocial distress through the life-history of one woman. She is separated from her husband and is bringing up her two sons. Her life-history presents themes which have also come up in the lives of other women. In addition to being representative of the women around her, she is also different in the manner in which she has shaped her own life.

The concluding chapter summarizes the main findings and presents reflections based on the conversations, observations and readings.

ACKNOWLEDGEMENTS

As the understanding of psychosocial distress in Jahangirpuri began through observations and conversations, there are many people to thank for accompanying me on this journey. I have to begin by expressing my gratitude to all the women in Jahangirpuri, who opened their hearts and allowed me a glimpse into their lives. Deepshakti (name changed), the organization which helped me gain an entry into the field and all the workers there who gave me their time and provided me with a legitimate identity in the community. Radha (pseudonym), who not only shared her life-story with me but also her life. Arpita Das my editor, for believing that the stories of women from Jahangirpuri were important and giving them a space in the sun, and also for her insights in helping me to rewrite the chapters. I have been fortunate in having an excellent doctoral supervisor Prof. Nilika Mehrotra. Her insights into the world of women and institutions have helped me in making sense of chaos. She has been a constant support in various stages of my career. Her encouragement and belief in my work has helped me to keep my faith in it. Thanks to all the editors from *Eastern Anthropologist, Indian Anthropologist, Psychology and Developing Societies, Social Action, Sociological Bulletin, Urbanities,* Women's Link and Prof. Asha Hans for all the copyright permissions.

To all my friends from various spheres of my life including school, college, Nimhans, TISS (as a student and an employee), Swanchetan, JNU, Silvassa—thank you all for supporting me, inspiring me and always being there. Tatha and Athamma, who are no more, for providing a home for Avnee and including us in their family. My entire family for arguing, pushing, advising, always believing in me and being ever present. My parents and sister for helping me start this journey, my in-laws for travelling with me and Aditya and Avnee for enriching my life by helping me and also creating chaos while completing this circle.

Introduction
So What is Abnormal?

Abnormality is defined by its context; it has no meaning without a background. Depending on the historical period, region and the person, rules of conduct are defined and expected to be followed. Madness or any kind of distress (mental or physical) is also a form of abnormal behaviour. It symbolizes difficult experiences that an individual experiences. In everyday usage, madness does not necessarily translate into illness, it is also used as a metaphor for any behaviour that is considered away from the norm. The sociocultural context of the individual, to a large extent, determines the experience of madness and distress. Increasing psychosocial distress is being seen as a result of the health transitions[1] that are taking place. Along with acute and chronic illness, behaviour pathology has become one of the 'triple burdens' in the developing world (Christakis, Ware and Kleinman, 2001: 143). Prevalence varies by WHO Region, from a low of 2.6 per cent among males in the Western Pacific Region to 5.9 per cent among females in the African Region. Depression is more common among females (5.1%) than males (3.6%) across regions. Anxiety disorders are also found to be more common among females than males (4.6% compared to 2.6% at the global level) (WHO, 2017).

Lifetime prevalence of depressive disorders was found to be 2.97 per cent in females as compared to 2.37 per cent in males. It was recorded at 5.17 per cent in urban metros as compared to 1.90 per cent and 2.15 per cent in urban non-metros and rural areas respectively.

---

[1] Health transitions refer to the ongoing worldwide increase in life expectancy that has occurred since the beginning of the twentieth century, especially since the 1960s.

For neurotic and stress-related disorders, prevalence rates for women were much higher at 4.29 per cent as compared to 2.72 per cent in males. Urban metros again displayed higher rates (nearly 7%) for these disorders as compared to around 3 per cent (approx.) in urban non-metro and rural areas (Gururaj et al., 2016). These figures indicate that being a woman and living in an urban metro area led to increased risk of depression, neurosis and stress-related disorders. Paykel (1991) identified four possibilities for this: the different health-seeking behaviour of the sexes; biological causes; social causes; and the differential acknowledgement and direction of distress. Literature exploring the possible causes of common mental disorders emphasizes on the importance of social and environmental factors and the relatively minor role played by biological factors (Cheng, 1989). In order to understand the complex and multi-layered relationship of 'women and psychosocial distress', it is important to understand the social and environmental factors that influence women's health in general and mental health in particular.

HEALTH AND SOCIAL LOCATION

In many low-income countries, over half of the population lives in poverty, which does not include those who are not considered 'poor' but live under impoverished conditions and are likely to suffer from poor health (Leon, Walt, and Gilson, 2001). Women represent about 70 per cent of the poor (UNDP, 1995), and are particularly vulnerable to health problems due to persistent gender inequalities. Existing statutory and customary laws continue to restrict women's access to land and other assets, and women's control over household economic resources remains limited (World's Women's report, 2015).

Health, in general, comes about as the product of many factors: biological, psychological, social, political, cultural and economic. Women's health refers to a state of 'complete mental, physical, spiritual and social well-being' for all female infants, girls and women regardless of age, socio-economic class, race, ethnicity and geographic location.

Both international and national policies for women's health have been strongly driven by definitions of women's health that are closely tied to biological reproduction, thus, deflecting attention from women's subjective experience of health and illness (Kielman, 2002: 128). Using biological difference from men as the chief organizing principle, women's health, in the past, was seen to fit within the ambit of obstetrics and gynaecology. Within this biomedical framework, women's health was confined to such biologically based issues as breast and cervical cancer, pre-menstrual syndrome, contraception, pregnancy and childbearing, psycho-endocrine problems, post-natal disorders and disorders of menopause (WHO, 2000). In their influential report on World Mental Health, Desjarlais, Leonberg, Good et al. (1995) pointed out that many of these programmes define women's health as reproductive health and that sometimes the health of children is seen as a proxy for the health of the mother.

The emphasis on women's reproductive biology is likely to stem from the view that women's health is synonymous with and reducible to those illnesses or conditions related to women's reproductive health. The splitting of body from mind and the identification of women and their health with the body, in general and in the case of reproductive functioning in particular, has led to a neglect of women's mental health and its social structural determinants. Das and Das (2005) urged that the definition of women's health includes effects of workload, nutrition, stress, war, migration among others. Historically, women have been absent from most health research as maleness has been regarded as the norm whereas women's female characteristics constitute deviations. A feminist critique of medicine is concerned with issues of power, both, as it shapes health, illness and recovery, as well as in the way it determines forms of and access to healthcare and research. It begins with the recognition of dominant and subordinate social roles in society; male and female social roles are unequal, and men's gender roles are more highly valued than women's (Hamilton, 1994: 60). Unequal gender roles have a profound effect on women's physical and mental health. Women's resistance to their social roles has been met with the introduction of a new set of social diseases such as hysteria, agoraphobia and anorexia nervosa. When illnesses are defined as medical problems which can be resolved with medical solutions, women lose control of fundamental aspects of their experience—fertility, sexuality, menopause and ageing (Oakley, 1984).

Feminist health sociologists have argued that medicine and patriarchy have sought to control women by focusing on the individual rather than their social location. The medical set-up reproduces situations which reinforce passivity, dependence and submission as appropriate feminine traits. For example, treating depression with drugs reinforces the traditional role of women (as daughters, wives and mothers) that they are seeking to escape (Seaman, 1997). Women's illnesses are both a consequence of, and response to a patriarchal society (White, 2009: 133). Problems of violence against women and its links to poor mental health have largely been ignored. The rise of second wave feminism and activism around women's rights has highlighted and focused society's attention on the widespread social problem of violence against women. Women who have experienced violence, whether in childhood or adult life, have increased rates of depression and anxiety, stress-related syndromes, pain syndromes, phobias, chemical dependency, substance use, suicidal tendencies, somatic and medical symptoms, negative health behaviours, and poor subjective health. Accumulating evidence suggests that the relationship between violence, depression and anxiety is causal. Controlled studies from a variety of settings have consistently found increased rates of depression and anxiety in women who have experienced childhood sexual abuse, childhood psychological abuse, and/or physical and sexual violence in adult life (Goel and Goel, 2008: 325). With the broadening of the concept of women's health, many issues which had been previously neglected have came into prominence.

Studies of social trends and epidemiological issues have established that women beset by a lifetime of social and psychological disadvantage, coupled with long years of childbearing and neglect, often end up experiencing poverty, isolation and chronic psychological disability. Poverty, discrimination and possible violence towards the female child have longlasting, debilitating and other adverse effects on women's physical as well as mental health (Craft, 1997). The forces of liberalization, privatization and globalization (LPG) have resulted in economic changes which have further increased the burden on women. Recent research has demonstrated that life circumstances often concomitant with poverty (e.g., living in disadvantaged neighbourhoods, reduced access to educational and employment opportunities, perceived neighbourhood disorder, food insecurity) also have negative effects on mental health and that these effects occur above and beyond the effects of personal poverty (Stafford and Marmot, 2003). Although poverty has negative health outcomes for both men and women, the greater burden falls on women. Therefore, it can be understood that women with mental disorders or psychosocial disabilities have to deal with multiple issues which are related to the difficulties that they face in everyday life.

EPIDEMIOLOGY OF MENTAL DISORDERS

It is generally accepted that in Europe throughout the eighteenth and nineteenth centuries more women than men were diagnosed with and treated for 'mental illness' (Ehrenreich and English, 1974; Showalter, 1985). And for some diagnoses, this gender difference constituted a near-total monopoly; hysteria, neurasthenia and chlorosis, for example, were very rarely diagnosed in men (Showalter, 1985). Current epidemiological statistics demonstrate the continuation of this preponderance of women in overall diagnoses of mental health problems (Ussher, 1991, 2000) and, in particular, diagnostic categories. Depression, for instance, appears to be twice as common in women as men (Culbertson, 1997), while girls and women represent 95 per cent of those diagnosed with eating disorders. Depression has a significant impact on women's well-being and productivity (Paltiel, 1993).

Women's higher rates of 'mental illness' are seen to reflect gender differences in help-seeking behaviour because women have a greater willingness to admit to psychological distress and to seek treatment. For example, women have been found to seek help from primary care services more often than men when experiencing distress; a gender difference which may be due to differences in help-seeking behaviour and expressing emotional dis/content, as much as to gender differences in levels of distress. This, in turn, often leads to women's subsequent referral to specialist psychiatric services, particularly when general practitioners' interpretation of the nature of their distress is medicalized (Johnson and Buszewicz, 1996). This argument receives considerable support from studies that have shown that women are more likely to recognize a psychiatric problem in themselves (Horowitz, 1977) and more likely to consult their general practitioner with psychological and emotional problems (Corney, 1990). Also, where 'women' are interpreted as a homogeneous category, overall gender differences in referral rates obscure other issues: the tendency towards presentation to medical services by women is not uniform, as women from some minority racial/cultural groups were found to have little faith in conventional medical services, and therefore, tended to be under-represented in statistical data (Nasser, 1997).

To focus entirely on DALYs,[2] a measure of disease, as an indicator of women's health, both in its biological and gender dimensions, is to lose sight of the definition of health including well-being as a quality of health. Increasingly, as one examines the gender aspects of how health and disease are perceived by women, and how the healthcare system and professionals perceive the health needs of women, one sees the discordance of the medical and the social models of health. In addition to this, another issue which comes up is that 'woman' is not a homogenous category; there are differences of caste, class, race, location and so on. In spite of this, a consideration of the statistics about women's mental health problems clearly represents a logical

---

[2] Disability Adjusted Life Years.

starting point in considering the nature of the relationship(s) between women and mental health problems.

Mental Disorders in India

The Bhore Committe (1946) showed that Indian women exhibited more psychiatric morbidity than men (Carr-Harris, 1992, c.f. Kishwar-e-Narmada, 1999). In general in medical clinics, 10–14 per cent are mental health patients with psychosocial problems, with a preponderance of females between 16 and 45 years of age. They have 'greater number of spontaneous complaints (more than four), larger duration of illness and come to the facility from greater distances (five kilometres); 60% of the causes were due to personal and family life'. The most common complaints were sleep disturbances, tiredness/weakness, body ache, decreased appetite, headache, backache, sadness, and pain in the abdomen, limbs and diet. The common sources of stress identified were family and social (50%), financial (19%), health (18%), marital and sexual (10%) and bereavement (10%) (Srinivas-Murthy, 1992: 405). Sarin (1989) in a study of rural households in Solan (Himachal Pradesh) pointed to the problem of male alcohol abuse to the extent of driving the women to suicide. Many studies on health have pointed to stress, fatigue, rape and community (male) violence and riots, as contributing to the emotional instability of women in rural, urban and poor urban areas (Kishwar-e-Narmada, 1990: 21).

When considering epidemiological issues in women with mental health problems, one needs to take into account that some psychiatric problems and diagnoses deserve attention because of their differing clinical implications for women and some psychiatric diagnoses are exclusive for women (Kishwar-e-Narmada, 1990). On the basis of a field study conducted in Kolkata, Chakraborthy (2001) reported some important correlates of common mental disorders in women. Age, marital status, economic status, occupation, education and family roles were these correlates. Neuroses increases with age for both genders but women have a much higher rate. It has been well established that women have a higher prevalence of depression, dysthymia, deliberate self-harm, seasonal affective disorder, generalized anxiety disorder, panic attacks, social phobias and eating disorders (Kohen, 2000: 3). Higher prevalence has also been reported in other urban studies (Sethi and Rajkumar 1967; Verghese et al. 1973; Nandi et al. 1980 and Premrajan et al. 1993). Sen et al. (1984) opined that social roles played by women in a mosaic of many ethnic and cultural groups might be responsible for this. Nandi et al. (1980) suggested that sex differences in the vulnerability to 'mental illness' might be biological rather than influenced by cultural factors. However, looking at the work profile by gender, it is seen that women in low income localities are more stressed than the men (Joshi et al. 2009). This happens because in a patriarchal set-up, while men are involved in generating household income, women are engaged in household chores as well as working to provide an income to the family. They face a double burden which can lead to adverse mental health consequences.

FROM ILLNESS TO DISABILITY

Over time, different terms have been used to describe behaviour which appears away from the 'norm'. 'Madness', 'mental illness', 'mental disorders', 'psychosocial disabilities', 'mental or psychosocial distress' are just some of the terms used. In this research, the model of distress and disability has been followed. This is because a notion of 'mental illness' will always remain a medicalized one, linked to psychiatric labelling, over-determined by law (Dhanda, 2000), and linked with negative social descriptors alienating women from themselves, their mind-bodies, and their life worlds. The gender discourse could look at 'disability' as an alternative way of constructing identities of persons and women who experience psychological distress and disability (Davar, 2000). The use of disability language over a 'mental illness' language helps in remaining close to the personal experience of the woman.

Feminist literature has pointed out the need to examine all the ways in which disability is socially constructed: the need to explore the interaction of disability with race, gender, class position. C. Wright Mills (1959: 14) argued in his essay on sociological imagination that, sociology has a particular contribution to make in helping us see how many seemingly 'personal troubles', which affect individuals and their immediate relations with others, are more appropriately understood as 'public issues' which link the institutions of society as a whole. Hence, it is a primary goal of sociological imagination to detail the connections between personal biography and wider historical and political circumstances. This becomes extremely important to understand in terms of women with psychosocial disabilities, as their identity in society as well as in their own homes is mediated by how society perceives them and what are the conditions prevailing in society which contribute to the development of psychosocial disabilities/mental health problems in the first place.

Addlakha (2001) in her study depicted how patriarchal standards of femininity condition the illness experience, perception, articulation and behaviour of the individual patient and her significant others. Women themselves internalize the gender-based evaluations in the evaluation of abnormality both within the family and in medical discourses. Mental health professionals, often unconsciously, carry the gender and class biases that they have been socialized in, into their practice. This is turn creates a vicious circle whereby women are judged through erroneous means. Mehrotra (2006) through her study of intellectually disabled women in rural Haryana showed how the position of women with intellectual disabilities becomes even more vulnerable. There is no clear recognition of intellectually disabled women as being 'disabled' as there is no physical impairment. Feeble-mindedness as deviance is associated with hot temper, erratic behaviour and impotence, and people manifesting such characteristics are described as mad or *pagal*. A disabled woman is usually married to a disabled man, a widower or into a household whose economic condition is lower than her natal home's, or to a man who cannot find a spouse due to any reason: illiteracy, low income or caste endogamy. There are also reports of heavy dowries paid by parents of disabled girls (ibid.). Their traditional gender roles as producer and reproducer are strictly enforced as in the case of non-disabled women. After marriage, disabled women perform the usual household chores: fetching water from the well, cutting fodder, cooking, cleaning, etc.; domestic violence is a routine occurrence, and disability gives another excuse for wife-beating, since the negotiating power of disabled women is even less than their non-disabled counterparts. These studies show that several social indicators combine to make women with psychosocial disabilities even more open to abuse.

It is important to look at disability at different levels: micro (individual), with regard to social rules and norms (social construction), and at the societal level (systems of health, education, social welfare and state policies). These levels define at a particular point in history what is considered normal and therefore what is abnormal. Therefore, in understanding mental distress it is important to draw on a broad spectrum of competing theoretical perspectives and paradigms. Bourdieu (1984) spoke about a dialectic interaction between the habitus and the situation that is the field that the individual finds himself/herself in. He views the individual as drawing on a wide repertoire of possible transformative and constraining courses of action. He has argued that 'habitus is not the fate that some people read into it...it is an open system of dispositions that is constantly subjected to experiences, and therefore, constantly affected by them in a way that reinforces or modifies its structures. It is durable but not eternal' (Bourdieu and Wacquant, 1992: 133). Therefore, there is a need to establish links between the individual level and social construction of psychosocial disabilities together with broader analyses of societal power and social inequalities. The next section explores different theories of mental disorders and examines the concepts of 'normality' and 'abnormality'.

THEORETICAL APPROACHES

The literature on mental illness, mental health and distress reveals that 'madness' has been interpreted in diverging ways depending on the era, the ideology and so on. Benedict (1934) states that, if we are interested in human behaviour, we need first of all to understand the institutions that are provided in any society. This is because human behaviour is influenced by these institutions without people even realizing it (ibid., 218). For a valid comparative psychiatry, the disoriented persons who have failed to adapt themselves adequately to their cultures are of foremost importance. This issue in psychiatry has been too often confused by starting from a fixed list of symptoms rather than the study of those whose characteristic reactions are denied validity in their society (ibid., 239). She pointed out that certain behaviours are considered normal in American society while they are regarded as abnormal in others and vice-versa. For example, ambitiousness is a valuable trait in American society whereas it is perceived negatively by the Zuni Indians of New Mexico. Therefore, psychosocial distress has to be understood in the context within which an individual is placed.

Sociological Perspectives

Some of the earliest theories related to deviance, mental illness and social causes of diseases came from the structural functionalists like Durkheim (1858–1917) and Parsons (1902–79). Durkheim (1964[1895]) argued that the rules and standards that define what is pathological help to reinforce the norms and values of society. The normal and the pathological are mutually constitutive, and societies and social groups define the pathological in order to sustain and strengthen the normal. This was done to maintain cohesion and smooth running of society. These concepts of social rules laid the foundation for other concepts such as the 'sick role' developed by Talcott Parsons. Parsons' basic argument is that sickness is a social and not a purely biochemical condition. He argued that whether illness is cured by magic, science or religion, the cure may take place and the system will be legitimated, or death occurs and nature, the devil or lack of knowledge are invoked and the legitimacy of the system put beyond question (White, 2002). He pointed out that people often get better because they expect to do so, rather than anything to do with the treatment: he made this point reflecting on the placebo[3] effect on which research had been carried out in the 1950s.

Research on the placebo effect led to the development of psycho-somatic medicine, this along with Parsons' argument that individuals have choices to make about their social relations and experiences, led to the conceptualization of the sick role. The development of psycho-somatic medicine emphasized the importance of the doctor's attitude rather than his science to the recovery of the patient and undercut any clear distinction between physical and mental illness. This implied that all illness had a motivational aspect (therefore, was also a form of deviance) and the doctor had to work with both the universality of science which focused on the illness and not the person, and the emotions arising out of the patient's unconscious will to be ill and dependent. This ultimately pressured the doctor to collude implying that doctoring served the social role of controlling this form of deviance (Figilio, 1987).

Within structural-functionalism then, the sources of psychological distress are identified in the characteristics of the individual's social life rather than in his/her personality. It emphasized that normal and accepted social structural arrangements can have dysfunctional as well as functional consequences.

Another way of understanding distress came from the symbolic interactionists' perspectives who emphasized the nature of interaction that the person has with other people. This perspective focuses on the 'micro level' social processes of health and healthcare and the important role that patients and healthcare providers play in the creation, development, and transformation of the larger healthcare systems of which they are a part.

---

[3] Individuals who believed that they were being treated with medicine respond as if they were, even when they are not.

Erving Goffman (1922–82) was one of the key interactionists who worked on mental illness. Goffman (1961) presented a bleak picture of the mental patient as he equated mental hospitals with total institutions such as prisons, concentration camps, orphanages and so on. Total institutions are places of residence and work where a large number of individuals are cut off from wider society for a period of time. Human needs are handled in a bureaucratic and impersonal way. According to Goffman (1968), mental hospitalization changed the way patients perceived themselves and others. When a person goes from being seen as a whole person to one who is tainted or discounted, then this attribution is stigma. Stigma is a societal reaction which 'spoils' normal identity. He introduced another concept called the 'courtesy stigma' which meant that stigma often spread from the stigmatized person to his or her connections as well. For Goffman the normal and the stigmatized were not persons but perspectives. A variant of symbolic interactionism following these studies by Goffman was the *labelling theory*. This posits that the impact of labelling a person as ill or deviant means that others will respond to him or her in accordance to that label, which will be very difficult to shed (Bourgeoult, 2006: 39).

Thomas Scheff (1966) explained how the process of labelling was related to mental illness. Society contains what Scheff calls the 'residual rules': rules of conduct which are expected to be followed in social situations that are not covered by specific religious, legal or moral constraints. If these residual rules are broken frequently and this comes into public knowledge then people are more likely to be referred to the police or a psychiatrist. Those of lower social status especially those in the margins of society are more likely to be dealt with by the official system (police, psychiatrist). Once someone has been referred to the system, it is likely that they are going to be officially labelled as mentally ill. The theory is that it recognizes the problematic aspects of reaction to mental disorder and explains how people labelled as mentally ill may be forced into a deviant role because of how people respond to them (Cokerham, 1996: 122).

Post-structuralism critiqued any attempt to formulate a macro theory of society and emphasized the importance of subjectivism and micro-sociological analysis. It stresses cultural relativism and plurality of viewpoints and argues that there is no 'truth' that can be uncovered or known; only different knowledge that can vary tremendously over time (Bourgeoult, 2006: 49). Michel Foucault and Pierre Bourdieu have helped medical anthropologists to find a path between approaches stressing either the semantics of illness and disease or the political economy of sickness and health. Their concepts help in understanding how the structures of societies influence and form individual lives, and how power can never be seen as a thing in itself, but always as a relational phenomenon working on all levels of social interaction (Samuelson and Steffen, 2011).

(a) Michel Foucault: The origin of madness

Foucault (1972) conceptualized madness as mental disease as a product of the Enlightenment project. According to him there was a rise in 'madness' towards the end of the fifteenth century. One of the reasons was because of a desire to organize society in a rational way instead of basing it on faith and the church. The other more compelling reason was the economic one. Madness was perceived, as was poverty, as incapacity to work and inability to integrate with the group. According to him increase in the number of 'mentally ill' or in the number of people who were confined was related to the economic crisis in the western world. Concepts of 'mental illness', mental health and madness are largely embedded in the historical and socio-economic position of a community, at a particular point in time. For Foucault, 'mental illness' was not an objective fact; it was only after a certain definition of 'madness' was put into practice that the appropriate subject, the 'madman' as current medical and psychiatric knowledge defined 'him', could appear. He considered the development of the modern social and medical sciences as the development of sophisticated power/knowledge of social control. This knowledge works through professional groups of helpers and healers and are internalized by us as subjective realities. The new disciplines of psychology, psychiatry and medicine established the 'scientific' criteria by which we distinguish categories of people: the sane, the insane, the disabled, the deviant, the criminal and the sick (Foucault, 1967). However, the concepts of 'mental illness' and distress are not just determined by the structures present in society but are also mediated by the interaction between the structures and individuals.

(b) Bourdieu: Habitus, field and symbolic power

Bourdieu did not directly talk about mental illness but his theory of practice allows us to understand both microcosmic and macrocosmic factors which arise while discussing mental disorders or distress. His concepts of habitus, symbolic power and different forms of capital are important conceptual tools which provide the link between the individual and the structures surrounding him/her. From a Bourdieusian perspective the mental health system can be conceived of as a 'field' in which competing agents have sought to establish a monopoly of expertise, authority and rights of treatment (Porter, 1987; Scull, 1993). In its early stages of development this was a struggle between medical, legal and religious groupings. Moreover, it entailed a struggle between these various groupings and a wider public who needed persuading of the value of their interventions. By the end of the nineteenth century, however, the medical profession had won the aforementioned struggle for monopoly and succeeded in securing hegemony for its practices and schemas of classification (ibid.). That madness is 'obviously' an illness, which requires the intervention of trained medics, had become a largely unquestioned assumption ('doxa'). The recognition and cooperation of both the public and parliament, which the symbolic power of psychiatry presupposes for its effective operation, was, attained (Crossley, 2010). Psychiatry became a taken-for-granted feature of life which could rely upon the habitual complicity of most social agents for its effective operation. The power of psychiatry is, among other things, a symbolic power to define, name, categorize and diagnose; to locate particular types of mental distress and deviance within a medical model of illness and to ensure, on this basis, that individuals falling within these categories are treated 'appropriately'. This is a power which depends ultimately upon 'belief'. This power leads to the symbolic violence of stigmatization and disqualification.

Mental distress is pre-defined in western culture by the discourses of psychiatry, whose reach has extended beyond the realms of a professional clique into the domain of everyday discourse. Being 'mentally ill', from this point of view, with whatever organic and psychological states it may also entail, is both a social position and a socially shaped disposition or habitus. It entails the incorporation of a social identity and a process of secondary socialization (Crossley, 2010).

(c) Anti-psychiatry movement

Anti-psychiatry was the criticism of psychiatry that emerged in the 1960s and 1970s. Anti-psychiatrists questioned the very basis of psychiatry itself: its purpose, its foundational conception of mental illness and the very distinction between madness and sanity (see also Tantam, 1991). Moreover, they examined and criticized the social control function which it performs within the society, arguing that even those techniques of psychiatry deemed more humane, such as psychoanalysis and psychotherapy, may in fact be subtle control mechanisms. A further distinguishing feature of the anti-psychiatric critique is its rootedness in a wider critique of society, which, it was argued, is oppressive and requires the distortion and repression of human potentialities for its effective functioning. This wider societal focus linked the anti-psychiatrists, conceptually, to other political movements of their time and these conceptual links were often consolidated through more practical cooperation (Crossley, 1998: 878). Thomas Szasz (1970) viewed 'mental illness' as the breaking of social, political and ethical norms and not as something which can be explained in medical terms. Szasz (1961, 1994) argued that 'mental illness' is a myth, since the concept has no literal application. He proposed that mental disorder be viewed within the framework of 'the game-playing model of human behaviour'. He then describes hysteria, schizophrenia, and other mental disorders as the 'impersonations' of sick persons by those whose 'real' issues concern the 'problems of living'.

Anthropological Explanations

Cultural traits and norms influence how we think, how we respond to distress, and how comfortable we are expressing our emotions (Eshun and Gurung, 2009: 4). Culture influences how individuals manifest symptoms, communicate their symptoms, cope with psychological challenges, and their willingness to seek treatment. It has been argued that culture and mental illness are more or less embedded in each other (Sam and Moreira, 2002). The modern ideas of psychiatry and psychology originated largely in the academic and clinical discourses of America and Europe. Because these discourses originated in these continents, these were usually applied in the same form in the South Asian context which was problematic. The disease perspective came largely from the west. For example, Dysthymic Disorder in DSM III(or neurotic depression in ICD-9) represented the medicalization of social problems in much of the rest of the world (and perhaps the west as well), where severe economic, political and health constraints create endemic feelings of hopelessness and helplessness, where demoralization and despair are responses to real conditions of chronic deprivation and persistent loss where *powerlessness is not a cognitive distortion but an accurate mapping of one's place in an oppressive social system* and where moral, religious and political configurations of such problems have coherence for the local population, but psychiatric categories do not. Usually this is found in people who have anaemia and other physiological effects of malnutrition and chronic tropical disorders that mirror the DSM III symptoms of Dysthymic Disorder (Kleinman, 1987).

Anthropology of Mental Health and Illness in India

Srivastava (2002) identified different ways of understanding mental illness in India which range from the 'supernatural theory' at one end of the continuum to the bio-chemical theory on the other. This continuum overlaps that of the societies; at one end are the tribal and peasant societies, at the other the complex, industrial and post-industrial societies. One explanation given is that as societies change from simple to complex, the theory of causation of mental illness also changes from the supernatural to the bio-chemical. However, one comes across these ideas (supernatural) not only in small towns but in metropolises also (ibid.: 151). Urban Indians, including those belonging to highly educated, upper classes, often attribute mental illness (and also, some other problems) to supernatural causes. This would explain the roaring success of supernatural healers, popularly known as *tantrik, sufi, gunia, ojha, siyana, bhopa, jankar* in urban India (ibid.: 152).

Fabrega (2009) argued that studying mental illness in the Indian context requires an understanding of medicine as well as of India's diverse intellectual and cultural traditions and social practices and institutions outside of medicine. All these were involved in formulating, appropriating, 'domesticating', coping with, and in the final event, healing. The advent of westernization and modernization created many changes in Indian society. The spread and growth of new ideas and values which challenged established customs and practices created instabilities and contradictions in thought, behaviour and experience, thereby creating vulnerabilities (ibid., 10). India's philosophical psychology concentrated on normal, desirable, sought after goals that directed a way to connect people's identities with the verities about the nature of the universe and the corresponding spiritual, religious and psychological values. This intellectual tradition did not signal disease or pathology per se as a major focus. Deviations in experience and behaviour were neither seen as sickness in the conventional sense nor were they condemned or stigmatized (ibid.: 248). Any anomalies in behaviour were considered to be limitations that needed to be overcome; human failings, weaknesses or mistakes were not seen as diseases.

Psychiatric symptoms have many different meanings. Kakar (1982) stated that in the Indian context psychiatric difficulties are seen in the context of healing rather than that of the medical model. Healing in its manifold aspects is a central individual and cultural preoccupation. In India, there are a wide variety of people involved in the tradition of psychic healing which include besides the few psychiatrists, *vaids* and *hakims,* many of whom practise 'psychological medicine'. There are also palmists, horoscope specialists, herbalists, sorcerers and a variety of shamans whose therapeutic efforts combine elements from classical Indian astrology, medicine, alchemy and magic, with beliefs and practices from the folk and popular traditions. And then, of course we have the *sadhus, swamis, maharajas, babas, matas* and *bhagwans,* who trace their lineage to the mystical-spiritual traditions of Indian antiquity and claim to specialize in the restoration of moral and spiritual well-being (ibid.).

When psychiatric difficulties are seen in the context of healing then there is an acknowledgement that the suffering is real. This can be further understood by examining the concept of *spirit possession.* This is the idea that supernatural personalities can enter, own and use people while they are in an 'altered state of consciousness' or trance state. Women are frequently associated with spirit possession; one theory talks of women trapped by the double standards of male-female relationships or by the socio-economic conditions of colonialism. The use of spirit possession as a means of resistance shows that since woman's choices are located within their everyday experience, they speak from within the multiplicity of their experience and location. They use several and varying acts of resistance that need not necessarily fall into a universal pattern but remain embedded in local acts or modalities of agency evolving from individual ways of perception and action (Thapan, 2006). These cults are seen as ways in which powerless people work out their anger of and fears about more powerful people. Kapadia (1995) in her ethnographic study carried out in South India examines the marginalization of women even in terms of possession. She says that among all the castes in south India, malign possession is mostly experienced by women which is why far more women than men are possessed by *pey* (evil ghosts). But even when this is the case, women who become possessed may legitimately behave in a manner that would be considered improper or even obscene in normal circumstances (ibid.). Therefore, spirit possession and local explanations of 'mental illness' can be seen as women organizing their agency to make spaces for themselves within the existing structures. With the advent of scientific realism, there has been a decrease in the usage of traditional healing practices. However, in the area of 'mental illness', there is increasingly a recognition of the need to understand and use the traditional myths, legends and stories of the communities as they play a large part in determining the kind of symptoms and illnesses that come up within members of the community.

Consequently, it becomes important to understand the mental health problems in the context of the geography and the culture of the area. Sujatha (2003) in her study of health practices in a village in Tamil Nadu found that villagers point out only one explanation for mental illness which was 'brain problem'. Erratic and obsessive behaviour was explained as 'deviant behaviour' and not as illness of the mind. The causes outlined by them which lead to 'mental illness' included anxiety, family quarrels, differences between parents and children, loss of property, betrayal by friend and so on. Obeyesekere (1985) argues that sentiments of sorrow and revulsion towards one's body in South Asia are irrevocably rooted in Buddhist cultural traditions, and are in fact, highly valued by some Buddhists who meditate on these sentiments in order to seek a more enlightened understanding of the world. Anything that might be labelled as depression in the West, therefore, assumes radically different sets of meanings among Buddhists in South Asia.

Other factors to consider are the culturally constituted 'idioms of distress' that pattern how people signal and embody distress.

Presuming limits on the ability of south Indian women to ventilate or verbalize 'distress' within or outside of home, Nichter (1981) finds a somewhat broader range of alternative idioms of distress in addition to 'illness idioms': eating disturbances, obsession with purity, reports of evil eye, spirit possession and involvement in *Bhakti* cults. In other studies that combine psychoanalytic and anthropological theory, Obeyesekere (1990) documents the ways in which the unconscious sentiments of desire and guilt motivate the lives of Sri Lankans and sometimes lead to situations of distress, illness, or frail cures as manifested in demonic attacks, divine possession, and ritual practices.

Feminist Perspectives

Women and psychosocial distress: Historical developments

The concept of mental health encapsulates psychological well-being and psychological problems. Since statistics were first recorded in the early nineteenth century, women have outnumbered men in the population treated for mental health problems (Showalter, 1987). According to the data both from community surveys and hospital statistics, women are two to four times likely to be identified as having neurotic disorders (anxiety disorders, depression, phobias) and depressive disorders. Feminist critics have argued that women are labelled mentally ill when they present a challenge to patriarchy (Ussher, 1991). The history of psychiatric disorders and psychological differences between men and women has been longstanding. Madness in women has been recognized in all cultures and mad behaviour has been attributed to different causes including divinity, passion and alcohol. Hippocrates in the fourth century BC described madness in women as related to the womb or 'hysteron' in Greek and hence, the term 'hysteria'. According to this belief all madness in women stemmed from the womb and womb-related functions. The idea that the womb increased women's vulnerability to mental dysfunction and mental weakness continued for centuries. In the Middle Ages and later, women were either deemed psychologically lesser and weaker creatures and therefore, not deserving equal rights or if they diverted from the norm, they were seen as dangerous and burnt as witches. Menopause was thought to be a period of great irritability and distress. In 1890 Kraepelin coined the term 'Involutional Melancholia' for a syndrome describing agitated depression, hypochondriasis and delusion in menopausal women (Kohen, 2000: 2). In classical times the female sex was identified with the unknown, mysterious and fearful. The Furies who brought madness to others were female, as were the Maenads, expressers of ecstasy. These characterizations were linked with the irrational in the rational/irrational dichotomy that characterizes Western thought (Holmshaw and Hillier, 2000: 41).

Towards the end of the eighteenth century there was a significant change wherein lunatics were viewed as sick human beings, objects of pity to be cared for. However, it was not until the Victorian era that madness itself became firmly conceptualized as 'mental illness' under the jurisdiction of the rising medical establishment, and the close association between femininity and pathology became firmly established within scientific and popular thinking. In the nineteenth century, a number of circumstances led to the concentration on the mental susceptibility of women (ibid.: 43). In the mid-nineteenth century women were deemed to be highly susceptible to becoming 'mentally ill' as they did not have the mental capacity of men, and this risk grew greatly if the woman attempted to better herself through education or too many activities. In fact, women were seen as most likely having a mental breakdown sometime during their life as 'the maintenance of [female] sanity was seen as the preservation of brain stability in the face of overwhelming physical odds' (Ussher, 1991: 74). Thus, women often suppressed their feelings, so as to not appear mad and reassumed the passive, housewife role. The idea of the 'Wandering Womb' developed during this time, as madness was associated with menstruation, pregnancy, and menopause. The womb itself was deemed to wander throughout the body, acting as an enormous sponge which sucked the life-energy or intellect from vulnerable women (ibid.).

Cultural associations between women and 'mental illness' have, of course, only been possible since the emergence of the scientific and medical discourses in which concepts of 'mental illness' have been formulated (see Foucault, 1967/1985). However, cultural representations of 'woman', primarily in terms of her body, particularly her reproductive body, have a considerably longer genealogy (Choi and Nicolson, 1994; Malson and Swann, 2003; Marshall and Woollett, 2000), as does the notion that female embodiment is risk-laden. It has recurred in some form or another across history and throughout most if not all cultures. As de Beauvoir (1953/1984) illustrated, since the Roman Empire up to the twentieth century, woman was represented, at least in European cultures, as the other of man and as lesser in her otherness. In addition, analyses of science, art, religion and popular cultures (Foucault, 1979/1990; Jordanova, 1989; Riley, 1988; Sayers, 1982; Walkerdine, 1988) demonstrate a similarly systematic 'other-ing' of women and women's bodies up to the present day.

Women became synonymous with madness, as they were deemed to be emotional and unstable. This understanding of women's distress as emotional instability was a reflection of how women's health in general was being perceived during the 1900s. This was the time when there was a gender shift in provision of healthcare. Female healers and midwives who had been caring for women and men for centuries had been displaced by male physicians, many of whom campaigned to exclude women from formal medical training (Walsh, 1977). This also indicated a shift from natural non-invasive methods to surgery drugs and other new technologies. Ultimately, in western societies male domination and gender-specific views created conditions for women's dissatisfaction and struggle for change. Therefore, the women's health movement emerged out of the socio-political relationship between men and women that, in terms of health and healthcare, became accentuated with industrialization, the growth of technology, and the rise of 'scientific' medicine in the nineteenth century (Zimmerman, 1980: 453).

Contemporary explanations of women's mental health problems are more likely to focus on endocrinal disorder than on 'wandering wombs', 'delicate nerves', suppressed feelings or 'mental weakness' (Malson, 1998). Yet the Victorian notion of 'woman' as naturally nervous persists even today, albeit, in a different form. As Gannon (1998: 287) argues: 'The primary difference between the 19th- and 20th-century account is that, in the nineteenth century, a woman's uterus and ovaries were the essence of her psychological and physical well-being whereas, today, the focus is on hormones.' In the twenty-first century, women's distress has been redefined in terms of common mental disorders.

(a) Phyllis Chesler: Women and madness

Chesler's analysis was built from two foundations: writings of anti-psychiatrists (emphasis on madness and mental disorder as labels and theme of social control) and the theorization of social roles, including gender relations, derived from structural functionalism (sickness and disorders as failures of role performance). According to her, 'What we consider "madness" whether it appears in women or men is either acting out of the devalued female role or the total or partial rejection of one's sex role stereotype' (Chesler, 1972: 56). Chesler argues that women's behaviour is typically devalued, rejected and pathologized: 'women, by definition, are viewed as psychiatrically impaired—whether they accept or reject the female role—simply because they are women' (ibid.: 115). It is primarily for this reason that women are overrepresented in mental patient populations.' As patients women face psychiatry which is numerically dominated by men and acts upon 'traditional myths about "abnormality", sex-role stereotypes and female inferiority' (ibid.: 61) and which mirrors female experience in patriarchal society. Women, therefore, seem to be in something of a double bind, since conformity to role expectations puts them closer to behaviours which/are defined as pathological by overall standards of adult behaviour, whilst rejection of these same expectations may itself be judged pathological. Chesler has been criticized for making incorrect assumptions about the nature of relationship between sexism and psychiatry. However, her theory helped in questioning the existing structures that had the power to define madness at a certain time.

(b) Dorothy Smith: Relations of ruling

Smith (1975)'s model assumes that mental illness is an objective social state which exists prior to treatment. She proposes a different model in which mental illness is not seen as a distinct disease or an entity. It is the last in a chain of events and results from a definition by the social control agencies involved. She explains that the position of women is not a product of something biological, but a product of socio-historical circumstances and their relationship with the relations of ruling. She further adds that the category 'women' is not all-embracing, exclusive or fixed. Its limits are constantly transcended as each woman brings a unique perspective (Smith, 1987). Smith argues that all formal institutions, whether private or state-sponsored have developed various techniques and procedures for the accumulation and interpretation of data regarding the 'correct' versus 'aberrant' behaviour of individuals. This includes institutions like mental hospitals which are supposed to serve a therapeutic function in society. Doctors, nurses and administrators learn and reproduce a particular set of bureaucratic and professional practices and terminologies that become part of their essential frame of reference. Through the application of this system of reference, 'local' events and phenomena—for instance, the subjective sufferings of disturbed or distressed individuals—are transformed into a set of neutral 'facts', which can then be effectively categorized, and 'dealt with 'by the organizational apparatus' empowered to handle such cases (Smith, 1990). Although Smith's analysis pertains specifically to western (white) capitalist patriarchies, her conceptualizations of 'relations of ruling' can be viewed as a significant theoretical and methodological development, which can be advantageously used to specify relations (Mohanty et al., 1991).

(c) Feminist perspectives from India

Mental health of women in India has always been linked with their social position, usually accorded to them by the family and kinship structures to which they belong. Academic discourses have explored the interface between gender and kinship and concluded that kinship structures present in the society have a substantial effect on the way women are treated. Male and female psychology is shaped by the patriarchal culture and its devaluation of women. Ganesh (1998) states that domestic violence cuts across classes; activist struggles reveal the extent of tacit acceptance of male violence on close kin, within the setting of the household-family. The public discourse on such violence suggests that it is part of an unarticulated 'common sense' in which the person of a woman can be rightfully invaded in the familial context; there is an endorsement of the right along with a condemnation of violence. Women face violence in a number of situations; in fact, many of their physical problems have roots in the stress that they face in their daily lives. A recent study of 1,853 persons who came to a general health facility found that 193 persons (10.4%) had psychological problems. Most were women in the age group of 16 to 45 years who had come to the facility from a far greater distance than those with physical disorders. For a majority of the group 'the cause of stress lay in personal and family life' and specifically for 10 per cent, marital and sexual reasons were the main cause of distress. It would be fairly safe to hypothesize then that while a sizeable percentage of women's health problems lie rooted in familial dynamics and tension-ridden relationships, more often than not they get treated for physical disorders (Karlekar, 2005). Changes in family situation also led to a lot of stress for women; for example, loss of the husband makes the woman's situation extremely precarious in the family. Increase in workload, loss of self-respect as well as tendency to neuroses was observed in a study of 350 widows in Haryana, which also found that most felt that survival and accommodation were major problems (Sandhya, 1994).

As a category, women have not controlled the means of production or of reproduction; in addition, they have routinely been sexually abused as well. Rape has been systematically used by men of every class and race to destroy women within their family or community and during wars, wives, mothers and daughters of the enemy. In India, sexual abuse of women has implications for the maintenance of caste boundaries as well. The mechanisms for the functioning of the principles of hierarchy, separation and interdependence characterizing caste operate not through individuals but through units based on kinship. Control over female sexuality is critical to purity and boundary maintenance between castes. Women are guardians and conduits of purity and honour of the caste. But to achieve this goal at the level of institutions, the family-household is important. *Purdah*, restrictions on mobility, stress on virginity before marriage, anxiety regarding early and appropriate marriage of girls, stigma of illegitimate offspring and abandonment, and ideological valorizing of chastity and fidelity are connected to the exigencies of boundary maintenance, and symbolized through notions of purity and honour. While these restrictions affect upper caste women in more stringent ways, they constitute a generalized set of norms which serve as a reference point even if not practised by all castes. Socialization towards these and mechanisms of monitoring, control and punishment are vested in the family-household (Ganesh, 1998: 122). Thus, for a woman in the Indian context the household itself becomes a place of control and threat. Even when they are suffering, the ways in which their distress is interpreted is mediated by the structures present in the society.

As a result of this, in India, the women's movement itself was seen as a mental health movement as this allowed women to challenge the social institutions as well as cultural and political structures which had a direct impact on the mental health and well-being of women (Shatrugna, 1999). The challenge to the medical model of psychosocial distress or disability and the view that women's health was being viewed from a patriarchal lens came from the women's movements which recognized that health was being used as a means towards the goal of controlling women's actions. A common assumption shared by various women's movements on women's health was that it had been medicalized in the past, and the gender-biased medical knowledge, diagnoses and treatments decided by biased male physicians had resulted in the overtreatment of women documented in high surgery rates for hysterectomies and mastectomies, and overuse of drugs, especially psychotropic drugs. Women's movements at that stage sought to halt the further medicalization of women's bodies by a redefinition of what is healthy. During the 1970s, women's organizations directly challenged the patriarchal social order while rallying around issues of violence against women, like dowry deaths and rape cases. The backdrop of this was constituted in a specific socio-economic and political context. Civil rights, women's and students' movements in the west precipitated the situation (Mehrotra, 2002). It was feminism that provided spaces for women to engage in the mental health discourse. It was later feminist disability studies that gave new and alternative ways for theorizing about 'mental illness' from a feminist perspective (Donaldson, 2002). The women's movement gave 'mad' women a chance to locate their lives within patriarchy, understand their powerlessness, and engage with re-scripting their identities from a political perspective. The women's movement which promoted the values of social justice, equality and empowerment viewed personal struggles, loss of identity and living in difficult circumstances as reasons for psychological and emotional distress (Davar, 2008: 264). Vindhya (2001) pointed out that women's problems were more due to distress than illness and therefore, the ambience of care and support that a woman's group could create could be rewarding for the women seeking support from the group as well as for the group members.

Psychological Perspectives

Within the psychological perspectives, mental illness has often been seen as a bias—sampling bias, self-report bias, diagnostic bias, and construct or criterion bias. Criterion bias occurs when the criterion for a particular disorder are themselves 'male' or 'female'. Measures such as the General Health Questionnaire (GHQ) when used as an index of psychiatric disorder in the community can lead to the over-representation of women as 'cases', as they include symptoms of distress which are common in women and exclude symptoms such as heavy drinking which are common in men (Newman, 1984).

In classical psychoanalytic theory feminine development could only be understood in terms of a *lack* of something. In the first instance it was the lack of a penis, but, as a result of the consequent difficulties in coming to terms with this in the Oedipus complex, initial disappointment was followed by a lack in other areas, such as, super-ego development, capacity for sublimation and moral judgement. Freud felt that feminine development predisposed women to hysteria and depression. Since women have suffered a narcissistic blow to their ego in discovering their castration, they are more likely to form over-dependent and narcissistic love relations and more likely to suffer melancholia on the experience of their loss. Freud also characterized hysteria as a 'feminine' neurosis and related it to the difficulties women had in negotiating the Oedipus complex and transferring their love from their mothers to their fathers. In contrast to classical psychoanalysis, psychoanalytic feminists explain women's oppression as rooted within psychic structures and reinforced by the continual repetition or reiteration of relational dynamics formed in infancy and childhood. Because of these deeply ingrained patterns, psychoanalytic feminists wanted to alter the experiences of early childhood and family relations, as well as linguistic patterns that produce and reinforce masculinity and femininity. Critical of Freudian and neo-Freudian notions of women as biologically, psychically, and morally inferior to men, psychoanalytic feminists addressed political and social factors affecting the development of male and female subjects. Like radical feminists, they saw as key issues sexual difference and women's 'otherness' in relation to men.

During the 1960s and 1970s coinciding with the rebirth of the feminist movement, analysts came up who placed the mother in the central position as the most powerful, enviable and influential parent. Feminist psychoanalysts spoke about issues of identification and separation from the mother as the key to understanding both men's and women's development. Psychoanalytic feminism claims that the source of men's domination of women is men's unconscious two-sided need for women's emotionality and rejection of them as potential castrators. Women submit to men because of their unconscious desires for emotional connectedness. Feminist psychoanalysts spoke about issues of identification and separation from the mother as the key to understanding both men's and women's development. Chodorow (1978) has argued that as a result of 'asymmetrical parenting' both girls and boys come to define themselves in relation to the mother. Girl's psychic structure develops within a context of identification on the basis of *similarity* with the mother, whereas boys construct their identity on the basis of *difference*. This negation is held to create difficulties for masculine identity which is seen as being threatened by experiences that re-evoke early maternal identifications, whereas, girls are seen as being more secure in their positive identification. Since women come to define themselves in terms of relationships, they are consequently more dependent on them, more vulnerable to their loss and less likely to express their dissatisfaction and anger towards their love objects. A non-autonomous self concept of this kind will lead to helplessness, self denigration and depression. Further difficulties arise for girls as a result of the need to identify with a figure that is devalued by societies that place a higher value on the male. In their articles on love and violence, Goldner et al. (1990: 555) suggest that this identification with a less valued figure creates problems for women's sense of power and agency rather than their gender identity as girls must 'struggle to claim for herself what mother was denied: a voice of her own, a mind of her own, a life of her own'.

Psychoanalysts continue to argue that passivity, narcissism and masochism on the one hand and dependency and the inability to find a voice of one's own on the other, pose particular problems for women. They also argue that these personality styles are associated with the 'feminine' (internalizing) disorders such as depression, somatic disorders, eating disorders and aggression against the self. However, contemporary analysts allow for the formulation of construction of gender identity which is based on the incorporation of identities of both parents.

Diathesis-Stress Model

'Mental illness' is seen as the result of interaction between biological and psychosocial perspectives. It involves a relationship between vulnerable predispositions (diathesis) and stress as contributors to the development of psychopathology. The theory posits that stress may serve as an activator of the diathesis, leading to the development and manifestation of psychopathology. Using this model the greater incidence of women's mental health problems can be explained as either occurring due to the greater vulnerability of women or because of their greater stress. Women's engendered role can be seen as adding to both greater vulnerability and greater stress. Women's social role makes them more vulnerable to developing mental illness, especially depression and anxiety. Women's lives are mainly lived in areas of experience where opportunity, autonomy, creativity, stimulation and acknowledged success are limited leading to frustration and tension.

Biological Model

The social, psychological models have not gone unchallenged. The alternative medical model posits firm biochemical origins for both forms (severe and common mental disorders) of mental illness. This model places mental illness within the realm of the internal biology of the body. Essentially mental illness is a malfunctioning of an individual's biochemistry. Currently, however, there are no neurobiological markers that define psychiatric disorders (First and Zimmerman, 2006; Heninger, 1999); diagnoses are still defined by clinical symptoms that seem to cluster and form similar patterns that may help predict course and treatment response (Robins and Guze, 1970; Sadock and Sadock, 2003).

The physiological perspective explores the influence of female hormones on mental health. Female hormones are known to influence certain neurotransmitter systems that have been implicated in psychiatric disorders and also to impact the hypothalamic-pituitary-adrenal (HPA) axis, the core endocrine stress axis in man (Sleye, 1974); the sex differences in stress system responsivity may be partly explained on this basis. In the case of the reproductive syndromes—pre-menstrual syndrome (PMS), post-natal depression and climacteric syndrome—the problem is located within: endocrine or neurotransmitter dysfunction, or 'female sex hormones', a pathology within the woman, outside of her control (but within the control of medical experts, we are assured). Indeed, fecundity is positioned as so detrimental to women's mental health that it is blamed for women reporting higher rates of depression than men, the 'sex hormone', oestrogen, positioned as the cause. The reproductive syndromes have become catch-all diagnostic categories that conveniently attribute female distress and deviance to the reproductive body, legitimating medical management of the reproductive excess, and implicitly of the monstrous feminine (Ussher, 2006: 16). In short, 'women continue to be defined in terms of their biological functions' (Phoenix and Woollett, 1991: 7) and their/our bodies defined as 'biologically labile' (Ussher, 1991) causes of mental health problems.

Currently, another model which has made an effort to combine several varying theories is the bio-psychosocial model. This approach holds that biological, psychological, and social factors combine to influence behaviour. Although the utility of taking a bio-psychosocial approach has already paid dividends, there is still a need to better incorporate research on diverse cultural backgrounds. A bio-psychocultural approach (Gurung, 2006) might provide clinical psychology with stronger direction because it not only incorporates the social nature of our interactions, but explicitly acknowledges the role that culture plays in our lives.

Psychosocial distress is often defined by who you are: man, woman, child, senior citizen; where you are: continent, country, region, caste, class, tribe; religion that you belong to and the era that you have been born in. One way then to understand concepts of abnormality, 'mental illness', mental health and distress would be to study them at a particular point of time, but this would leave out the historical development of these concepts which would again limit our understanding of these concepts. Usually everything which is away from the norm is categorized as 'illnesses'. The concept of mental health then becomes even more complex as it is about health and not just about being 'normal'. The placement of the individual on the continuum of illness, normalcy (with some amount of required stress) and health is a difficult process influenced by multiple factors. Normal is usually defined as what the average number of people experience or how they behave. Then, does distress become normal if a large number of people experience this state and are troubled by it?

Culture, Context and Distress*

The nature of the space inhabited affects the sense of well being that a person has. Every individual is, to a certain extent, shaped by the structures and systems that surround him/her; this is because these structures either restrict their freedom or enhance it. The macro forces provide the boundaries within which people live and negotiate their lives. The 'culture' of an urban resettlement colony is unique as it is actually an amalgamation of cultures—people from heterogeneous backgrounds (regions, religions, class, caste) live in proximity and create a different dynamic. It is important to explore this social space and its impact on women.

SOCIAL SPACE AND GENDER REGIME

The social space that a person inhabits has an impact on his/her everyday life and is instrumental in determining the course of his/her life. Social space can be broadly defined as, a practised place, a place where people encounter and interact with each other and where the quotidian activities of everyday life take place. It is also a theatre where individuals play out and perform various social roles. Social space is not a homogenous or a fixed entity. Instead, a complex ensemble of factors eventually contributes to the construction of social space. There

---

* Certain sections of this chapter have been published in the book *Disability, Gender and State Policy* by Nilika Mehrotra, Jaipur 2013 and as part of a chapter in *Disability, Gender and Trajectories of Power*, Asha Hans (ed.), SAGE Publications, 2015.

is an abstract component of social space that gets constructed based on the mode of practice which an individual engages in (Bourdieu, 1977). An individual may, therefore, engage in multiple social spaces depending on circumstances. It is not merely a material or geographical entity; instead several factors, both material and abstract, fixed as well as circumstantial, contribute to its construction. In Bourdieu's analysis, physical space plays an important role in determining the hierarchy and symbolic power relations that exist in society. Although physical space is simply a material disposition, social space gets constructed through meanings and actions of the actors in it. Bourdieu's notion of organization of space naturally leads to the question of whether space is something that already existed or one that was created according to the individual actors. He gave importance to both structure and agency.

He attempted to reconcile social structure and individual agency and how the 'outer' social and 'inner' self help to shape each other (Maton, 2008: 50). He defines 'habitus' as a property of social agents (whether individuals, groups or institutions) that comprises a 'structured and structuring structure' (Bourdieu, 1994: 170). It is 'structured' by one's past and present circumstances such as family upbringing and educational experiences. It helps to shape one's present and future practices (structuring). It is also systematically ordered rather than random or unpatterned (structure). This 'structure' comprises a system of dispositions which generate perceptions, appreciations and practices (Bourdieu, 1990: 53). Habitus also links the social and the individual, the objective and subjective, and structure and agency. Habitus is, 'a socialized subjectivity' and 'the social embodied' (Bourdieu and Wacquant, 1992: 127, 128); it is in other words, internalized structure, the objective made subjective. This concept also helps us to understand how the personal plays a role in the social—its dispositions underlie our actions that in turn, contribute to social structures (Maton, 2008: 53). It brings together both social structure and subjective personal experiences.

The physical and social spaces people occupy are structured and the relation between these two structures gives rise to practices (ibid.: 52).

The experience of doing gender is in part a result of the internalization of objective structures. Attention to gendered meanings of space have allowed scholars to move away from the determinism of a universal patriarchy (Acker, 1989; Smith, 1983) and towards understanding gender relations as specific to particular places and times (Bondi, 1993; Rosaldo, 1980; Walby, 1989). Risman (1998) explained the importance of addressing the intersection of 'institutional gender stratification, situational expectations, and gendered selves' and that 'even if individuals are capable of change…the influence of gendered institutions and interactional contexts persists' (ibid.: 30). Risman's work identifies the need to address the intersection of process and structure. These intersections can be understood with the help of the concept of gender regime. Connell (1987) defines gender regime as the 'structural inventory of a particular institution' (ibid.: 99) that represents 'the state of play in gender relations in a given institution' (ibid.: 120). He points out that gender relations constitute a social structure. This definition of gender regime highlights the time- and place-specific aspects and attitudes of gender and the fluidity of gender structure. Studying the gender regimes in a particular community reveals the ways in which structures intersect with processes to shape the experiences of women living there. The concept of gender regime provides a framework to identify gender meanings that are attached to specific locations. Some variations in gender relations are tied to economic structure and opportunities. Other differences are rooted in local culture and values (Williams, 2002: 32). Local gender regimes capture meaningful differences in ways communities organize gender relations and reveal how structure intersects with process to shape the experience of women. This is further mediated by the cultural transformations that take place in Jahangirpuri because of its interaction with the globalizing world.

CULTURE[1] AND MENTAL HEALTH IN THE GLOBALIZING WORLD

If environment is broadly the entire context of human experience—geographical, physical, social, psychological and economic aspects of life—then we can talk about culture as acting as an intermediary between human and environment. Culture may, thus, be viewed as both a product and a producer of urban environment (Schell, 1997). Urbanization has brought its own set of problems pertaining to mental health and well-being. Mostly because of increased speed and decreased costs of communication and transportation, cities are growing increasingly diverse in their population. Consequently, cultural factors have taken centre-stage in the understanding of urban mental health. In exploring the relationship between culture, mental health and globalization, the conceptualization of culture given by Appadurai (2004) is used. This includes aspiration as a strong feature of cultural capacity. Aspirations are related to wants, preferences, choices and calculations; globalization has created gaps between aspirations and realities which is leading to different kinds of mental health issues.

During the last few decades, the quality of life in most countries has been greatly affected by economic disintegration, social disruption, disordered urbanization, political repression, huge migrations and many other destructive processes. For example, 'structural adjustment programmes' (SAP) in many countries have led to increased rates of malnutrition and unemployment, generating psychosocial problems of individuals and families (Chosudowsky, 1994). Mental health disorders now loom as a worldwide problem of enormous proportions that cannot be dissociated from the highly complex macroscopic context of globalization that frames our life (Bibeau, 1997). Since the mid-1980s, India has pursued a policy of economic liberalization,

---

[1] Culture should be regarded as the set of distinctive, spiritual, material, intellectual, and emotional features of society or a social group, and that it encompasses, in addition to art and literature, lifestyles, ways of living together, value systems, traditions, and beliefs (UNESCO, 2002).

which was a dramatic reversal of earlier policies of protecting domestic industrial capital. It has been argued that the privatization of public sector enterprises, reduction in public sector investment, and lower government expenditure on poverty eradication programmes have not served the interests of women (Panini 1995: 57). As a result of globalization attitudes, practices and beliefs of different places have come together and evolved. Globalization means the import and export of cultures as well. Culture is reflected in the learned shared beliefs, values, attitudes and behaviours characteristic of a society or population. It is dynamic and ever-changing and, it is the way people structure and adapt to their internal and external environments. The process of globalization has largely consisted of spreading the hegemony of the dominant cultures, that is the culture and lifestyles of the 'developed' nations is being copied and followed by the rest of the world. This process is carried out especially through the media which is one of the major mechanisms of globalization. The homogenization of cultures across the non-industrialized world in the past decade is a marker of the vulnerability of cultures to the onslaught of modern marketing and global media networks (Patel, 1999). Although there have been concerns that globalization will eventually lead to the homogenization of culture and identity, there is evidence that this process is being opposed by the tendency for communities to retain or assert their ethnic identity—in its extreme form leading to the rise of neo-nationalist and fundamentalist movements (Bibeau, 1997). Despite evidence that all mental disorders are psycho-biosocial in origin and that the quality of social environment is related to the risk of mental illness, it is difficult to predict the impact of globalization on the prevalence and course of psychiatric disorders. What is certain, however, is that mental disorders can no longer be dissociated from the global context that frames our lives.

According to Kirmayer and Minas (2000), globalization affects psychiatry in three main ways: through its effect on the forms of individual and collective identity, impact of economic inequalities on mental health and through the shaping and dissemination of psychiatric knowledge itself. They identify both the tendency for communities to reassert their distinctive ethnic identity, i.e., the 'creolization' of identity and of the cultural idioms through which emotional distress is communicated. One of the key factors of globalization is urbanization which is explored next.

URBANIZATION AND MENTAL HEALTH

Globalization has clearly brought with it rapid urbanization (World Bank, 2000: 9). Urban environments encompass a great deal of economic and social difference. Socially defined groups (e.g., ethnic groups, the poor, minorities and homeless) are created through cultural consensus about what is acceptable, right and normative. There is economic variation across these groups of people and urban environments are the loci, where there is great disparity among groups of people living in proximity (Aday, 2001; Nguyen and Peschard, 2003). Disparity in the urban environment leads to relative poverty leading to discontent among people. Although these characteristics have been present for a long time and this relationship between urban living and well-being has been explored extensively, globalization has accelerated these effects.

Historical Perspectives

Rousseau studied the relationship between socio-environmental factors and mental health and well-being (Marsella, 1995). He launched a battle against society's contributions to crime, injustice, political corruption and so on. He attributed poor health to social corruption and inequity. He stated:

> The greater part of our ills are our own making, and we might have avoided them, in nearly all, by adhering to that simple, uniform, and solitary manner of life which nature prescribed. When we think of good constitution of the savages. At least of those whom are troubled with hardly any disorders save wounds and old age, we are tempted to believe that in following the history of civil society, we shall be telling that of human sickness. (cited in Durant and Durant, 1967: 29)

Although Rousseau presented a romanticized version of a simple life, to a large extent, his work anticipated the public health and social medicine movements which followed later. Social theorists spoke about traditional and rational society (Weber), and societies based on mechanical or organic solidarities (Durkheim, 1893). Ferdinand Tonnies (1887) distinguished between *gemeinschaft,* a community based on kinship ties where people knew one another and cooperated with one another, as against *gesselschaft,* a community based on common political, economic and social interests where trust and cooperation were absent and there were few ties among residents.

The Chicago School and its predecessors proposed that cities were subjectively alienating. According to Wirth (1938), urbanism leads to weakened social ties to a place and to the breakdown of informal social control, which produces alienation. Wirth (1964) contended that urbanization led to extended differentiation and separation among occupational, familial, recreational and institutional aspects of life. This resulted in poor social integration with consequent alienation, aberrant behaviour and social withdrawal. Simmel (1969) argued that urban areas harm residents' mental states by exposing them to high levels of negative stimulation: the chaotic sights and sounds of the city, such as contact with strangers, crowds, noise, sirens, dirt and garbage, and the disorder, crime, and danger that result from a breakdown of informal social control. The distinctive features of the urban mode of life have often been described sociologically as consisting of the substitution of secondary for primary contacts, the weakening of bonds of kinship, and the declining social significance of the family, the disappearance of the neighbourhood, and the undermining of the traditional basis of social solidarity. In recent times, there is a recognition that it is not the place where the person is located but the kind of resources and life that a person lives, which makes the difference. Inkeles and Smith (1970, cited in Ahmeida-Filho, 1998) noted that the issue is not rural or urban life, but rather the existence of stress regardless of where it is located. Studying mental health issues in cities becomes important because most of the population is moving there which leads to conflicts related to resources.

Early Studies

The work of Faris and Dunham (1939) first looked at the relationship between living in a particular area and mental illness. They reported that first admission rates for schizophrenia were particularly high in certain areas of inner city Chicago and decreased towards the periphery. Within the inner city itself, rates were higher in the more disorganized areas, irrespective of deprivation and ethnicity. They suggested that the nature of living conditions in certain neighbourhoods, in particular, the experience of extended isolation, produced abnormalities of behaviour and mentality that led to mental illness. Their theory was called the 'social drift' and 'social isolation' hypotheses.

Hollingshead and Reslich (1958) propounded the 'social class' hypotheses wherein the spatial distribution of mental disorders in urban areas was seen as a function of concentration of poverty in city centres rather than the geographical location. They found a correlation between social class and mental disorders. They reported increased rates and severity of mental disorders for lower socio-economic class members. Schizophrenic disorders were inversely related to social class membership, while depression was found to be higher in upper social classes (Marsella, 1995).

Another group of studies led to the formulation of the 'sociocultural disintegration hypotheses'. Leighton (1959) argued that sociocultural milieu can interfere with basic human needs thereby increasing the risks of mental disorder. Sociocultural disintegration characterized by family and marital disintegration, few social networks and associations, few and weak leaders, weak and fragmented communication networks, and high levels of hostility and similar traits, disrupted psychological homeostasis, thereby increasing the risk of mental disorders. These are more likely in communities with extensive migration and poverty, cultural confusion and rapid social change.

'The socio-environmental stress, resources and psychopathology hypothesis' given by Marsella and his co-workers (1969) provided a conceptual framework which considered the stress associated with problems related to housing, work, marriage, child rearing, security and related urban problems, in simultaneous interaction with the resources available for their resolution or attenuation. These early studies launched an era in which social causation of mental disorders gained prominence; this was required to understand mental disorders from a broader framework.

Later Studies

With the current rate of urbanization, there is a growth in the number of neighbourhoods which are characterized by disorganization. Visible signs of social disorder include fights and trouble among neighbours, people hanging out on the streets and the presence of people drinking, taking drugs, panhandling and creating a sense of danger. Physical disorder refers to a neighbourhood's overall appearance. Places with high levels of physical disorder are noisy, dirty, and run-down; many buildings are in disrepair or abandoned; vandalism and graffiti are common. Social and physical disorder are conceptualized on a continuum, with order on one end and disorder on the other.

According to Massey (1996), neighbourhoods with concentrated poverty engender violent behaviour in their residents. In these neighbourhoods, where informal social control is weak and violence is common, residents adapt to violence by becoming violent themselves. Perceived powerlessness is another response. Although no direct empirical comparison exists between the prevalence of violence and the prevalence of perceived powerlessness in disordered neighbourhoods, we think that few people in these neighbourhoods will become violent (ibid.).

Blue (2001: 219) argued that it was poverty rather than urban or rural residence that played a role in creating high levels of stress and subsequent mental ill health. The need to focus on urban areas arose as a majority of the world's population will live there in the future and urbanization would have resulted in changes in social structure which have an impact on mental health. Between 1991 and 1992, the 'Brazilian Multicentric Study of Psychiatric Morbidity' was carried out. It was found that prevalence of mental disorders was highest in the lowest socio-economic districts and lowest in the highest socio-economic sub-districts in Sao Paulo (ibid.: 220). Vikram Patel (2001) argues that in the Asian context, there is a cycle of poverty and mental ill health. Poverty causes emotional distress due to insecurity: the stress of making ends meet, coping with emerging difficulties and crisis, indebtedness, and dependency on moneylenders. Therefore, in the case of common mental disorders, with their vast array of associated social and environmental determinants, it is important to go beyond the individual-exposure risk model. Lacking the basic goods and facilities for quality of life to be maintained is only one aspect of poverty; how people relate to the deprived circumstances that they find themselves in and the social circumstances is another, less well-analysed, aspect.

Urbanization is not inherently positive or negative. Underlying drivers, also referred to as social determinants, converge in urban settings which strongly influence the health status and other outcomes. These determinants include physical infrastructure, access to social and health services, local governance, and the distribution of income and educational opportunities.

Life in an Urban Slum in India

World over, urban areas are growing very fast and every week nearly 1.3 million population get added to already overcrowded urban settlements. The urban population of developing countries is projected to grow at an average annual rate of 2.4 per cent, twice the annual population growth rate of 1.2 per cent in the developing world (United Nations Population Division, 2002). Because of this rapid population growth, rising poverty levels, weak policy frameworks and inadequate public institutions, urban areas in developing countries face an enormous challenge to provide adequate infrastructure; shelter; basic services including access to safe water, sanitation, education and basic health services, employment opportunities; and ensure food security. Growing urban poverty is becoming a major concern. The magnitude and extent of urban poverty can be understood largely by looking at the conditions prevailing in urban slums. A slum may be regarded as the physical and sociocultural environment of the poor (D'Souza, 2012: 32). Slum areas are generally characterized by overcrowding, poor environmental sanitation and lack of infrastructural amenities. The inadequate public facilities and the unhygienic conditions of the slum environment have severe consequences on the overall health of the community (Basu and Basu, 2000: 181). Health conditions of the urban poor are sometimes even worse than those of the rural poor (World Health Organization, 1998). One of the reasons for this is because people in slums live on the margins of society. D'Souza (2012) explains how slums are usually located in places which are unsuitable for more profitable use and so some of the slum conditions are inherent in the physical location of the slum itself. He argues that since slums are marginal in the ecological structure it follows that slum-dwellers also occupy a marginal position in the social structure of the community. This sociocultural marginality becomes the real cause of their poverty (ibid.: 37). It is not the 'culture of poverty',[2] rather the disadvantaged conditions of the slum-dwellers are forced upon them by the dominant sections of the community to serve their own interests (Valentine, 1973: 166–67).

While slum population in general constitutes an underprivileged group, slum women, in particular, suffer from far more disadvantages than men. This has been emphasized by WHO (1978): 'malnutrition,

---

[2] The concept that poverty and slum life have a number of associated traits related to family structure, interpersonal relations, time-orientation, value systems and spending patterns that are handed down from generation to generation along the family lines (Lewis, 1961).

poor housing, overcrowded living conditions and insanitary surroundings exert their harmful effects, particularly on the health of women and children, who constitute a highly vulnerable group among the slum population in urban areas of developing countries.' Within the urban poor, women are likely to be more affected as they have less access to resources, lower employment opportunities, and face greater restrictions in accessing credit (Arun, 1999).

Social exclusion and lack of voice for poor urban women increases their vulnerability to ill health and violence. This also has a significant impact on their mental health. Another aspect of slums is the number of migrants living there. Migration, urbanization and globalization bring about rapid changes in an individual's society. Migratory populations find it strenuous to adapt to the changes and the culture shock they receive; many ailments occur as a result of having to adjust to a new social environment. In urban slum areas, migrants find the patterns of behaviour in cities conflicting with what they know from their traditions. Schwab and Schwab (1978) noted greater mental illness under social, especially metropolitan conditions of instability, turmoil, adversity, corruption and social disintegration. Basu and Basu (2000) describe how in order to reduce the distress associated with migration, migrants settle down in areas where they have established networks. Families having common ties (same village/caste/linguistic community, kin group) generally cluster together in such a way that in times of need they provide social support to each other. They observed that this social support was essential for slum women who play a major role in the family's efforts to cope with conditions of poverty. Being an underprivileged group, slum women, in particular, suffer from far more inequalities than slum men. They accumulate within themselves all the disadvantages of being low caste, poor, rural migrant and above all, women (ibid.: 190).

WOMEN, SOCIAL SPACE AND DISTRESS

An examination of women's position in society reveals that there are sufficient causes in current social arrangements to account for the surfeit of depression, anxiety and distress experienced by women. Traditional intrapsychic, biomedical approaches to mental illness have not taken into account the impact of social factors on the mental health of women. It is feminist research rather than mainstream psychological research that has demonstrated the ways in which social inequities and social assumptions about womanhood influence different aspects of women's lives, and thereby their physical and emotional health.

Following this approach has led to the realization that other disciplines apart from psychiatry require an understanding of the mental health of women. Because of this there has been an increased focus on understanding the social and anthropological factors that influence the mental health of women in the community. The most important contribution towards understanding the social origins of depression has come from the work of Brown and Harris (1978). They view depression as the central link for many kinds of problems: those that lead to depression and those that follow it. The four vulnerability factors identified in this research are: early loss of the mother (before 11 years), the lack of a confiding relationship, the presence of three or more children under fourteen, and the lack of employment. The causality between self-esteem and these four vulnerability factors could work either way. The authors suggest that depression can be best understood in terms of the contribution of current environment relative to other influences. The vulnerability factors might be evident for many women, but the current environment with new role identities and opportunities to find new sources of positive value can lessen the risk of depression.

Recent research has demonstrated the impact of social circumstances upon women's private experiences and actions. Whether it is denial of economic resources or education, legal and health services deprivation, lack of physical and mental nurturance, exhaustion from overwork, or sexual and other forms of physical and mental abuse across the life span, research corroborates that it is women who are at greatest risk. These issues not only fall within the fabric of human rights, but are also those which understandably affect mental health. In addition, the routine of women's lives render them at risk to experience more stress than men (Eichler and Parron, 1987). This reflects the greater number of social roles women fulfil as wife, mother, daughter, care-giver and an employee. Furthermore, women's reproductive role as bearer and nurturer of children produces a unique potential for stress-related effects. Thus, the well-documented higher morbidity in women's health across the life span has clear underlying biosocial causes (Vindhya, 2001). Community-based studies of mental health in developing countries suggest that 12 per cent to 51 per cent of urban adults suffer from some form of depression (see 16 studies reviewed by Blue, 1999). In India and other low-income countries, common mental disorders were about twice as high among the poor than the non-poor and there is higher prevalence of these disorders among women, especially women with lower levels of autonomy (Patel et al., 1999). As different community studies show, in India, common mental disorders were found to be associated with economic difficulties, limited decision-making agency and low levels of family support.

Religious fundamentalism and neo-liberal economic reforms are converting poor grassroots-level women in India into both agents and instruments in a process of their own disempowerment (Dhanraj, Battliwala and Misra, 2002). Though these forces are not necessarily in concert, they are, nonetheless, reconstructing gender and other social power relations. There is accumulating evidence that links mental disorders with poverty, powerlessness and alienation, conditions most frequently experienced by women. There are two main routes through which women's position in society might contribute to poor mental health outcomes, one indirect and the other more direct and extreme. The first is concerned with role-related stressors including multiple role strain, role overload and role conflict. The second includes actual sexual victimization whether through brutal stressors like rape, battering, or other forms of violence against women. While experiences of gender oppression, ranging from employment discrimination and sexual violence to trivialization of women's work, occur with regularity, the accumulation of such experiences help account for mental health risks that disproportionately affect women, such as depression, anxiety and phobic disorders (Russo and Green, 1993).

Living space referring to women's diverse locations in terms of class, caste, region and religion also determine the kind of problems and discrimination they will face. In urban spaces, where the struggle for survival is continuous, women often find themselves in spaces which by their very nature are oppressive. One of the determinants of health is poverty. The attention to the poverty-health nexus can be attributed to a broadening conceptualization of poverty, accompanying a renewed commitment to poverty alleviation (World Bank, 1990). Poverty is now viewed as multi-dimensional, embodying more than material deprivation. Raising living standards may not be sufficient to combat poverty if the health of the poor does not also improve (Wagstaff, 2001). Previously, it had been thought that absolute poverty rather than relative poverty was the only robust social determinant of ill health and that this effect was unidirectional, affecting those lower on the social ladder. Also, that health outcomes with regard to those who live in non-egalitarian societies are inferior to those who live in more egalitarian societies has led to the observation that some societies are indeed 'unhealthy' (Kawachi and Kennedy, 2002; Wilkinson, 1996).

The concepts of mental illness and distress are not just determined by the structures present in society but are also mediated by the interaction between structures and individuals. Bourdieu's work on the interaction between field and habitus offers explanatory potential. The concepts of field and habitus offer the possibility of exploring the significance of power relations in the details of ordinary lives and of understanding how structural realities of the economic, cultural and social are internalized over time to become habitualized, unconscious practices. According to him, social structures inculcate mental structures into individuals; these mental structures in turn reproduce or change social structures (Bourdieu, 1988). In a study of Mumbai, Parker et al. (2003) give an account of the stresses that affect men and women in a slum community in the north of the city. Men in this community are deeply frustrated by the lack of work and seeing few prospects of improvement, many of them fall into a pattern whereby idleness is mixed with helplessness and hostility. This has increased the burdens on women, especially, when their spouses retreat into alcoholism or lash out in episodes of domestic violence, infidelity and deliberate humiliation. Women face violence in a number of situations; in fact, many of their physical problems have their roots in the stress that they face in their daily lives.

In developing countries, women bear the burden of responsibilities as wives, mothers, educators and carers; at the same time they are a part of the labour force. In 25–33 per cent households, they are the prime source of income. Significant gender discrimination, malnutrition, overwork, and domestic and sexual violence add to the problems. Social support and the presence of close relationships (more commonly observed in rural society) appear to be protective against violence. Women do have a greater role to play in the urban set-up, but the rise in the scale of social hierarchy that should rightfully accompany this increased demand on them is still missing (Trivedi et al., 2008). Therefore, the existing social structures have an impact on the mental structures of individuals living within that social structure. Another example of how habitus influences mental health can be seen through the concept of 'caste'. Caste impinges on women's lives, intersecting with poverty and their autonomy (Deshpande 2002; Dube 1996). Lower caste women are vulnerable due to their lower socio-economic status and social exclusion, whereas high caste women have lower autonomy and less control over their lives (Mohindra 2009: 32). Therefore, the caste of women can influence the levels and kinds of distress they face.

Work and Distress

In 1988 the *Shramshakti Report* on self-employed women and women employed in the informal sector was published. It highlighted the extremely vulnerable working conditions of women, high levels of discrimination, and the health hazards they faced. It also made certain recommendations for the improvement of the working conditions of women. The World Bank's *Gender and Poverty Report* which followed a few years later made use of the data collected during the formulation of the *Shramshakti Report*. But this report reworked the findings and presented them in a different light highlighting facts like the incredible range of tasks that poor women perform, their often greater contribution to household income in spite of lower wage earnings, and their ability to make scarce resources stretch. In spite of the deteriorating conditions, the report presented these findings through a different lens: not as arguments against exploitation but rather as proof of efficiency. The report agreed with the *Shramshakti Report* that poor women required more access to resources but it said that they did not need the conditions of employment available in the formal sector as that would stifle productivity. The *World Bank Report* concluded that poor women are clearly better and more efficient economic actors with greater managerial and entrepreneurial skills than men. The dangers of this kind of perception have been pointed out by John (1999) who explains how the message that is sent across by such a presentation is that if poverty cannot be eradicated in the medium-to long-term, it can perhaps be endured through better management. And poor women are made out to be more promising managers of poverty than their men (ibid.: 113–14).

This indicates how the apparent strength of women is often used against them yet again, making them responsible for a large number of things, thereby increasing the levels of stress on them further. A study conducted in the Olinda region in Brazil found that women working in the informal sector were more likely to be a case of CMD than formal workers; no difference was found for informally working men. This implies that working outside the protection of employment legislation and with limited opportunity for skill use may be a risk for women's mental health (Ludmir and Lewis, 2005). Many studies have looked at the stressors of urbanization and industrialization; they found that spirit possession became the affliction of young, unmarried women placed in modern organizations overnight, drawing the attention of the press and the scholarly community (see Teoh, Soewondo, and Sidharta, 1975; Chew, 1978; Lim, 1978; Ong, 1987). Anthropologists studying phenomena related to spirit possession have generally linked them to culturally specific forms of conflict management that disguise and yet resolve social tensions within indigenous societies (Crapanzano and Garrison, 1977; Firth, 1967; Lewis, 1971).

A focus on the effects on women's lives underlines the paradoxes of global restructuring; deregulation has been accompanied by an increased regulation of reproduction, austerity by consumerism and a feminized workforce with increased levels of malnutrition and violence against women. When the globalization of industries (electronics, textiles) occurred, young women were preferred workers because they could be forced to accept low wages and submit to the employer's strict work regimes. Mies (1986) noted that processes are similar in developed and developing countries in this regard; they involve deregulation, flexibility of labour, 'housewifization', and an increase in informal sector work and home-based labour. The poor economic status of women increased their dependence on state welfare policies; in the late twentieth century government policies of privatization have eroded such welfare provisions. Reduced work opportunities for women without the safety net of state welfare have led to increased poverty among women. This has increased their participation in marginal unregulated activities such as street vending, working as domestic servants, prostitution, and so on. The new emphasis on cost-efficiency in different fields has led to more exploitation of women's labour, for example, hospitals becoming 'more efficient' means that patients are discharged earlier and medicines are not available for free, and women's invisible family labour is compensating for this situation. The stretchability of this invisible labour resource has its own limits; i.e., women's health gets ruined in the process. It can be seen that although globalization and urbanization increased opportunities of work for women, this has happened in a manner which is not beneficial to them. Instead of increasing their status it has mostly increased the burden on them. Being employed does have beneficial effects but only when this employment is provided in the current environment which takes care of the basic rights of women.

Households and Distress

The household, in more ways than one, is located at the centre of women's lives, being both the object of and the locale for a large chunk of their daily activities. Historical, social, cultural and economic factors directly or indirectly influence a woman's position in the household. When there is a macro change in the environment, the domestic unit as a collective, consciously or unconsciously, adopts a strategy to adjust. Women's spaces are defined within the parameters of the macro changes as also the context of the domestic strategy adopted (Deshmukh-Ranadive, 2002: 80).

Often a sharp distinction is made between the domestic and public spheres and since women are identified with the domestic, the larger macro forces are somehow delinked from their lives, hence, their lives are considered less important as compared to those of men, whose lives symbolize the public sphere. By situating analyses of mental health in terms of women within households, this research emphasizes the political nature of the household and how this influences the well-being and emotional health of women. Households are important in feminist analysis because they organize a large part of women's domestic/reproductive labour. As a result, both the composition and the organization of households have a direct impact on women's lives, in particular, on their ability to gain access to resources, to labour and to income (Moore, 1988: 55). Caste norms determine the woman's behaviour both within and outside the household. The same norms even decide her entry into the labour market and the place where she can seek employment (Deshmukh-Ranadive, 2002: 99). The roles of women within the household became even more complex with the global changes that have taken place. The structural adjustment programmes (SAPs) that were imposed on the indebted third world countries in order to bring their economies under the discipline of the neoliberal 'free market', have had disastrous consequences, particularly for poor women. The austerity programme that IMF prescribes under SAPs usually consists of devaluing a country's currency, privatizing state-run enterprises, dismantling social programmes for the poor, such as primary healthcare, free education, subsidies for basic food items and promoting export-oriented production. Increased poverty and social polarization, sparked off by neoliberal austerity programmes, have led to more violence against women, social strife and even ethnic, religious and racial war (Chossudovsky, 1994).

In a poor urban household, these and other issues combine to make life more difficult for the women. Mehrotra (1997) describes the life of a woman in an urban slum in Delhi where the husband is regarded as the head of the family. He expects to be obeyed, served and well-looked after. Women are required to keep busy with completing domestic chores or engaging in home-based production activities while men go out to earn, make purchases, gossip, play cards, consume liquor or gamble. Whatever earnings women or men have, the latter exercises more right over it. Domestic violence, particularly in the form of abuse and wife beating, is a regular occurrence in most families (ibid.).

Focus on poor women as better managers has created more difficulties for women, as was evident in the workshop 'Rethinking Microcredit' held at the World Social Forum in Mumbai. Rural women from different parts of the country spoke about how their multiple debt burdens and repayment had increased their loads to inhuman levels. Meanwhile, men in the areas where these projects were being run had become sullen and resentful as women handling so much money had become a source of humiliation. They neither understood nor acknowledged the women's onerous workload or the debt trap. Thus, apart from being overworked and anxious about mounting interest and repayments, women had to deal with this growing hostility (and possibly violence) from men (Battliwala and Dhanraj, 2007: 24).

Economic and social policies that cause sudden, disruptive and severe changes to income, employment and social capital that cannot be controlled or avoided, significantly increase gender inequality and the rate of common mental disorders. Trends have shown that the migration of women has increased in the last decade because of increasing feminization of labour. More women than men are said to suffer from mental disorders. And yet psychological distress of women has not been articulated as a distinct agenda either by the academia or the women's movement in our country (Vindhya et al., 2001).

POLICIES RELATED TO MENTAL HEALTH

Health is determined by the interaction of economic, political and social forces. Understanding the significance of this interaction means an appreciation of the interconnectedness between models of development pursued around the world and systems of domination which reduce the capacities of people, especially, poor people, to sustainably lead their lives (from the Copenhagen Conference Statement, 1992). In the fifth International Conference on Women's health issues held in 1992, it was recognized that the Structural Adjustment, now operative in about 80 countries, has increased the caring burden on women by the state withdrawing service provision in many areas. There is an erosion of women's access to food, shelter, occupation and education resulting in a deterioration in women's health. Policies related to different social issues have an impact on the level of distress that people face. Discussing all the policies is beyond the scope of this book but the Table 2.1 briefly presents the different committees and their recommendations related to mental health.

Mental health policies have changed and developed according to the prevailing notions of mental illness in the society. Before independence, the focus was on custodial care rather than therapeutic or rehabilitative care. With different committee recommendations, mental health came under the purview of the general healthcare services.

Table 2.1 *Committees and Recommendations (in relation to mental health)*

Committees	Recommendations
Bhore Committee Report (1946)	Creation of mental health organizations as part of establishments under the Director of Health Services at the centre and the Provincial Directors of Health Services in the states.
	Improvement of 17 existing mental hospitals from British India and establishing two new ones.
	Provision of facilities for training in mental health of medical professionals.
	Establishment of a department of Mental Health in the proposed All-India Medical Institute.
Mudaliar Committee (1962)	The recommendations were made under three heads: general, training and research.
	Setting up of inpatient and outpatient departments at lay hospitals, independent psychiatric and mental health clinics and institutions for the mentally ill.
	Need for training mental health personnel, orienting professional groups (like paediatricians, school teachers, nurses and administrators) in mental healthcare, and orienting medical and health personnel in mental health.
Srivastava Committee (1974)	No specific plans or proposals for developing mental health programmes.
	Important recommendations for the Community Health Volunteer (CHV) whose training had a component of mental health. CHV manual also recognized and spoke about the management of mental health emergencies and problems.
National Mental Health Programme (1982)	Ensuring the availability and accessibility of minimum mental healthcare for all, particularly the most vulnerable unprivileged sections of the population.
	Encouraging the application of mental health knowledge in general healthcare and social development.
	Promoting community participation in developing mental health services and stimulating efforts towards self-help in the community.

(Continued)

Table 2.1 *(Continued)*

Committees	Recommendations
National Health Policy (1983)	A special well-coordinated programme be launched to provide mental healthcare as well as medical care and also physical and social rehabilitation of those who are mentally retarded, deaf, dumb, blind and physically disabled, infirm and aged (GOI, 1983).
District Mental Health Programme (1996)	Providing sustainable basic mental health services to the community.
	Integrating these services with other health services.
	Early detection and treatment of patients within the community itself.
	Ensuring that patients and their relatives do not have to travel long distances to go to hospitals or nursing homes in cities.
	Taking the pressure of mental hospitals.
	Reduce stigma attached with mental illness through a change of attitude and public education.
	Treating and rehabilitating mental patients discharged from the mental hospital within the community itself.

Source: Kumar, 2005.

The National Mental Health Programme (Government of India, 1982) was the outcome of developments in providing mental healthcare through different methods as well as overall healthcare goals. The need for improvement of mental health services was emphasized in all the committee reports but there was no serious attempt to improve these services. Problems in the implementation of NMHP eventually led to the formation of the District Mental Health Programme (henceforth DMHP) (Kumar, 2005).

Currently with increase in focus on healthcare, mental health is also getting more funds and attention. One of the results of this is the enactment of the Mental Healthcare Act, 2017 which has enlarged the definition of mental illness and provides specific rights to certain groups like women and children. Although there are gaps in this Act as well it is an important step. The Act recognizes that all individuals in the country who are suffering from mental disorders have a right to get treatment, support, and lead a normal life free from discrimination and injustice. It also describes the responsibilities of various public agencies, such as the police, judicial system, and the public healthcare system, in protecting these rights; it sets goals of public mental health programmes, and determines the role of DMHP. The national health policy and mental health act both recognize the lack of good healthcare management systems, and propose systematic solutions that can rapidly improve the provision of healthcare (Mirza and Singh, 2017).

District Mental Health Programme (DMHP)

The District Mental Health Programme (under the National Mental Health Programme, 1996–97) developed in the Bellary district of Karnataka was to be implemented in several districts in all states. In Delhi, it has been started in only a few places. The first being the psychiatric OPD at Babu Jagjiwan Ram Memorial Hospital in a single room in the general ward of the hospital. Kumar (2005) studied the implementation of the DMHP in Jahangirpuri. He states that there is no signboard where the service is presently given, which leads to a lot of running around for the illiterate population, trying to locate the doctor or the room where the service is provided. The room allotted for the purpose is very small. However, the room is used for the treatment of patients as well as for distribution of medicine by the social worker. The resident doctor coming from IHBAS (Institute of Human Behaviour and Allied Sciences) in Delhi to assist the main doctor also uses the same room. With so many officials operating from the same room and in the presence of waiting patients, patients find it difficult to share their problems with the doctor. Presently the service is available twice a week. The social worker is supposed to take care of the social aspects of mental health problems, which include preparation of case history, giving insight into the sociological causes of a patient's problem to the psychiatrist, visiting patients at home, rehabilitative measures, and follow-up at the community level. It is his/her duty to arrange and organize community mental health awareness programmes along with other measures, which will enhance the coping mechanism of the community. Unfortunately in reality, the social worker just does the work of distributing medicines. The study shows that the DMHP has a curative and a bio-medical approach. The holistic approach to mental health is completely missing. Based on this study it can be reasonably established that since its inception, the DMHP was not found to be sensitive enough to these cultural variations, needs and cultural intricacies. There is no integration of mental healthcare with primary healthcare either.

In 2002, a 're-strategized' National Mental Health Programme was unveiled. But not much changed in the implementation. Jain and Jadhav (2009) describe similar practices (as mentioned in Kumar's study in Delhi) in DMHP clinics in Kanpur, where 'pills' constitute the main service that is provided by the clinics. They argue that community psychiatry has become administrative psychiatry focused on effective distribution of psychotropic medication. They attribute the practical failure of the NMHP to the disjuncture between the articulation of policy objectives and the implementation of concrete programmes.

While monitoring and evaluation activities are required to be conducted by DMHP, such activities are largely missing in all states (Gururaj et al., 2015–16). The NMH Survey finds that the financing of mental healthcare is in a state of total disarray, and there is lack of clarity about the sharing of responsibilities between central and state governments and among the various state-level departments, which also leads to large underspending of resources; for example, in 2012–13, only 42 per cent of the total funds allocated for DMHP were spent (Patel et al., 2017). The NMH survey (Gururaj et al., 2016) reports that the budgeted funds for mental health-related activities do not have clear specification, justification, and/or timely allocation, and are thus difficult to spend, and that most states were unable to utilize even clearly available funds due to the lack of clear mechanisms, guidelines, and a shortage of human resources. Convergence between programmes related to the Mental Health Act (2017) and the National Health Policy (2016) would help in addressing many gaps of implementations. According to Mirza and Singh (2017), addressing psychiatric and medical aspects of issues as well as those of management and administration of the system would help in providing quality mental healthcare. This would go a long way in addressing some of the mental health needs of women.

Finding a Way through the Labyrinth*

A group of men and women sit in a congested and poorly lit room holding their monthly team meeting. Discussions about self-help groups, problems, finances and conflicts end with the programme coordinator introducing me and saying, 'Introduce her to the Dukhyari[1] women in your groups'.

The health worker takes me to a one-room house where several women are sitting and waiting to hold a meeting. Some are sitting on the floor and some on a single bed which is the only furniture in the room. We are followed into the room by a disabled man (who I am later told is the gatekeeper for the community as he cannot travel far and therefore is responsible for the surveillance of the women there). The health worker then introduces me as someone who wants to talk to 'pagal' women, i.e., women who mutter to themselves when they are alone, keep sitting alone, and never laugh.

Research follows a trajectory, a part of which is planned and the rest gets dictated by the field that the researcher is trying to study. At various points, I was introduced in ways similar to the one quoted above; that I was someone who wanted to talk to poor women or women whose husbands hit them. When I explained that I wanted to talk to women who were distressed or depressed; they usually responded by assuring me that none of them had such problems and they were all happy and cheerful women. After which I would sit in one corner and

---

* Some sections of this chapter were originally published in the Journal *Urbanities*, Vol. 2 No. 1, May 2012, pp. 68–79 under the title, 'The Power of the Field: Reflections on Field Work Improvisations' and *The Eastern Anthropologist*, 65(2), 157–169, 2012.

[1] Suffering, Distressed or Sorrowful are the various translations that I could come up with to explain this concept based on further discussions.

listen to them while they spoke as they carried on with their work. These animated conversations of women I was privileged enough to be privy to revealed distress related to continuing aches and pains, about the problems related to being separated or widowed, about the loss of children and the sadness that followed such loss. The content of their conversations revealed their many problems and how they were having trouble coping with things but again they were not ready to talk about them with me. Although in the first couple of months everyone was welcoming they were reluctant to talk. With the exposure to many people from different NGOs, funding bodies, government officials and others coming in to ask questions, they had mastered the art of giving exactly the information that they wanted to give and nothing more.

Ideas related to using mental health screening tools were dropped at this stage and I had to do a lot of unlearning. At the outset I was still a psychiatric social worker attempting to study common mental disorders in a clinical way. Although from the beginning there was an awareness that being trained in a set-up where the main emphasis was on bio-medical care would colour my perceptions, it was only in the field that I realized just how deeply ingrained that training was. Initially, I started talking to the women in the hospital but in order to understand the high prevalence of common mental disorders in the community it was important to move out of the hospital. As a tentative step towards moving into the community, I first visited the community mental health programme of the hospital. There I found that the women came from different places and talking to women in that set-up would make it difficult to link the geographical, environmental and sociocultural factors and psychosocial distress faced by women. Therefore, a decision was made to carry out research in the community which also had access to some psychiatric facility so that the choices that women made (when they had several options available to them) could be explored. Another reason for this was that there were already existing studies (Addlakha, 2008; Vindhya, 2001) that explored the experience of women within hospital milieus, but the experience of women undergoing psychosocial distress within the community had not been explored extensively. While working in the community, reflective practices had to be employed as there was a need to guard against the automatic medical explanations arising from the researcher's training. Another area of concern was of the interviewer's effect (gender, class, caste, marital status) on the responses of the informants. An embodied perspective emphasizes how the researcher's social positions influence what questions we ask, whom we approach in the field, how we make sense of our fieldwork experience, and how we analyse and report our findings (Naples, 2003).

This study aimed to explore the reasons for psychosocial distress of women in an urban resettlement colony and therefore, followed a qualitative research paradigm. Frequently, the terms used for describing distress include: mental illness, mental disorders, mental health and psychosocial disability; each emerges from a certain world-view. Initially some of these terms were used in this research because the idea was to study common mental disorders. As the research progressed, the researcher began to question the use of these terminologies and decided to use the terms distress, psychosocial disability and mental health to more appropriately capture women's experiences. In order to present the experiences of women in their own voice and relate them to the larger macro forces, there was a need to use different theoretical perspectives and hence the approach used was multi-dimensional.

Reflexive ethnography and feminist approaches were used to carry out the research. These methods are important in this kind of research as distress (as mental illness) has largely been understood from a biomedical viewpoint, overlooking the impact of sociocultural factors on a person. A multi-disciplinary approach requires greater awareness of the field work strategies employed. It was also important for the researcher to be aware of the disciplinary influences on her observations, choice of topic and so on. Reflexivity therefore, became even more essential. An ethnographic research strategy with observational methods as the central plank was used. Participant observations enabled the researcher to record the social setting in which the participants lived, the interactions, actions and behaviour of people, as well as understand how people interpret these actions and act on them. In-depth interviews helped in generating narratives which facilitated the exploration of the links between everyday life experiences and broad-based social structural processes (Campbell, 1998).

Tenets of institutional ethnography[2] have been used to explain the linkages between psychosocial distress in the everyday lives of women and their larger social context. Smith (1987) argues that the position of women is affected by their socio-historical circumstances and their relationship with the relations of ruling. She further adds that the category 'women' is not all-embracing, exclusive or fixed. Its limits are constantly transcended as each woman brings a unique perspective (ibid.). According to Smith, 'standpoint' as the design position in institutional ethnography creates a point of entry into discovering the social that does not subordinate the knowing subject to objectified forms of knowledge of society or political economy. It is a method of inquiry that works from the actualities of people's everyday lives and experiences to discover the social as it extends beyond experience. The institutional ethnographer works from the social in people's experience to discover its presence and organization in their lives and to explicate or map that organization beyond the local of the everyday.

In order to understand these linkages between micro and macro experiences, basing the study in a resettlement colony was important, as the impact of macro-level policy changes is reflected starkly in these places. Jahangirpuri became the appropriate place to carry out the study as it originated as a part of the government's policy of moving slums to the peripheral areas of Delhi in the 1970s and had a varied

---

[2] This examines the dialectical interplay between the relations of the ruling as expressed and mediated through texts, and the actual experiences of people as they negotiate and implement those texts. It is a method of elucidating and examining the relationship between everyday activities and experiences and larger institutional imperatives (Smith, 1987).

population facing different kinds of stress. Since the District Mental Health Programme was located there, it was also a space which had access to different kinds of avenues (ranging from bio-medical, counselling to traditional healing practices) for seeking mental healthcare. Within Jahangirpuri the household is the structure which has seen multiple changes over the decades. Women's distress and how they cope with it is determined by the structure of the households and interactions with people within it. Theoretical and practical insights from across disciplines (sociology, anthropology, social work, psychology and psychiatry) were used in the formulation of the questions as well in conducting research. Social and anthropological methods were emphasized rather than purely clinical methods in conducting research related to mental health and distress. The interdisciplinary nature of the research made this engagement more difficult as well as more enabling.

JAHANGIRPURI:
MULTIPLE VOICES, MULTIPLE REALITIES

In the 1970s, slum rehabilitation schemes were launched as a result of which several resettlement colonies were built; Jahangirpuri, in the north of Delhi, was one such. Such colonies were virtually turned into new slums due to insufficient basic services and little planning and lack of control on the further development of the allotted plots (Gupta, 1983: 210). Jahangirpuri is situated in north-west Delhi. It represents a mixture of slum characteristics and refugee resettlement pattern. The colony suffers from space congestion, has only few civic amenities, poor sanitation, unauthorized constructions and rampant encroachments of land. There is a mix of permanent housing structures and small, precarious, unstable hutments (*jhuggis*) set up as part of a resettlement drive to shift slum dwellers in 1976. The economic condition of the slum dwellers worsened due to the occurrence of floods in 1978 and the burden of poverty was hoisted onto women who took up the task of looking after the family and children. The slum is divided into eleven blocks. It largely consists of rural migrants from various states (Gujarat, Uttar Pradesh, Bihar, Haryana, Madhya Pradesh and

Rajasthan) who entered various areas of Delhi in search of work. Earlier they lived in *jhuggi-jhopri* clusters or hutments in different areas and were later shifted to such resettlement colonies. Notably the migrants were overwhelmingly poor, generally belonging to deprived sections of society. They were allotted plots in the colony. A majority of them, however, sold off the plots in the course of time and returned to building *jhuggis* in the same colony (Mehrotra, 1997: 22).

Although Bhalswa Jahangirpuri city has a population of 197,148, its urban/metropolitan population is 16,349,831 of which 8,750,834 are male and 7,598,997 are female (Census, 2011). The population structure reflects heterogeneity in terms of ethnic, caste and religious differences. Each block consists of people who live together bound by ethnicity, religion, caste and kinship considerations. The key informants of the study divided the population of Jahangirpuri into 60 per cent Hindu, 30 per cent Muslims and 15 per cent Scheduled Caste. These figures are supported by the 2011 Census data as well: Hinduism is the majority religion with 76.47 per cent followers, Islam is followed by approximately 21.57 per cent, Christianity 0.29 per cent, Jainism by 0.08 per cent, Sikhism by 1.51 per cent and Buddhism by 1.51 per cent. The Scheduled Caste segment makes up 21.9 per cent of the population.

The occupational structure is quite diverse. There are people working in government services, private services, sales, production, labour, self-employed services, and petty business (around 30%).[3] Basically the population is involved in the informal sector for bare survival. A large number of them belong to the categories of drivers, mechanics, ragpickers, brushmakers, factory workers, rickshaw pullers, construction workers, or house cleaners, etc. (around 70%). Homemakers too are often engaged in home-based production of items like iron-edges and other packing material; they are also engaged in activities where contractors give them certain vegetables to separate from the crop for

---

[3] Figures are based on a socio-economic survey conducted by the organization Deepshakti between 2010 and 2012.

around ₹25 per day. There are certain blocks (C, CD Park, G *jhuggi*) where the main occupation is ragpicking—men, women and children all are involved in this activity.

The total literacy rate of Bhalswa Jahangirpuri was 77.66 per cent in 2011 which is less than the average literacy rate (86.21%) of Delhi. The male literacy rate was 84.21 per cent and the female literacy rate was 69.93 per cent (Census, 2011). Rana (2001) in her study of Jahangirpuri found that 91 per cent of the female population in the high- and middle-income families were literate as compared to only 16 per cent in the low-income group. In certain blocks, children go to the small schools run by various NGOs and are often helped by them to enrol in the MCD[4] schools. Overpopulation, poverty and illiteracy are the factors behind the high crime rate in the colony. Gambling and alcoholism are highly prevalent which leads to violence within the households. During the day, groups of men can be seen gambling at most street corners. Drug addiction has been increasing among adolescents and even among pre-adolescent boys in certain areas. Although men are considered the heads of households, the responsibilities lie basically with the women who look after the household and are also often working to financially support their families.

Population density is quite high with five to six people living in one room. Dwellings are small—on an average about 2.5 m wide and about 3 m tall. A majority of dwellings are built of brick, some to a good standard. Some dwellings have a second storey where the access is either by a steep and narrow staircase or by a crude ladder with widely spaced rungs which is frequently placed externally to save on internal space. The houses are self-built and owner-occupied. Most households (median of five persons) live in one or two rooms with a median of 16 square metres of floor space and eight square metres of dedicated living space (i.e., only about two square metres per person) (Kellet and Tipple, 2000). There are some small open spaces on the

---

[4] Municipal Corporation of Delhi.

streets, but there are a few more formal community spaces, such as temple courtyards.

The houses that I went to were different depending on the socio-economic background of the woman concerned. Although most houses had two rooms on one floor, the differences appeared in the manner in which the houses were set up. In a few of the houses, there was very little furniture and there were mattresses rolled up on the side with one bed in the room; all houses had a television. We usually sat on a mat on the floor. There were few items on the walls and all that could be seen were utensils and things needed for daily activities. In most of the houses the kitchen was installed in the first room and the internal room was used for sleeping, watching TV and receiving any visitors. Toilets were usually outside the house in a corner next to the main door. The relative financial condition of the families could be assessed from the furniture that they had; for example, in a few houses there would only be a bed in the second room whereas in others there were chairs along with the bed.

Some of the families lived in a one-room set-up with no furniture or TV. Everyone would carry out activities in the same room, in other words, the room would serve multiple purposes. Some people would be sleeping, children studying, and older girls doing some household work or some part-time work that they had taken on. There were also houses that just had a curtain on the side and a wooden wall in front of the door. Inside was a two-room set filled with items of everyday living (utensils, clothes); electric wires were hanging at the entrance, there was usually one single bulb in the room and no fan. There were no windows and the walls were unpainted. For this kind of dwelling, the family would have to pay ₹800 as house rent and an additional ₹200 for electricity; electric metres had not come to this part of the colony.

In contrast to this, there were also households where the family had multiple floors so I met them in a sitting room which had a TV, chairs and centre table—obviously this was a place to receive visitors.

The different kinds of housing were often determined by the blocks. Slightly more space in the house as well as furniture (beds, chairs, cupboards) would be there in most houses in I-block which being closer to the main road was also known as a 'good block'. Some places like C-block and CD Park were considered to be in a very bad state. They had the reputation of being dirty and difficult places to live in. C block with its high density of population and migrant people (who were considered to be from Bangladesh) was considered an unsafe place where crime was high because of the *'Bangali Log'* as the people living there were called. Chaudhuri (2005) in her research on identity formation amongst Bengali migrants in a Delhi slum used the term Bengali Muslims (which is used by the people in the community). She explains that it remains an unresolved issue whether they are residents of Indian or migrants from Bangladesh (ibid.: 284). She further says that everyone assumes that the migrants are from Bangladesh but no one ever said that they were from Bangladesh (ibid.: 294). The situation in Jahangirpuri is similar.

One of the workers who lived in C block told me that 'I block *acha hai kyunki wahan Hindu log rehten hai'* (I block is good because Hindus stay there). This was a sentiment that I was to hear again as another woman told me that places inhabited by Punjabis and Banias were clean and relatively crime-free as compared to places where Telis, Kolis and Muslims lived, which were full of crime and were dangerous. I heard this many times in the period that I spent in the field from both Hindus as well as Muslims. The difference would be that Muslims would hold the people from *Bengal* (Bengali-speaking Muslims), who they said kept coming in every year, responsible for the filth, fights and crime. On the surface, caste and religious differences were brushed aside. But a little probing revealed the existing biases. This is elaborated on later in the book.

Other explanations were given such as the one about many meat shops in C block which led to an increase in problems as they were not always kept very clean by their owners. There were some lanes which most of the workers avoided; I realized the reason for this when I walked into the wrong lane and was unable to see for a few seconds as my face was covered by flies which got inside my glasses as well. Those few seconds frightened me and I walked very quickly out of the lane stopping to breathe only when I was out of there. Looking back at my reactions I realized that the narrowness of the lane along with the darkness (multiple floors led to restricted light in the lane), with the flies and dogs next to the meat shops leads to constriction of space for walking. This is turn can create an illusion of being trapped which is likely to activate the latent stereotypes. Blaming the other reduces our fear and helps us in overlooking the fact that 'the other' whom we want to blame is forced to live in these surroundings because of lack of choice. This was apparent in what many women had to say who despaired at the places where they had to live. Places by their very nature exert a strong influence on the way our lives are structured. Thus, 'Places have multiple meanings (for their inhabitants) that are constructed spatially…(and) need to be understood apart from their creation as the locales of ethnography… (more crucial is to) raise questions about how the anthropological study of place relates to experiences of living in places' (Rodman, 1992: 641).

STARTING OUT:
COMPLEXITIES IN CONVERSATIONS

The nature of the research and the place meant that the best collection of data would happen by following the conversational style for an interview. However, there were difficulties in accessing women, time, space as well as the place of interview.

Initial interactions were through focus group discussions with women who had come for their self-help group meetings. Here, I learnt about the history of the place from the perspective of the women living there and I also started becoming a familiar figure. In this phase I began to gradually understand some of the dynamics and the use of language that was required. In some group discussions, the women turned their faces away when I tried to talk to them, a signal that they had no interest in me and were suspicious of my motives. These groups were usually comprised Bengali-speaking Muslim women; they described their place of origin as Kolkata. Categorization of all Bengali-speaking Muslims as Bangladeshis is one of the 'secrets' of Jahangirpuri; they were covertly held responsible for the high rate of crime in the area. Because of this strong bias many of the Muslim women in the area made sure that they mentioned their region of origin (especially if they were not from Kolkata) within India. It appeared that this emphasis was to illustrate their legal status and right to live here. When I too spoke about 'Bangladeshis', the programme coordinator reprimanded me. According to him, many of the Bengali-speaking Muslims had been living in the area for decades and if I talked like that no one would be willing to talk to me. This helped me understand the reasons behind the women's reluctance in talking about their background. I could have been and was probably perceived as a person from the government who wanted details about their citizenship. As a researcher I was trying to understand the background of the women I was talking to but too intense an inquiry into the antecedents of the people could raise suspicions very easily; I learnt over time that asking too many questions led to fewer answers. Naples (2003) speaks about reflective practices being employed throughout ethnographic investigation and implemented at different levels, ranging from remaining sensitive to others and how we interact with them to a deeper recognition of the power dynamics that infuse ethnographic encounters.

My initial idea was to have at least two interviews with each of the women. I would have the first interaction in the school or office where they came for the meeting. Subsequently, I would meet them in their homes so that they could talk in privacy. I had not taken into account that I was imposing my ideas of privacy and confidentiality on them. This idea was not met with enthusiasm; in fact, the idea of me coming to their homes might have deterred women from talking to me. One of the women explained to me that it was better for them to talk in the meetings surrounded by other women. She said that she felt more secure talking about her life with the women around her. In her house if someone heard her speaking about her difficulties it might be construed as criticism and she would have to face the anger of her family. Therefore, she had to be very careful while talking to me in her house whereas she would be much more comfortable outside her house. Another woman who spoke to me while sitting outside on the steps of a school where a camp was going on pointed out her husband and said:

> *Woh soch raha hoga main aapse kya baat kar rahin hun, usko lagta hai ki main hamesha uski burai karti hun, isliye main kisi se zyada baat nahi kar sakti.*
>
> (He must be wondering what we are talking about; he feels I am always criticizing him which is why I can never talk for long).

These explanations highlighted the fact that for women often there were no spaces that they could call their own and the concept of privacy was secondary to the concept of safety. There were some women whom I met several times and they even invited me to their homes to talk, but I learnt to check with them properly which was the best place to talk. By becoming more open about talking in the time and space that the women were comfortable talking in, the places for interviews became unorthodox: corner of a small room which was filled with other women, waiting area of a dispensary, nurse's station at a community health centre, steps outside the centre, standing at the door of the house in the street, and many more. All the women helped me to rework my concept of privacy; privacy from my point of view was akin to safety from the gaze of others whereas for some women the presence of others (other women) provided safety. The notions of privacy differ from woman to woman; I had to learn to adapt to the situation wherein they were comfortable rather than imposing my own ideas of privacy on them. Unlearning habits of thinking and social practices that are taken for granted helps to facilitate the unfolding of the phenomena of everyday life in their own frame, uninhibited and undisturbed by the presence of the fieldworker. The 'manner of their unfolding' is thus the appropriate subject and the appropriate object of inquiry in fieldwork. The practice and discourse of unlearning is concerned with the manner in which phenomena become accessible for inquiry. It seeks to minimize distortions introduced on one hand by conducts that inhibit openness in discourse and on the other hand by social practice that generate different conflicts. In this way it opens up social spaces closed by the hegemony of method (Savyasaachi, 1998: 85).

The initial plan was to identify women who were known to be more distressed as compared to others with the help of NGO workers and group leaders. Then I would screen them with a standardized questionnaire SRQ-20[5] (self-reporting questionnaire) and women who fell in the distressed category would be interviewed in detail. In most studies the cut-off point for the SRQ-20 used for differentiating probable cases from non-cases was 7/8 (Blue, Ducci, Jaswal, Ludermir and Harpham 1995: 85). Das and Das (2005) outline how in the literature on psychiatric epidemiology caseness can refer to three things: (1) A case that is typical of the symptoms for a particular diagnostic category; (2) that is exemplary with regard to a set of symptoms; and one (3) that represents a cut-off point of a distribution that represents the scores on a set of symptoms. Since this is not a clinical study, the last criterion would be used. The fundamental point here is that sadness, anxiety and fluctuations in mood are part of normal life but can be seen as symptoms of a mental disorder when they interfere with normal functioning,

After my initial experiences and after speaking to many women and reworking my ideas of privacy and confidentiality, I decided to bring in the questions of the screening tool within the purview of the narratives and subsequently focus on those narratives in which

---

[5] Instrument developed by WHO to screen for psychiatric disturbance especially in developing nations. It consists of 20 questions such as: Are you frightened easily? Do you sleep well? Is your digestion poor? Do you feel unhappy? These questions can be answered with a Yes or No.

the criteria of common mental disorders were matched. A decision was made to spend the initial months in attending the meetings and observing; I did not remain an observer for long. I was often given files of some group to collect money, count money for the workers, and help them out with the work. As I performed these activities, I gained more acceptance; none of this was planned, rather it happened organically. I gained greater insight into the reasons why I was accepted by them when one day one of the workers introduced me to some of the students. She told them that I spend a lot of time in the field walking around the various blocks in the hot summer months with them and therefore I was like them. As a researcher we often like to think that we have planned many things and have thought of various strategies to gain acceptance in the field; in that assumption we forget the agency of the people whom we interact with. When and how they give us space is dependent not so much on our strategies but more on their judgement of us. While we go into the field with some criteria in our head, we often fail to take into account that we will also be judged and evaluated. And it is only when we pass their evaluation which is based on their criteria that we are given a chance to get a deeper look at their everyday lives.

Another important aspect of gaining acceptance in the field consists of our attire, speech and eating habits. In the NGO, eating lunch on the first floor (with the administrative staff) or downstairs (with the community workers) was also one of the determinants of acceptance by the workers who took pride in being the real link to the field. With increasing acceptance, the workers who belonged to the community told me more about it, and introduced me to their groups in a manner which made me more trustworthy. The workers often took me for meetings where they thought that there was a woman who needed to 'talk'. After months of observation I learnt that if I explained my research and then listened, women told me many different things which I would have never thought to ask. I still asked my questions but learnt to frame them in a different manner and to time them appropriately. I acquired a new language which was more in keeping with the style of communication of the women in Jahangirpuri.

Changing my manner of communication ensured that women approached me rather than the other way around. One day while I was sitting in the government dispensary a woman approached me and asked whether I was the person talking to women about their difficulties. She had heard about me from her son who worked in Deepshakti and expressed the wish to talk to me. This was important as talking about personal distress and about one's life is an exhausting process. Women who did not want to share their life story could not be singled out even if they did appear to be going through a difficult time. The nature of the community being what it was, most people were soon aware of what I was doing, and talking to me could soon 'label' women as explained at the beginning of the chapter. Sometimes samples have to be self-selected because of the nature of research and this appeared to be one of those instances. I had to wait for the women to approach me after I had explained the nature of my research. This strategy was not without its difficulties. It meant that things took longer; some women came to talk to me because of their own agenda. Most of the women were exposed to many government and non-government programmes. Many of them asked me what they would get after talking to me; when I explained that they would not get anything material, they would walk away. It was only women who were genuinely distressed and wanted to share their experiences who stayed behind to talk about their lives. They felt that I was talking about them when I explained my work. Some of the women wanted referrals to adequate services, others just wanted to share.

In order to contact women who were not a part of any SHGs, I also went through one of health centres run by MCD. The ANMs working there took me to the *jhuggi-jhopri* (JJ) clusters where they provided services. In one of the centres, I was able to talk to women with the help of the nurses and paramedical staff. Along with an allopathic doctor, these centres provided homeopathic and Ayurveda treatment as well. Many of the women consulted two of the specialists or sometimes even all three. I was able to interview the homeopathic doctor who sat in the centre; he spoke to me for some time but asked me to come back if I wanted to talk to the women. I was refused permission after that as I was told that I could not be allowed to talk to women in a government facility. I was unable to meet the Ayurvedic doctor as whenever I visited the centre he was unavailable.

BACKGROUND OF THE WOMEN

In addition to the focus group discussions, informal conversations and interviews with the health providers, in-depth interviews were conducted with 42 women. The age of the women interviewed ranged from 16 years to 78 years. Most of the women interviewed were in the age group of 20–50 years. The largest number (n=14) were in the age group of 30–40 years. There was an effort to include women from different age groups so that stresses faced during different life and family stages could be understood. It was difficult to get the women in the younger age group to talk; power dynamics present within the community could have prevented many of them from talking to the researcher. Among the age group of women that I interviewed, education had never been a priority. Out of the total women interviewed, 23 had never gone to school, ten of them reported studying till Class V to X, some of them said that they had gone to school till sixth or seventh standard and then left schooling. Some went to school irregularly for several years and then cleared class X through an open exam, one was still in school, her education had been delayed because of her disability. Three women had completed studies till the tenth standard and three of them had studied till the twelfth standard. The occupation details of the women are presented in Table 3.1.

Although there are some women who are listed in the category of homemakers, it must be remembered that all of them were carrying out household work as well. The categorization is for women who were exclusively involved in this, but categorization here is difficult as the status would change frequently. Nineteen of the women reported being homemakers but many of the women in the area often took seasonal work which they did from home. Some of them said that they

Table 3.1 Occupational Details of the Women

Occupation	Number of Women
Home makers (many took on seasonal work at home)	19
Home-based work (papad-making, mending clothes, straightening wires)	4
Rag-picking	4
Housemaids	2
Peons	2
Running tea stalls	2
Health workers	2
Masseuses	1
Teachers (crèche)	1
Vegetable sellers	1
Construction workers	1
Factory workers	1
Unemployed*	1
Students	1

Source: Compiled by author.

Note: *She has been listed under unemployed and not under homemaker as she was actively looking for work outside the house.

had never worked because in their kinship groups, it was considered derogatory for women to work outside the house even if there was an income crunch. Two of the women from Gujarat reported the same but said that because of financial difficulties they were forced to work sometimes, this was usually when the families had to repay loans which could get accumulated because of losses and health problems.

Four of the women were involved in ragpicking and four said that they did home-based work (*papad*-making, mending clothes, straightening aluminium wires), three were going to the flats for daily work, two as maids and one as a masseuse. Two of the women worked as peons in offices and two ran tea stalls. The two women who were running their tea stalls had worked as ragpickers and had also worked in a factory; with the help of money from the SHG they had started their own tea stalls. Two of the women worked as health workers, one in an NGO and the other as an ASHA worker.

Marriage is considered a very important event in the community. Twenty-nine of the women were married and living with their husbands at the time of the interview, seven were separated and four were widowed, two of them were unmarried. Two of the women who were separated were making efforts to reunite with their husbands, one through family intervention and the other was planning to take some legal action. The reasons for this were related to pressure from the community, inability of the natal family to support the women and so on. One woman's husband wanted to come back to her after his other wives had left him but she was refusing to take him back. One of the women believed that her husband might come back to her because of her two sons but she was unsure whether she could trust him again. Being married and living with their husbands provided a status to women and gave them a certain amount of permissiveness. For example, women who dressed up in the absence of a husband were often commented on. Although some women reported that their husbands had been in out-of-marriage relationships, they chose to stay on in the relationship for various reasons.

Out of all the married women, 10 had husbands who were unemployed. Reasons for unemployment ranged from addiction to health problems. Ten were working in 'private' jobs (electrician, driver, *mistri*, tailor, cook, supplying goods to companies), five were self-employed and three were working in factories. The work of self-employed men ranged from selling vegetables and utensils to owning small jewellery shops. One of the husbands was a landowner and they received rent from their lands while one worked as a ragpicker and one was working in the Sub-divisional magistrate's office. The employment details of only those husbands were taken who were living with their wives or contributing to the family income.

The household income described by the women was not really a stable income wherein a fixed amount came in every month. In most households one income would be the stable income and others would supplement it and this could differ from month to month. Either the husband or the wife was in a stable job or one of the older children was working which ensured that a certain amount of money came into the house every month. In some cases, children were going for ragpicking even when they were supposed to go to school. Most women took on some temporary work at home and earned some money by that. In some households, the husbands were in regular employment but got very little money home as it was spent on alcohol or gambling. Some men were also maintaining two households which would further decrease their contribution to each house. Eleven houses (of separated and widowed women) were solely female-headed and supported by the women themselves with a little support from their natal families. In one of the households, the two grown-up sons were not contributing to the family income and the woman was also bringing up her two granddaughters as their father refused to take responsibility for them.

Twenty households were in the income bracket of ₹5,000–10,000, eleven were earning less than ₹5000 a month. Four households were in the bracket of ₹10,000–15,000; two in between ₹15,000–20,000 and two were earning more than 20,000. Three of the women were unable to describe the actual income as they were dependent on their families for meeting their basic needs; two women were supported by their natal families and one woman described how her sons paid for basic needs like electricity, food, water, clothes as well as for their sisters' education.

With respect to children there is a marked preference for sons within the community and being the mother of a son elevates the status of a woman. One of the women described how after the birth of her son, the abuse and violence that she had faced from her husband and mother-in-law had stopped. One had a son after five

Table 3.2 Number of Children

Number of Women	Number of Children
3	0
5	1
6	2
8	3
10	4
6	5
2	6
1	7
1	8

Source: Compiled by author.

daughters and said that she had been forced by her mother-in-law to have the last two children. Table 3.2 shows the number of children each women had. These do not include the children who had already died. One of the women had recently lost her grown-up son because of health problems. One had lost her child and did not have any children at the time of interview. One woman was pregnant during the interview.

With respect to region of origin, 21 women belonged to Delhi, 10 to Uttar Pradesh, five were from West Bengal, two from Gujarat and one each from Haryana, Rajasthan, Bihar and Madhya Pradesh. 23 women were Hindu, 17 were Muslim, one was Sikh and one Christian. Eight of the women belonged to the Dalit community (they have been included among the Hindus in religion as the women wore symbols of marriage worn by Hindus and often followed similar religious practices). Caste identities in the area were difficult to access; as a researcher I found it difficult to probe beyond a point. When women introduced themselves, they would only mention their first names. In the SHG registers also only the first names of the women were mentioned and even when they were asked their full names, they would repeat their first names. Grover (2011) talks about the disguising of caste identities in her field site; she describes how people introduced themselves with incomprehensible and multiple caste names. This is indicative of how caste remains a strong social marker and continues to play a central role in Delhi's low income neighbourhoods (ibid.: 104).

RECIPROCAL RELATIONSHIPS: FINDING AN ANCHOR

Talking about distress, eliciting information about its causes is not easy for a strange person in a community which is suspicious of strangers. I was able to meet a lot of women and talk to them because of the support of the women working in Deepshakti. But the woman who became one of my key informants and gave me insights into the workings of the community and allowed me to 'see' her life as well was Radha. Radha was a health worker in the community and was assigned to help me in my initiation into the community. She took me under her tutelage and through her I was able to access many spaces and gain acceptance. The decision to record her life history was not mine but hers. Life histories represent the lives of exceptional rather than representative or average persons in the community. They are people who are usually eloquent and sensitive in their presentation of personal and cultural data. L.L. Langness (1965, cited in Pelto and Pelto, 1970) argues that very often the chief anthropological concern is the patterning of people's beliefs and conceptualizations of past events, rather than the truth and falseness of these accounts. They become important in examining patterns of general values, foci of cultural interests and perceptions of social and natural relationships rather than as true life histories. After observing my interactions with other women in the community, Radha asked me to record her life history. I met Radha regularly and she started talking to me about her problems. But if I mentioned talking in detail for the purpose of research, she resisted. She would ask me what she would get out of it. When I could offer nothing concrete she would laugh and say that her case study had been quoted many times in the organization's success stories. I went through these success stories which were brief reports related to the impact assessment of programmes. They only gave an overview of her life. The reasons which led to Radha's life history being selected for detailed description are described in a later chapter.

As I became a regular visitor, Radha started involving me more in her work. She found ways of making the best use of resources that I had—language and writing skills. She would ask me to accompany her to the government offices and ensured that I did the talking. While taking me around with her on work, she observed me: my attitudes and ways of working. Gradually as the relationship evolved and there was increased reciprocity, she started talking more about her life, her opinions and what she wanted to do. There were times when she was better at eliciting information about me and my life than the other way around. For example, when she wanted to know more about my house and I was unable (and unwilling) to give her the size of the plot, she immediately asked me how many rooms there were. When I replied that there were four rooms her next question was *'kitchen, toilet aur latrine alag hai?'*(Kitchen, toilet and bathing area separate?). This assessment helped her in placing me in a social category and get more precise knowledge of the space in which I lived.

While taking me around the community Radha gave me details of the community and the changes that had occurred there; she gave me a picture of the community as it appeared to her. She took me to a woman's group meeting and initially introduced me as someone who wanted to talk to 'mad' women—women who screamed, shouted and cried. I had to intervene and clarify that that was not all, and I wanted to talk to women who were going through difficult times and were distressed. The clarification of my research objectives was also one of the reasons that motivated her to talk to me. Radha's life history which is presented later focuses on the discourse of distress and ways of coping with it.

Information about Radha's life was gathered by using the method of triangulation, a mixture of observation and almost casual chats with me taking notes. In addition, information about her was obtained from her colleagues through 'fragments of narratives' by different people at different points of time.

HEALERS AND HEALTH WORKERS

In an attempt to understand the mental health problems of a community it was important to meet the people who were accessed by the women in case of difficulties. It is not easy to approach anyone in a place where divisions are clear and there is suspicion about the other's actions. It was through the introduction given by the NGO that I was able to access many of them.

The medical practitioners (doctors) in the government facilities had no hesitation in talking to me as they were in secure positions and I could pose no threat to them. They were also the ones who took most time to understand what I was trying to do and even when I explained, did not see much relevance in it. They presented their view of the community but were not very concerned about the daily lives of people. Their responses and positions will be discussed in a later chapter in detail. One of them was waiting impatiently for a transfer to a 'better' place; she was in fact transferred some time after I spoke to her. For a long time, the health centre did not get a replacement and was managed exclusively by the nurse and ANMs. More insights about the place and people were given by the other staff: nurse, lab technician, and ANMs. They were the ones who had better interactions with the local people and were more involved in their lives. They had a good idea what was happening in the lives of the people, especially the women who came to the centre.

The other two, a *maulvi* and a registered medical practitioner (RMP), only spoke to me because of the association with the NGO. The RMP was hesitant initially which was probably because many places had been shut down after the crackdown by the police. There was an effort being made in the community by the authorities to shut down the places which were being run by 'quacks' (as the medical fraternity would call them) or 'private doctors' (as the people in the area called them).

Since the concept of 'mental illness' and distress varies within communities, the narratives of women have to be analysed in the context of the community. The views presented here are predominantly from the women in the community. The accounts of men are mostly from the prominent men in the community (programme coordinator, RMP, Homeopath, NGO workers). This was also a result of the choice of gatekeepers: the NGO wherein most of the workers were women as well as a dispensary which catered to the reproductive health needs of women. Naples (2003) explains that some perspectives might not surface during the course of the research study, therefore 'findings' are always partial and unstable, and most research efforts remain a work-in-progress. The presentation and interpretation of findings thereby become even more difficult. During the initial period, the information gleaned might be generic because the subjects remain alert about the status of the researcher. But when the relationships deepen, the boundaries become fuzzy; although to a certain extent that is the aim of the researcher, it also creates a dilemma for the researcher in terms of presentation of data. Wolf (1992) asks whether by studying subjects and exploring their lives and by attempting to improve women's living situations, researchers are imposing another (powerful) society's values. The researcher must therefore maintain a delicate balance between imposing her/his views and completely repressing what she/he believes in. Interpretation of interviews was done within a reflexive frame as often it is during the process of interpretation that the researcher silences the voice of the informant and their own voice takes over. Behar (1993) discusses her inclination to fit Esperanza's story into the prevailing model of feminist studies of Latin American Studies but concluded that the ethnographer's desire to produce stories to empower the people she studies must be grounded in allowance for the way women in other cultures 'misbehave'. There must be respect for the different ways of making sense. This was especially important as I had learnt from the field that when my voice was the primary one (approaching people, asking questions) there were no other voices. When I learnt to be silent, that is when I could hear the voices of the women. The voice of the informants must be primary as what people present in their interviews is after all the results of their perception, their interpretation of the world, which is of extreme value to the researcher because one may assume that it is the same perception that informs their actions.

Deconstructing Madness

Possession and Pains*

The construct of madness has changed over the years theoretically and also in the everyday lives of people. The understanding of madness in a community is influenced by the structures present therein. In India for example, far less attention in paid to 'mental illness' as compared to physical illness (Srivastava, 2002). This is also because illness and disability are understood through the theory of *karma* (if one has committed misdeeds in the previous birth, one has to inevitably bear the consequences). If illness or disability is a result of the sins of the previous birth then one is called upon to accept it as divine retribution (Mehrotra, 2004: 37). While studying these cultural meanings, however it is important to keep a few things in mind. Culture is not understood as static or homogenous. Anthropologists emphasize that culture is not a single variable but rather comprises multiple variables, affecting all aspects of experience. Culture is inseparable from economic, political, religious, psychological, and biological conditions (Kleinman and Benson, 2006). It is dynamically interactive and a developing socio-psychic system. At any point in time the culture of a community is engaged in the joint production of meaning (Douglas, 2004: 88). It is through this joint production of meaning that the findings in this chapter are presented.

---

* Some sections of this chapter have been published in the *Sociological Bulletin*, 64 (3), September–December 2015, pp. 341–55.

CONNOTATIONS OF MADNESS

Behaviours which are away from the 'norms' of a society are given varied meanings depending on the cultural context. Rivers (1924) names three sets of explanations which are seen by people as causes of disease: natural causes; human agency; action of some supernatural or spiritual being. According to him these three sets are so closely interrelated that disentanglement of each from the rest is difficult or near impossible. In spite of this difficulty, an effort has been made to disentangle the findings and present them in a manner which is comprehensible.

Here the explanatory models of 'madness' that exist in the community are explored. An explanatory model is a symbolic representation of distress applied to a particular case of human suffering or illness. It is a culturally based, cognitive attempt to cope with questions regarding the aetiology, onset, manifestations, treatment and prognosis of the particular illness or suffering (Good and Good, 1986; Marsella, 1993).

All human societies frame the bodily and behavioural manifestations of sickness and distress within the contours of some symbolic map (Bilu and Witztum, 1993; Obeysekere, 1970). This shift from immediate experience to symbolic representation is universal. The symbolic representation of distress is grounded in a wider cosmological context: in the symbolic reality (Budman et al., 1992; Kleinman, 1980). In many non-Western societies, the symbolic representations from which idioms of distress are derived tend to be grounded in external realities, which are often ultra-human and metaphysical (Al-Krenawi and Graham, 1997; Ben-Ezer, 1992; El-Islam, 1975, 1980; Kiev, 1972; Leff, 1981). Designated as myth, magic, mysticism, and religion, they identify and map entities and forces with special ontological status: for example, divine energy, moral sins, demons, and sorcery as agents of affliction and empowerment (Bilu and Witztum, 1995; Parson and Wekely, 1991). Within Jahangirpuri as well, there were different explanatory models for understanding madness or mental disorders.

Member 1: Why do people mutter to themselves?

Member 2: And if you ask them, they deny it, it's soft muttering, not loud.

Member 3: It's probably because of alcohol....

Facilitator: Sometimes it's because of alcohol, other times there are different reasons.

Member 1: We think it is because of 'excessive thinking'.

Member 2: Must be because of putting pressure on the brain (*dimag par zor dalta hoga*).

Member 4: 'Something' happens to their brain, therefore they mutter.

This discussion took place amongst a group of boys (18–20 years); they were attending a group discussion on 'positive attitudes' facilitated by a NGO worker. Alcohol, stress (excessive thinking) as well as unexplained factors ('something') came out in the discussion as causes of madness. Other behavioural manifestations of madness which were frequently mentioned were 'being isolated', inability to laugh, and so on. The informants spoke about mental distress in a variety of ways. One aspect of mental distress included bizarre behaviour (talking to self, muttering, running away), behaviour which was present for long

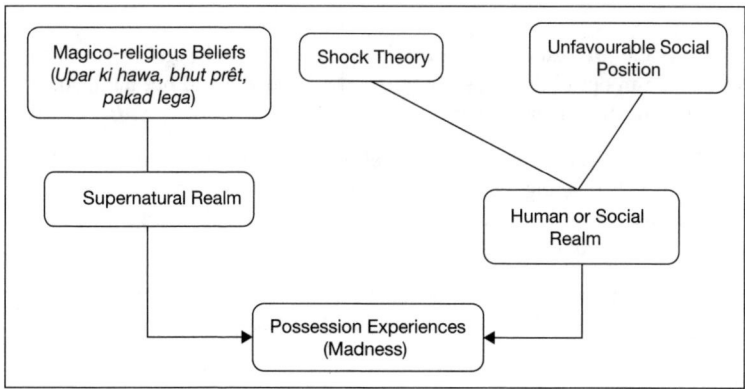

Figure 4.1 *Explanations of Madness*

Source: Author.

periods of time. Another aspect included behaviour which lasted for short periods of time after which the person went back to their usual ways of functioning. These explanations have been discussed in the following manner.

Supernatural Realm

The unexplained 'something' which one of the boys talked about in the group is a fairly common explanation for any kind of unexplained illness in the community. Usually people in the community refer to it as *'upar ki hawa'*. *Hawa lagna* or the individual being affected by air[1] is a common way of explaining bodily deformities. Disability caused by this is natural and does not connote the cosmic arena. The origins of this are not known but it is related to temperature and seasonal changes (Mehrotra, 2004: 40). While explaining any kind of 'bizarre' behaviour the *'upar'* (above) is added to the concept of *hawa lagna*. With the addition of the word *'upar'* the connotations change and imply the supernatural realm. The extent of possession differs in different cases. The main symptom of the illness caused by malignant or nefarious supernatural entities is possession in varying degrees; it may be grotesquely violent or perceptibly docile (Srivastava, 2002: 151).

> Bhagwanti (42 years): *Usko upar ki hawa lag gayi thi, woh pagal ho gaya.* He would run out of the house or sit quietly; usually he did not hit anyone but sat quietly in one corner.
>
> Chanda (60 years): My daughter was okay but the day when Ganesha drank milk, she kept going there to offer milk to him and something happened after that. From that night onwards she kept singing *Jai Mata Di*, we did not understand what had happened.
>
> Salma Khatoon (42 years): My daughter also forgets things now; we are all going mad. My husband has been mad for a long time; he shouts and

---

[1] The explanation for Hawa Lagna given by people includes the idea that air enters the body and impacts the heart and brain causing problems in the individual.

beats everyone, *upar ki hawa*, in the village we have some enemies who have done something.[2]

Satwanti (49 years): No one wants to keep my second daughter; she is mad, she goes out of the house without telling anyone. Earlier she used to work and keep quiet; when she turned 18 she became even more quiet (*gumsum*). We did not notice anything at first, then she started going out of the house; I thought it is something to do with '*upar ki hawa*', something has become attached to her because she used to sing songs. I don't know how many temples I have taken her to, Balaji also, pir babas.

Running out of the house, talking to self, singing songs, not being able to do anything, becoming quieter were all seen as signs of 'madness'. Other behaviours categorized as 'mad' were walking up and down a street the entire day, muttering to self, repeating the same statement again and again. The behaviour which was vastly different from the everyday actions of the person and had come on suddenly without any apparent causes was more likely to be given a supernatural explanation. '*Pagli ho jana*', *gumsum rehna, dimag garam ho jana* were some of the other expressions used to describe 'mad' behaviour. These instances are usually attributed to possession caused by the 'malicious' actions of others (*bhut prêt, koi pakad leta hai*). This could occur because of some wrongdoing by the individual or because of enmity with others, who with the help of '*tantriks*' 'get something done' (*kuch karwa deten hain*). Beliefs related to *bhut prêt* (ghosts), *kuch karwa dena* ('someone gets something done' usually implying black magic), *koi pakad leta* (person is possessed), indicate the strong belief in witchcraft and sorcery within the community. Rosenthal and Siegal (1959) explain how witchcraft and sorcery can be seen as varieties of magic which aim at controlling the behaviour of persons. They suggest that magic arises as a symbolic means of handling important environmental influences which are not subject to empirical control, and also for dealing with the anxiety, frustration, or threat which may be the result of

---

[2] An effort has been made to present the text exactly as it was spoken by the women. Therefore, the sentence structure of the narratives is not always grammatically correct and often the linkages appear weak.

people being confronted with important environmental forces which they cannot master (ibid.: 144). Other people's actions that are seen as being responsible for the 'madness' or ill-health fall under the aegis of 'black or bad magic'.

> Kunti (70 years): My son was the best looking, tall and fair, earning well also; he worked as a DTC (Delhi Transport Corporation) conductor and on holidays he used to work in a TV repair shop. He died because someone did something, one *Pundit* did it. I had taken him to Balaji; there he said his name was Raju. *Bhangi ki aatma ghus gayi thi, pet gal gaya tha.* (A lower caste person's soul had entered him, his stomach had rotted away). He refused to get out and said that he had been sent by *Pundit Narayan*. These Pundits are like that, they are not to be trusted; we used to give him lots of clothes, food but it's like that.

Evans-Pritchard (1931) differentiated between good and black magic: good magic acts in favour of, and black magic acts against, justice and order. He explains how in the Azande culture, sorcery or bad magic is generally a personal weapon aimed at some individual whom the sorcerer dislikes, against whom he has a grudge but no case of even a quasi-legal nature. Its purpose is to injure those who are successful, the brave, the rich, the noble, the fair, and the powerful (ibid.: 35). In pain, sickness, fear of death, anxiety, grief, remorse, misfortunes and humiliations of every kind it is a great comfort to believe that these evils are not due to one's own carelessness, lack of ability and indiscretion, or that they are the inevitable workings of fate, rather they are caused by the jealousy, envy, malice, hatred and spite of others which surround us (ibid.: 53). This is evident in Kunti's narrative as she believes that the death of her son who was good in all spheres had been caused by the jealous or malicious actions of others. These magico-religious explanations as mentioned by Evans-Pritchard also bring some respite to the distressed persons.

Another explanation of 'good' and 'bad' magic was given by one of the healers:

> People become mad when a *jinn*[3] comes on them. See Mohammad could resist bad things but he had to use *Jadu (magic)* once to show people that *jadu* exists. Once I went to a village where there were many *jadugars* (magicians). I saw a tree with fruit and wanted to eat them so I washed up and came out but by that time the tree had become barren. Because a woman *jaadugar* saw that and did it. People would look at you and you would fall down. Some people are like that: we like to help and they like to spoil things for others. There are many kinds of jinns: *chudail, pahelwan*, Hindu and Muslim ghosts are different. Strong *pahelwan* ghosts are called *devs*.
>
> We find out whether people are faking problems by reading something; it tells us whether it is an act or *jinn*; in case it is a *jinn* it comes out. Sometimes *jinn* come because a person has urinated in the wrong place and his urine goes in the *jinn's* house which might be below the drain. You are not supposed to have sex with no clothes on; sometimes if *jinns* are flying overhead and look down and are attracted towards the body they might enter it. There are different ways to take out different *jinns*, some are easy and some are tough (Interview with a Maulana).

The Maulana again brings out the presence of 'benevolent' (we like to help) and 'malevolent' magic (they like to spoil things). He further explains that there are people who show similar symptoms, which he calls an 'act' as they are not related to '*jinns*' and hence they need to be treated differently. These behaviours occur because of some problem in the life of the person and this kind of 'madness' is attributed to human or social causes.

Human and Social Realm

Here 'madness' occurs because of certain conditions in a person's life. In this case, the 'madness' or 'mental illness' may be temporary. After the improvement in conditions, the persons usually go back to his/her previous ways of functioning. Here women talked about shocking incidents which led to a change in behaviour, as well as the societal reasons for madness.

---

[3] Jinn are entities that form part of the same cosmic order as Gods, Angels and Saints and since they are mentioned in the Quran, they constitute a part of the ecosystem of the Muslim faith (Senger, 2003: 23).

(a) Shock theory

According to Srivastava (2002), Indians believe that sudden shock—a failure in examination, loss in business, betrayal in love, death of a loved one—is enough to make an individual mentally upset that may in course of time lead to 'mental illness'. They also believe that sometimes a windfall, for instance, winning a huge sum in lottery, may also cause mental imbalance. Acceptors of this theory are definitely more in cities and towns but often observers have reported that tribals and peasants also speak of social and cultural shocks (ibid.: 151).

> Bela (55 years): My daughter took tea for her husband and found him dead. First time we ever saw anything like that (shaking her head). She went into a shock, used to sometimes laugh, sometimes cry. *'Pagli' si ho gayi thi*, never cared about food.
>
> Khalifa (36 years): *Mere saath hadsa hua hai jiski wajah se main bawali ho gayi* [She kept repeating that for some time]. My elder brother was jailed because of which I became mad with worry. I still keep feeling that my brother is in jail and keep getting upset—he specially came to meet me to reassure me—I felt better but still continued to be sad. I stopped speaking to others. My neighbours made fun of me and said that I had gone mad.

Bela and Khalifa talk about sudden changes which caused the madness. Bela refers to her daughter as *'pagli si'* (she behaved as if she was mad); Khalifa refers to herself as *'bawali'*. *Pagli* and *Bawali* are milder terms used to indicate behaviour away from the norm in everyday interactions when people rebuke each other. *'Pagal'* is seen as someone whose behaviour stands out as being out of the ordinary. This differentiation is apparent when Khalifa calls herself *bawali* but expresses resentment towards her neighbours who made fun of her and called her 'mad'. The movement from *pagli si, bawali* to *paagal* would imply moving from behaving a bit oddly to complete loss of control.

(b) Unfavourable social position

Another important reason identified as leading to madness was the social position of women. Marriage and poor marital relations could make women more vulnerable to breakdowns.

Deconstructing Madness

Leela (32 years): I had a fight with him and two months back I was on the streets screaming with my hair open, I was mad. I told my husband that I would leave with our three children, beg or do anything but I wouldn't stay with him; that's when he promised to stop the affairs.

Shabnam (26 years): The two of us sisters got married to two brothers. That family was like that, everyone was bad, used to hit us because of small things. Their sisters were at home so our *dahej* (dowry) was wanted for them, so they hit us again and again. Our mother is a widow so they troubled us more but our brothers supported us. My sister was like a madwoman, she was in a bad state, she would not speak, she would do just what they asked her to do, she would not say anything even to our mother. They had done some '*totke*' on her, science does not believe this but it happens, we brought water from the Maulavi and made her drink that; then in a separate room she told mother everything. When she was taken from the house to the doctor, he also said that in another couple of days she would have died. Sometimes I still remember those beatings, sometimes with shoes.

Leela and Shabnam's sister both appeared to be in a state of possession. Leela probably by a benevolent spirit who helps her to fight for her rights; Shabnam's sister by a malevolent one induced by her in-laws (through *totkas*). According to Sharma (2010), possession by malevolent or benevolent forces is a daily occurrence in rural society, a phenomenon which is transcultural in language and idiom and cuts across religious and caste hierarchy. This phenomenon is a powerful site of resistance and protest, a ritual formulation that is significant for our comprehension of the dynamics of rural society and its dominant belief and attitudes (ibid.: 198). These ritual formulations are usually carried into the cities by people who have migrated from rural areas or smaller towns. Leela's account and that of Shabnam's sister highlight the marginalization and powerlessness of the married woman. Both were in liminal states, one active, screaming with open hair (implying a state of undress); the other passive, not speaking, and withdrawn. Both active and passive behaviour forced people around them to effect changes. Leela's husband promised to stop having affairs and Shabnam and her sister were taken back to their natal home.

The use of possession as a powerful negotiating tool came out clearly in a focused group discussion among women:

Member 1: Aurutain phans jaati hain, ghar sambhalene padte hain unhe. Aadmi kuch nahi karte, upar se khane ke saath saath apne shouk bhi purey karwaaten hain; bidi, tambakoo, sharab ke paise bhi nikalwate hain, na karo to maar pitaai hoti hai.

(Women are trapped, households have to be looked after, the men don't do anything. They don't work, in addition to that they have to be provided not only with food but their demands of cigarettes, tobacco and alcohol have to be met as well; if you don't then you get beaten).

Member 2: Jab pareshanian had se bad jati hain toh auratain chandi ban jaatin hain. Log unhe paagal samajhte hain par yeh nahi dekhte ke woh aisa kyun kar rahin hai.

(When problems become excessive then women become like Kali, people think they are mad but they don't see why they are doing this.)

Member 3: Chandi banti hain aur chillati hain, unhi ko samajh aata hai jo khud musibaton se guzar rahen hote hain, baaki nahi samajhte.

(They don the role of Kali and scream, only those understand who are going through problems themselves, others don't).

Possession is often seen as a condition of strength. Bargen (1988) describes how in the Genji, monogatari-possessed women unwittingly manipulate their oppressors and wring from them hitherto denied attention and respect. The putatively supernatural event of spirit-possession momentarily reverses traditional roles and upsets the normal order of values so that victimized women temporarily rule over men. The event belongs, in Victor Turner's sense, to a 'liminal state' which simultaneously affirms and challenges the ordinary set of social relationships. When it is concluded, the process leaves no mark, or at most a healing 'scar', on the received hierarchical order of the society (ibid.: 95–96).

When problems cross a limit then women don the role of '*Chandi*' and come out in the streets. Bringing issues of the private sphere out into the public sphere is not approved by the community. By bringing out issues while in the liminal state of possession, they become publicly acceptable (their behaviour which is against the norms of the community is accepted because they are in the state of possession and therefore not responsible for it) and force public reflexivity. Turner (1979) explains that public reflexivity takes place as performance: the language through which a group communicates with itself includes 'doing' code-like gestures, singing, dancing, painting and so on. Possession seems to offer a brilliant metaphoric language with which to express the fundamental splitting that is imposed on the woman's capacity to move into the world. The ontological distinction between the woman's body via the agency and desires of a radically different being, the fracturing of the woman's voice by the narratives of others who must fill the gaps in the woman's narratives about her possession experiences—all seem like nothing more than heightened dramatizations of the existential condition of women in patriarchy (Ram, 2001: 208).

Through accounts of possession, women bring out issues related to dowry, domestic violence, property issues, extramarital relationships as well as the multiple roles that women have to fulfil. They are clear that although such women are called 'mad', these women actually convey the psychosocial distress in their everyday lives. In possession experiences, awareness of distress is created through the enactment of distress in a public place. But distress is also embodied in and suffering is expressed through illness and pain. This expression of distress is not usually categorized as madness (whether supernatural or social) and therefore it often goes unrecognized. The next section presents the psychosocial distress of women through their illness experiences.

ILLNESS EXPERIENCES/NARRATIVES

The way in which women express their distress is mediated by their cultural context. Illness experiences present the manner in which women understand their psychosocial distress. These explanations are important as they determine the actions that women take to alleviate distress. Illness is culturally shaped in the sense that how we perceive, experience, and cope with disease is based on our explanations of sickness, explanations specific to the social positions we occupy and systems of meaning we employ (Kleinman, 1975). It is shaped by cultural factors governing perception, labelling, explanation, and valuation of the discomforting experience (Fabrega, 1972), and processes embedded in a complex family, social, and cultural nexus (Litman, 1974). These have been shown to influence our expectations and perceptions of symptoms (Mechanic, 1972), the way we attach particular sickness labels to them (Waxler, 1974), and the valuations and responses that flow from those labels (ibid.: 74). Illness behaviour is a normative experience governed by cultural rules: we learn 'approved' ways of being ill.

Biomedicine has increasingly banished the illness experience as a legitimate object of clinical concern. This systematic inattention to illness is in part responsible for patient non-compliance, patient and family dissatisfaction with professional healthcare, and inadequate clinical care (Kleinman, 1974: 31–35; Stimson, 1974). This increases the role of traditional or folk healers in the lives of women as is evident in their narratives.

Suffering Woman: 'Dukhyari'

We feel scared because a few days back police came and took all the young men. We said that they were innocent. The police said that they would release them after questioning, but we were scared. I get headaches when so many women are talking, my heart starts beating fast, and I feel dizzy. Everyone has problems but when I go out I get tense. When I go to my daughter's place I take an auto although it costs ₹100 for one side but I can't take bus or metro; I feel very tense. I feel something will happen to me. So I don't go anywhere. I have been taking medicines for a long time, have gone to several doctors. When I keep taking medicines I feel better, when I stop, the headaches start again. Once a *pir* gave me a *taweez*; it did not help me at all. I run a tea stall to run the house. I have three daughters and one son; he sits in a DVD shop, his own. He is married with a three-year-old girl. I have been married for 30 years and my oldest son is 24. My husband used to drink from the beginning, he never did regular work. I used to segregate garbage or make *papads*. I had to bring up the children on my own. Now my older son helps, he gives me ₹150 when he can. I don't ask for more, I can't.

I underwent a full X-ray but nothing showed up. The doctor told me that my problem is *'chinta'* (worrying), it affects my body but what to do? I have to give money to my married daughters, their husbands ask for money, ₹1000, ₹1500. Then there is my 13-year-old daughter too, I have to save for her too. I keep thinking about that and my heart beats faster, I sweat. Sometimes I sit quietly when I am worried. As long as my husband is not drinking I am happy. My body feels light. Even if he drinks and then sits quietly, I don't mind, but when he talks too much, laughs, I don't like it. Then I fight; he never hits me, just becomes loud.

One of the main problems is that he steals money from the shop. I tell him to deposit money and he gambles it away. In the shop too if I have kept some material he will steal it. I keep thinking about it, suggest a good doctor to me, though doctors tell me that my problem is *'chinta'*. I have tried homeopathic, ayurvedic [treatment] but all the responsibility is on my head, so what do I do?

People used to tell me that another woman would have run away but I can't. When I went to my village, my body was light, my head was okay, I had no problems. So I know it is *'chinta'*. I have no problem in my body. When I am working I forget or when I am talking to people like I am talking now, there is no problem. In the shop when I am busy, there is no problem but when I sit alone then the thoughts come. Can't go to the village very often, it is expensive, ₹2000–3000 every time. My husband's mother is his stepmother so I feel sorry for him; after all he is my husband, he has no one but me. I can go to my sister's house; I have people but he has no one, so I have to take care of him. He is around so I am safe also. (Conversation with Suraiya, 45-year-old Bengali-speaking Muslim woman living in C block)

Suraiya's narrative is representative of the stories of many women in Jahangirpuri and depicts the manner in which distress is exacerbated by structural violence (Nayar and Mehrotra, 2017). Her narrative brings out issues related to the arbitrary nature of systems/administration (shown by local policemen arresting all the young men of the community), husband dependent on alcohol who gambles and steals to fund his addiction, meeting the dowry demands of her married daughter's households, as well as attempting to save for her youngest daughter's marriage. Suraiya's narrative at times appears to be abrupt as she moves from describing issues related to her family to symptoms of ill-health (for example, arbitrarily moving from talking about an arrest to the bit about getting headaches in the presence of women). In reality her distress is interwoven in her narrative and comes out metaphorically through the body. 'Heart beating fast', 'sweating', 'feeling as if something will happen to me'; 'dizziness' are all expressions of psychosocial distress. In psychiatric language, Suraiya might be categorized as someone having a panic disorder. She has been on medication for a long time without benefitting greatly from it. Her 'symptoms' are better understood via the lens of distress and in terms of *cultural idioms of distress*. Nichter (1981) refers to the use of a local, conventional mode of expression of distress (which can be verbal, gestural, or expressed through symbolic action) to convey suffering that may have different origins and locations. Intolerable social circumstances of marital or family conflict, poverty and oppression may be alluded to through talk about 'nerves' (Low, 1994), excessive heat (Jenkins and Valiente, 1994), or other bodily or emotional symptoms.

Women dealing with multiple burdens are often referred to as '*Dukhyari*'. The word *dukhyari* here implies a 'suffering woman'. One of the main reasons for labelling women as '*dukhyari*' was usually when a woman had suffered multiple losses: loss of husband, lack of adequate resources, poor health, child with a disability and poor social support. Suraiya had multiple responsibilities and poor support (since her husband did not contribute to the household) and therefore could be categorized as '*Dukhyari*'. Sometimes the label of *dukhyari* was given to women who themselves believed that they were more affected as compared to other women. Because of their circumstances, many of the women reported psychosocial distress. The Self-Reporting Questionnaire (SRQ-20) which is frequently used as a screening tool for psychiatric disorders in the community lists questions related to headaches, tiredness, poor appetite and digestion, nervousness, worries and sleeplessness. Many of these come up in the narratives of women as problems that they have had for a long period of time. If screened they would probably fall in the category of women requiring further psychiatric intervention. But within the community, the categorization of *dukhyari* took into account the social conditions of their everyday lives. This 'local' category of distress consisted of women seen as being vulnerable and requiring support. They were not stigmatized; in most cases, others in the community sympathized with them and made efforts to increase their resources.

Everyday Distress

This section presents the descriptions of distress which arose from the circumstances of their living conditions.

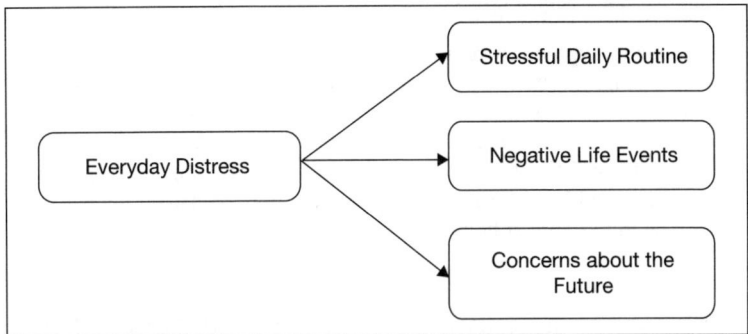

Figure 4.2 *Factors Responsible for Everyday Distress*
Source: Author.

(a) Stressful daily routine

Many of the women had gruelling everyday routines which tired them out. They talked about working for around 13–14 hours a day without rest. This often included house work, care work and paid work. In addition to the long hours of work, the monotony of the work unbroken by any leisure time activity added to their feelings of suffocation and being unwell.

> Kamala (50 years): In my house the only problem is that my sons and husband don't do any housework. They will not heat the tea themselves, they don't do anything. If I am busy they will say it's alright, leave it and they will not eat at all. Sometimes my elder son does not wash his socks for 3–4 days if I don't do it, they begin to stink [making a face]. Does not wash his undergarments also. My younger son at least does some

work. I have never worked outside. I can't, there is always something to do at home. I don't have much work but everyone has their different schedules and they all want 'hot' food so I am in the kitchen from seven in the morning till late at night although there are only four people in the house. If I don't serve hot food, my son will stop talking to me; once he did not talk to me for many days. The house runs only on his salary. So I keep doing that only, one household task after the other. I feel suffocated (*ghutan*). Because of this my health has also suffered; my body hurts, my limbs hurt. I take some medicines, but all my tests were done and nothing showed up. The doctor says that I take too much stress because of which I was having the aches. I never go outside if I have the time, I sleep and take rest.

Sita Devi (35 years): There is so much work at home. I get up by five in the morning; get the children ready for school; after they go, I clean the house, wash clothes. I have come here having left dirty clothes at home. Then children come for lunch, etc., and then it is time for dinner. I sleep by 11 at night. There is the worry about saving for my daughters also. My back hurts and I feel weak; my husband does not understand my workload; he thinks I am at home after all but he does not see the amount of work in the house.

Work inside the house remains invisible and therefore unrecognized and ignored. If women are unable to perform some task at home, it often remains unfinished till the time they can do it. Kamala's narrative brings out how no one in the household is willing to share her responsibilities. She lives with three men as her only daughter is already married. When her daughter got married it meant she lost her one ally. Time allocation studies from India indicated that no matter how much the burden of other work increased, time spent on domestic chores remained constant. Throughout the region, the only way in which women were able to reduce the burden on themselves was by distributing work among other female family members; more often than not, this meant depriving girls' access to school. Most studies also found that official classifications as well as women's own self perceptions led to their undervaluation as workers (Karlekar, 1988: 98). Researchers have suggested that it is the mundane work that women engage in which leads to their 'breakdown' (Miles, 1987). Oakley (1972) uses the example of housework to illustrate this. She argues that housewives work an average of 77 hours per week and the feelings of the women she spoke to were characterized by hopelessness at not being able to find a way out as well as guilt that in spite of all the work that they had put in, their efforts were inadequate.

For women, the work never ends and there is hardly any time for leisure; this picture gets more complicated when there are health issues in the family. Care for another becomes an additional burden for the mother. Satwanti who was a widow with poor support was unable to cope in a situation where her daughter's (person with schizophrenia) condition worsened.

> Satwanti: I wake up at four in the morning and finish all the work; she does not do anything although she can. Her medication being stopped has made things worse; she has become completely mad; keeps running away. She has not eaten in a week. I shifted just one month back; how many houses can I change? Everyone has come to know she is mad; every wrong thing is then blamed on her. I want a medicine so that she can die; then I can live in peace. My eldest daughter says that she cannot live with her; she says, Mummy how can you live with her? The second one came with her son to live with me for a month in his holidays; she had to leave in a day; my other daughter would not let her stay. She has become completely mad, I want her to die.

Satwanti was in tears while describing her daughter; she felt isolated and unable to go on. She wanted to end her own life as well as her daughter's. The burden of being a caregiver was too much for her at that time. When I met her after some time, her daughter's condition had improved with the new medication. At that time Satwanti was more cheerful and the extent of her distress had reduced. Very often caregivers are also given antidepressants or anti-anxiety drugs; what they actually need is improvement in the home situation which can bring down the level of psychosocial distress they are facing. Medicines play an important role as seen here where they have drastically improved the condition of Satwanti's daughter but they need to be used with caution.

(b) Negative life events

Life events involving the loss of some kind could trigger depressive reactions. Negative experiences in the lives of the people they were attached to would lead to psychosocial distress in women.

> Kunti: My health has become bad since my son died five years ago. I used to be very healthy, now I have become unwell. I have not been well after he died. I can't sleep at night, keep walking up and down. Thoughts keep running in my head, my youngest daughter has to be married and we can't find a suitable boy for her. I keep thinking about things again and again. My daughter-in-law does all the work, sometimes I help out but I am not happy anymore.

> Shilpa (50 years): I have difficulty in crowded places; if the bus is empty I can go in otherwise I keep sitting at the bus stop. Even if there is a *barat* (wedding procession) I say that let everyone go first. I can't be in the middle [of a crowd], my heart starts beating fast, I start sweating. I have palpitations if I am in the middle (*ghabrahat hoti hai agar main beech main hoti hun*). For Satsangs also I sit at the back when I go. This started only three or four years back. Of course, I have tension; they say that one's husband's money can be spent with pride, but one's son's money should be spent with care (*mard ka paisa chowde hokar aur bete ka paisa kone main kharch karna*) [she says this with tears in her eyes]. I lie awake at night thinking about the marriage of my daughters. All is good, my health has gone down in the past three years, but all is well.

Kunti experienced a loss through death. She is unable to stop thinking about her son who died at a young age. She describes the illness of her son as a result of a possession experience; her own distress on the other hand has become embodied. She describes a feeling of ill-health since he died signifying the inability to experience happiness after the event, sleeplessness and restlessness.

Many women talked about losing children through abortion and ill-health. But the loss was felt more when a grown-up child died. They usually described the personality and physical characteristics of the deceased child in detail. The unexpected death of an older child was often explained as a result of sorcery. '*Aatma ghus gayi thi*', '*devi daal di thi'* were the expressions used to describe the reason for the death. These reasons were followed by the expression *'gal gal ke mar gaye'* when the person was ill for a long time and died slowly. Watching a son or daughter die had obviously left a scar on these mothers who found it difficult to forget the long and protracted experience of losing their child.

Shilpa's distress is related to the loss of her husband's job which subsequently meant a loss of status for her. She and her husband have now become dependants. The trajectory of her problems started three or four years back which coincides with the time when her husband became ill and had to stop working.

Some women talked about events which changed the course of their lives. They spoke about feeling helpless and hopeless in the circumstances that they were in:

> Lata (35 years): I was married when I was 13; I had no understanding of anything at that time, by the time I was 18–19 the kids were born. Till then I used to tolerate everything. As I started growing up questions started arising in my mind. I was so distressed that I would keep crying, and could see no way out. My mother-in-law and husband used to beat me. Two or three times, I tried to kill myself, I took medicines but did not die, just kept lying on the bed for three or four days; once I even tried to burn myself. I was so angry and tired. Then I understood that all this is useless, there is no gain in dying. Things improved after I had a son.
>
> Nagma[4] (18 years): When I was small I had a problem with my legs but it was okay. At three I went to school but gradually I found it more and more difficult to walk so my schooling stopped. For several years I was at home because I was not able to go to school. I had nothing much to do, I was very sad and would keep crying through the day. I was a waste; many times I felt that life was useless, it should end. Everyone tried to take care of me, but I used to get very angry and it made no difference.

For Lata, life appeared to be a series of negative events till she gave birth to a son. Her position in the household improved and her

---

[4] Case study published in *Women's Link*, Vol. 18, No. 2: 15–19.

husband and mother-in-law starting respecting her. Nagma's Polio had restricted her ability to walk and therefore curtailed her movement. Fulfilment of an imposed social responsibility (giving birth to a son) improved Lata's condition. Nagma spoke about reduction in distress when she met the health worker of an NGO who helped her to start new activities and schooling.

(c) Concerns about the future

Most households survive on the income earned but are not able to save much. Since savings are poor, any crisis can push the family from a position of stability to instability. Because of inadequate social support systems women remain continuously apprehensive about the future.

> Rajwanti (78 years): I have become empty (*main to khali ho gayin hun*); I don't know why I am alive. Because of my son's accident our household has become difficult to manage again.
>
> Sanjeeda (45 years): I am running the house on a daily basis. I have to take my son to the hospital as well, I have never travelled so much; at this age I have to take [care of] my adult son all over again. So, I can't sleep at night. I also have to get my daughters married and I am very worried about that. At night I sit up and think about my daughters. My entire body aches and I hardly eat anymore.
>
> Zayeeda (20 years): My mother has money but will my brothers give me and my children any money after she is gone? I keep thinking about this all day. I am always having headaches; I can't sleep at night. I feel uneasy (*ghabrahat hoti hai*). I sit and watch TV or keep thinking these thoughts again and again till 2 or 3 in the night and then get up at 5 in the morning. My health is deteriorating.

Sudden changes because of death, sickness and accidents increase the vulnerability of the household. Rajwanti's statement that she had become 'empty' is both literal and figurative. Literal because she was in need of money which she was not able to get because of problems with her pension and also emotional because her son was unwell and immobile. To see him in this condition was upsetting her even more.

In most of the narratives everyday distress is expressed metaphorically through the body. The body represents the experience of the social world as felt by the women. In a study by Patel et al. (2007), the commonest category of symptoms reported by women in Goa were aches and pains, most commonly pain in the limbs and joints, and headaches. The next common category of symptoms was that of autonomic symptoms. More than half the participants complained of palpitations. Social and cultural attitudes and struggles are played out in the terrain of the individual body. The individual body and its sicknesses are not so much representations of the larger environment as a vital and inseparable part of it. In her research with the southern Sudanese refugees in Cairo, Coker (2004) found that they spoke about pain being everywhere and also nowhere at the same time. They feel it in the heart, the stomach, the head and the legs but particularly in the 'self' (ibid.: 17). Similarly, for the women in the field site, distress is lived out through the pain in their bodies. Embodiment of distress has implications in the way it is addressed. The next section continues this discussion to explore further the impact of biomedicine on psychosocial distress.

Terms of Distress

Articulation of distress through the body means that many of the women use medical terms to explain their problems. One of the reasons for the increasing use of biomedical terminology has been the extension of medical jurisdiction over health itself (in addition to illness, disease, and injury) and the commodification of health. That is, health itself and the proper management of chronic illnesses are becoming individual moral responsibilities to be fulfilled through improved access to knowledge, self-surveillance, prevention, risk assessment, the treatment of risk, and the consumption of appropriate self-help/biomedical goods and services (Clarke et al., 2003). Medicines now play a growing role in dealing with psychosocial stresses. As powerful technical devices and cultural symbols, medicines have acquired a status and force in society. Therefore, while women talk about psychosocial stressors as being responsible for ill-health, they often resort to medicines to reduce the distress.

> Bela: When I have pain, I have a medicine which is for one or two rupees. When my daughter was unwell, in the nursing home they did all the tests and told us that she had TB; her stomach had swollen but she improved in a year. That was a tough time for me. We felt we had done something wrong with our children [putting her hand on the stomach saying it was hurting]. While talking about this I feel sad, that is why it hurts (*yeh baat karte hue gam hota hai, isliye dard hota hai*) (tears in her eyes) I always have problems with my stomach now.

> Reena (25 years): My blood is less because I had three kids. I had less blood before also, then by this age we have three; doctors scold me if I tell them my real age so I never tell them. I sometimes get scared of myself; at home I am worried that something bad is going to happen. I have gone to the best doctors, they have done all the tests, scans, etc., and nothing showed up. They say I worry that's why I feel unwell; if one side hurts, I say my kidneys are not working, if it's the other side then it's my liver[laughs].

> Sangeeta (28 years): I am always tense (*mujhe bahut tension rehti hai*). I am always worried how drunk he will be when he comes back because that will increase conflicts. We fight and go to sleep. He never remembers anything if he is very drunk. But he is never sorry about anything. I have heard stories from other women how their husbands force them to have sex; at least my husband is not like that. I have lost a lot of weight, look at me now; I used to be much healthier, now often I don't eat. My health has become very bad.

> Sita Devi: My back is always hurting; the doctor once told me to get a thyroid test done but everything was normal. I think it's after my operation for the last child; it was in (a) private (hospital). I have too much anxiety, that is why I cannot sleep well (*Tension toh mujhe bahut hoti hai isliye main acche se so nahi paati*).

Women talk about their aches and pains and worsening health in the context of the situation at home: illness violence, financial problems and so on. At the same time, how important medicines are becomes apparent. The women attribute their problems to psychosocial causes but the treatment they have sought is medical. Reena's statement about having 'less blood' is a metaphor for the tiredness and weakness she feels. Based on research in rural south Karnataka,

Nichter (1989) noted that the term *nare nitrana* (nerve weakness), is often used to 'refer to general feelings of instability, lack of well being and lassitude. Physical weakness is often used as an expression of mental weakness' (ibid.: 95). A corresponding term, and common complaint, in Tamil populations is 'Shakti illai' ('strength is lacking'). The importance of this concept is manifested throughout India in the widespread use of tonics, which are purchased even by poor families in attempts to counter 'weakness' (ibid.: 246–51).

Pain in different parts of the body, especially in the stomach, which is described as occurring often is something which came up in the narratives of many other women as well. Categories of distress are borrowed from each other, compressing idioms which although hybrid, aim to convey shared meanings and similar life experiences. The principle underlying this analogical reasoning is one in which similar life circumstances are seen as producing a similar illness among people (Eskell-Blolkland, 2009). Many of them seem to be taking recourse to similar treatments as well; medicine-taking behaviour has been recognized as an important idiom of distress (Nichter and Thompson, 2006; Nichter and Vuckovic, 1994).

Distress may also be experienced as a subjective state of risk that leads one to seek diagnostic tests, and the taking of tests may be engaged in as a means of expressing distress to significant others. This is becoming a common phenomenon in India, catered to by both clinicians and a lucrative diagnostic testing industry readily available to the public (Nichter, 2002). Clarke et al. (2003) consider this an important dimension of bio-medicalization; this behaviour was evident in Jahangirpuri as well. It was found that women often spoke about getting MRIs and scans in an effort to diagnose their problems. This persisted even when they had been told by doctors that their problems were because of excessive anxiety. Conrad (1992) explains that medicalization has become a sociocultural process which may or may not involve the medical profession. The framework is so prevalent that women believe in it even if the agents of the system themselves do not propound it.

Kamala: My health has also gone, my body hurts, my limbs hurt. I am having some medicines but all my tests were done and nothing emerged. The doctor says that I take on too much stress because of which I keep having the pains.

Women were usually unaware of the name of the medicine that they were taking and the exact nature of the medicine; when asked they described the colour and shape of the pills. The picture becomes more complicated as many of the women were taking medicines for anaemia and vitamin pills because of nutritional deficiencies (as described by the health providers). Some of them who had prescriptions of psychiatric medication and were in regular follow-ups did not report many benefits. There were others who stopped medication because of its side-effects.

> Salma Khatoon: I have been worried for so many years; I have stones also. If I start telling you all my problems, I will not be able to stop. I can never sleep, I get up at 3.00 and sit and think about problems. I have been taking treatment *(showed me a prescription of Alprax and Fluxotine from a psychiatric hospital)* but I still feel tense all the time.
>
> Khalifa: I went to the hospital in the mental clinic but with those medicines I keep feeling sleepy, I keep having shocks which worry me more, so I stopped the medicine. I still don't feel hungry, I can't do the work because it will fall on my daughter to do everything and I want her to study.

Salma Khatoon was regularly going to the hospital for follow-ups but beyond changing the medication to a certain extent, it appeared that no other intervention was planned for her. She had multiple stressors in her life which included a son with intellectual disability, another suffering from tuberculosis, and a husband with a major mental disorder. Khalifa's problems had begun with her brother (to whom she was very close) being jailed (unfairly according to her) and her subsequent struggle to get him released. In both the cases, there were multiple stresses for which they require support. But the primary help that they sought, and which was given to them seems to be bio-medical. Ecks and Basu (2009) found that over the 2000s, the use of antidepressants had rapidly risen in India. They suggested a possible global rise of depression caused by rapid socio-economic changes and stresses. Another factor was suggested by Kirmayer and Minas (2000) who hold that the global spread of psychiatric disease classifications and diagnostic routines account for the increase in antidepressant uses. This argument is sharpened by the suspicion that the globalization of antidepressants is, by and large, the work of pharmaceutical marketing. This implies that biological idioms and treatments gain more prominence. Although these are gaining prominence, biomedicine has not replaced the other systems of healing present in this community; rather the two co-exist.

The everyday life of most women involved struggle and suffering. But they were not passive receptacles to these struggles. Their agency was revealed in the various strategies that they used in order to reduce their suffering. The strategies used depended on the way the struggles were understood and articulated. Women lived out their distress through the body, either through possession or pains. This determined the person that they approached for help: healer in the community or a certified doctor. This revealed the co-existence of different systems of healing. The following sections cover the ways in which women seek to manage their psychosocial distress—this includes the support that they seek and get from individuals as well as institutions.

SOCIAL CAPITAL AND PSYCHOSOCIAL DISTRESS

The ways in which women attempt to reduce their distress reveals their agency. Both formal and informal sources of help are accessed by women to cope with distress. The kind of help sought by the women is determined by several factors: a) whether distress is articulated through possession or pains; b) support systems present; c) nature of resources present in the area; and d) accessibility of these resources. This section explores the various avenues of help available to the women. These sources of help have been explained using the concept of social capital.

Bourdieu's (1986) view of social capital reflects an assumption that it is the property of an individual. But here the analysis is carried out by viewing social capital as ecological. This implies that social capital is embodied in relationships between individuals, between groups, and between groups and abstract bodies such as the State. A common distinction is made between informal and formal social capital (Ferlander, 2007; Putnam, 2000; Rose, 1998). Informal social capital is characterized by casual contacts with family and friends, while formal social capital comprises rule-bound networks, such as voluntary associations and state-level programmes in the community. Among informal networks, a further distinction can be made between contacts within and outside the family (Stone, 2001).

Informal Sources of Help

Within the household

During stressful periods, the main source of help that women talked about was their mother. In their narratives, women brought out how

Informal Sources		Formal Sources
Within Household		Healers
Mother		Private Doctors
Children	Distressed	Certified Doctors
Husband	Woman	District Mental Health
In-laws		Programme
	Outside Household	
	Self Help groups	
	NGOs (working on women's issues)	
	Religious Groups	
	Paid Work	

Figure 4.3 *Sources of Help Available in the Communities*
Source: Author.

Table 4.1 *Sources of Help within the Household*

Children	Husband	In-laws
Chanda: My elder daughter is the only support I have, no one else, the sons are useless.	Kamala: My husband tries to help out by wearing the same pants for 3–4 days to reduce my washing load.	Babita (45 years): My father-in-law helped a lot in the initial years after my husband left. I am happy that I managed to carve out a life for myself with his help.
Shahbano (36 years): I did not want any of my children to do rag picking. But we were in a very bad state so the eldest had to do that. The others are studying.	Neera (35 years): I was married young and soon after my husband brought me here—it was very surprising to come to Delhi from Ahmedabad; I did not even know the language. My husband is nice. I can only talk to my husband but my husband also gets worried, so I don't want to trouble him.	
My husband used to beat me but now he is scared of my son; my son has warned him [said with pride] that if he did anything we would shift elsewhere.		

Source: Compiled by author.

their mothers had been a source of both instrumental and emotional support for them.

> Chanda: After my husband's death my mother asked me to marry again, but with five kids my family was too big. Mother used to sell vegetables, she lived nearby, she taught me this work too and I ran my household with it.
>
> Mariam (45 years): For 15 years, my husband had been living separately; he left when my daughter was two months old. I have been used to work since them. My husband was living with another woman, he never visited, and only liked the eldest son. The other two children did not know him at all. My mother used to take care of me, she died three years ago. I felt I lost everything. She was my main support; now there is no one to talk to.
>
> Zayeeda: I am living with my mother and she arranges for my food and so on. Once a month I come here and I can talk to others but it's only once a month.

Reviewing literature on mother-daughter relationships across different societies, Chodorow (1974) describes these ties as being extremely close, composed of companionship and mutual cooperation and positively valued by both mother and daughter (ibid.: 62). The aspects of companionship and mutual cooperation are evident in the narratives as women learnt to cope with difficult circumstances and survive with the help of their mothers. Along with the support, mothers helped in honing the agency of their daughters by teaching them skills enabling them to manage households on their own.

Children, husband and in-laws represented other sources of help that women had within the households. Often grown-up children were the ones who actively intervened to stop the violence that their mothers were facing.

Outside household

(a) Sister to sister talk

Few et al. (2003) describe sister-to-sister talk as Afro-centric slang to talk about congenial conversation or positive relating in which life-lessons might be shared between Black women. A similar phenomenon can be seen in Jahangirpuri as spending time in the company of other women was mentioned as an important factor in dealing with distress. Many of the women derived a feeling of companionship through the SHG meetings that they attended. They were able to talk without fear in these groups. Attending meetings gave them breathing space and a legitimate space to relax and interact with others. '*Man halka ho jata hai*' (I feel lighter) was a statement made by many women attending the groups.

> Mariam: All day I sit at home now; when I come out for meeting I can talk.
>
> Neera: In the group we can talk to women; I feel lighter after that (*man halka ho jata hai*). There are many women who face more problems (than me).

Attending SHG meetings also provided exposure to the women there as information about new initiatives was provided through these groups. They were able to gain knowledge about the work of other NGOs as well. One of the informants spoke about taking women who were facing violence to Navjyoti (an organization working on women's issues). Another woman who herself had faced violence spoke about accompanying other women to the crime-against-women cell. Being a part of the groups increased the social capital of the women and made new avenues of help available to them. This is best summarized through Shama Devi's statement when she was in a NGO:

> Shama Devi (35 years): I like to spend time with educated women; we take on the colours of those whom we spend time with. If I stay with villagers, I will become like them. When I come here (NGO) and talk I feel lighter (*jiske saath rahte ho usika rang chadh jata hai, gawaron ke saath rahoongi toh unhi ki tarah gawar ho jaungi*. Jab yahan aake baat karti hun to *man halka ho jata hai*).

(b) Religion and well-being

Attending religious group events was another way of alleviating distress. *Satsangs*, performing *namaaz*, and weekly prayers helped women in coping with the everyday difficulties.

> Kamala: The only place I like to go is the *satsangs*; for what I really want to do I manage to take out time. Everything is (dependent) on god, my belief is firm, everything will be managed.
>
> Satwanti: Every Sunday, my daughter and I go for *satsang*, both of us feel better after that.
>
> Zayeeda: I feel better after performing *namaaz* or *dua*. I am feeling lighter after talking about this.

Participation in religious festivals and carrying out religious rituals (fasting) were found to be helpful in reducing anxiety amongst women. They spoke about following these rituals to ensure the well-being of their families. Numerous studies have found positive relationships between religious beliefs and practices, and physical or mental health measures. Studies have also shown a significant positive effect of religion on well-being (George, Ellison and Larson, 2002; Mohan, 2001). A review by Worthington et al. (1996) offers some tentative answers as to why religion may sometimes have positive effects on individuals. Religion may (1) produce a sense of meaning, something worth living and dying for (Spilka, Shaver and Kirkpatrick, 1985); (2) stimulate hope (Scheier and Carver, 1987) and optimism (Seligman, 1991); (3) give people a sense of control via a beneficent God, which compensates for reduced personal control (4) prescribe a healthier lifestyle that yields positive health and mental health outcomes; (5) set positive social norms that elicit approval, nurturance, and acceptance from others; (6) provide a social support network; or (7) give the person a sense of the supernatural that is certainly a psychological boost, but may also be a spiritual boost that cannot be measured phenomenologically (Bergin and Payne, 1993).

(c) Paid work

Paid work implies additional burden on women. This is because even if they engage in work outside the home; their unpaid work within the household remains the same. In spite of this, women spoke about wanting to work outside the house.

> Mariam: I miss work. I would share things, listen to others. At home I just worry about things like my son's poor health, prices of things.
>
> Neera: I also want to go back to work, it used to make me feel better. There is always something new to do; my head feels heavy when I don't go.

Women engaged in paid work generally have better health than full-time homemakers, yet women's experiences may vary in this regard and reflect variations in occupational roles, family demands and resources (Khlat, Sermet and Le Pape, 2000; Lahelma et al. 2002). Mariam and Neera speak about wanting to go back to work because it enabled them to interact with others, engage in different things, 'there is always something new to do'. Women spoke about increased social mobility and satisfaction as working outside the house enabled them to contribute to the household income. Moving out for work distracted them from everyday worries and struggles.

Informal sources of help outside the household enabled women to move out of the household and engage with others. This engagement reduced their isolation and subsequently helped in reduction of distress.

Formal Sources

Apart from the informal sources of help which are present for the women, there are other sources which women access to help them deal with distress. These exist in conjunction with the informal sources; often women are directed to formal sources of help through the informal sources. These sources deal with both physical and mental health. Here the dichotomy between mental and physical health is blurred. People seek to alleviate mental as well as physical health problems through similar avenues. Any kind of health service for women needs to encompass elements of both as often the physical presentation of symptoms and issues is linked to mental health problems. In the following section, the different kinds of formal sources of help are covered through narratives of women and key informant interviews. In addition, the views of different kinds of healers (including allopath, homeopath, nurse, private doctor as well religious healer) about treating the body and mind are discussed. This is important because some healers seek to heal only the body and its symptoms while others do not believe in the mind-body dichotomy and seek to heal the whole person through different ways. Their explanatory models of health and illness help in understanding the reasons for which they are approached.

Health and Healing

The narratives of the women made the pluralistic nature of help-seeking apparent. Medical pluralism refers to co-existence and syncretism among multiple therapies. It also refers to pluralistic settings within a given system of medicine. This means a plurality of medical personnel practising medicine. These include generalists, specialists and the RMPs (Registered Medical Practitioners) who have no training in allopathy (Bhardwaj, 2010). Kumar (2005) in his study in Jahangirpuri found that there is a substantial section of the population which visits various spiritual healers, priests, and mystics for solutions to their problems. Patients are taking treatment at the psychiatric OPD and simultaneously availing of treatment by spiritual healers.

> Chanda: Hospital people also do not explain anything, they give medicine and say that she will get well. Everyone says that, again we have thought of taking her to Balaji. First time when we gave her medicine she became worse, started shouting more, and then we took her to Santosh Hospital. Buses used to come (to take us there). The treatment was good there, but somehow it stopped. Once for six months she was absolutely all right; we had been taking her to one *pandit* who wanted her to marry his brother but his brother was too old so we refused. His brother died, so he got angry and refused to treat her further.
>
> Rubina (33 years): We went to *hafi*, because this was a case of '*upar ki hawa*'; he sent us to a doctor. So now I take him to both places, he is better but refuses to go to school.
>
> Salma Khatoon: I have spent a lot of money taking him to Maulvis, ₹200–300 every time. I am not going there anymore; he is being treated at IHBAS.
>
> Shahbano: I never used to believe in *taweez* but after my daughter's condition did not recover, I went to this woman who is possessed by the *pir*, and she told me that my daughter was trapped (*aapki beti ko band rakha hai*). All the family will be destroyed. When I asked for *upay* (solution) she asked for 16,000 rupees; we did not have so much money so we did not get it done.
>
> Suraiya: I keep thinking about it. Tell me a good doctor. Though doctors tell me that my problem is *chinta*. I have tried homeopathy and Ayurveda but all the responsibility is on my head, so what do I do?

Women access help through many quarters; sometimes they move from one to another and back, for example Chanda, who says that they are planning to go to the Balaji temple again. This is because seeking medical help has not been completely satisfactory. Her daughter has moved from functioning well to not doing any work, therefore the constant hope for improvement. Chanda's daughter showed negative symptoms of schizophrenia for which she requires rehabilitation rather than just medication. When I met Chanda, her daughter was not aggressive or actively symptomatic but she was unable to follow a routine. This is a common problem that many families face with people with schizophrenia. This kind of behaviour is difficult for family members to understand, and it leads to a search for different avenues. Periods of functioning well mean that families keep trying different healing practices because of the intermittent reinforcement that these periods bring. In other cases, Salma Khatoon and Shahbano talk about the expenses involved in accessing healing practitioners in the community, thereby making them inaccessible. Rubina is sent by the *'hafi'* to the doctor and thereafter continues to access both places. That the experience of the women mentioned here is representative of the community practices is supported by the accounts of the key informants:

> Both Hindu and Muslim women stand outside the mosque in the evening; after *namaaz* they blow air (*phoonk marte hain*). Women whose children are irritable take them there and believe that this will cure them. They also go to the Maulanas because they give tangible things like *taweez*. Poor Hindus usually go to them because Maulanas have a certain personality; they maintain a lot of hygiene, have incense sticks and create an atmosphere. Well-to-do Hindus, for example the Baniyas who live in Mahindra Park [area next to Jahangirpuri which is considered a better colony] will never go to a Maulana; they go to Pandits for *upay* (solution). Usually they are asked to fast, or get a small puja done; they approach Pandits in case of any family problem. Many people go to private doctors who are also called Bengali doctors. These are men who have passed class IV or V and with some training with doctors, open their own clinics. Nowadays police has closed down many of these clinics to try and stop quackery. Those who had Ayurveda certificates now function as Ayurvedic clinics and give allopathic medicine on the side. They are the lifeline of poor people because they give medicine for ₹4–5 and are available 24 hours. They also talk to the patient in detail and their medicine help the poor a lot. People think

it's more efficient to go to these private doctors than government doctors who hardly look at them; they just prescribe medicine and send them to buy medicines from outside.

KII[5]_PC[6]

The programme coordinator of the NGO states that 'Bengali doctors' or private doctors are the lifelines of people. This is because they provide cheaper services and are available whenever there is need. Because of their various attributes, people have more faith in them. People in the community consider the medicines prescribed by 'private doctors' as more effective because of the dyadic relationship between the patient and the healer. After many of them closed down, people started taking medicines from the chemists as they do not have the energy or the resources to go to a government doctor.

> Whatever the background, everyone first goes to the maulvis or the gurujis they believe in. I do not know of too many pandits who are consulted although there are many maulvis who are consulted. Uneducated people believe everything is *upar ki hawa*. Medicine do not work in two days, but they don't have the patience for wait longer. Go for exorcism, someone has done something (*Jhadhe ke liye jao, kisi ne kuch kar diya hai*), this is considered a faster cure.

KII_HW[7]

> Many women want to talk but we don't have time for them. They usually believe when anything is wrong that *upar ki hawa lag gayi hai*. They listen to us but hardly ever do what we ask them to do; they are always going to other places. There are Ayurveda and homeopathic clinics on the first floor in the afternoon; same patients go there as well. They take all the medicines together.

KII_HW2

The health worker's (HW1 who was Dalit) statement about being aware of more maulvis then pandits corroborates the statement made

---

[5] Key Informant Interview.
[6] Programme Coordinator.
[7] Health Worker.

by the programme coordinator about caste differences in help-seeking. Many of the women I spoke to talked about approaching maulvis for help rather than pandits because of the nature of my sample of subjects which consisted of more Dalit and Muslim women (around 60%) as compared to upper caste Hindu women.

Creation of 'atmosphere' and offering concrete symbols for help (in the form of *taweez*) are considered important in building faith. It is important to understand how this 'faith' is formed and the reasons for approaching multiple sources of help.

Continuum of healers

(a) The Maulana

The Maulana was a tall and well-built man, with a long beard. He would always wear *kurta*, *dhoti* and the traditional Islamic cap. He had a powerful voice and while talking would look straight into your eyes without blinking. He practised healing part-time as in order to run his household he was involved in several part-time businesses. He said that he was not so well-trained but he belonged to a family of trained maulvis who were experts in healing. Apart from being a healer, he introduced himself as someone who was engaged in helping people, taking them to hospitals and so on whenever anyone needed help. He described various instances of healing. According to him, healing required special skills and there were some people who misused this. He said that they conducted several raids to weed out conmen who duped people for money or lust. He gave instances of how they had caught a man who had sexually assaulted several women. He said this was important so as to retain the sanctity of the work. He felt that allopathic doctors were sometimes too distant from the people, *parchi likh di aur khatam* (write a prescription and that's all). There is a need to go to the root of the problem, he said. He gave an example of a case that he had handled of a couple who had come to him; the wife had been going for treatment for years with no help:

The woman used to hit her husband, tear her clothes and scream, pull her hair out; everyone thought she was going mad. I spoke to her for some time and then asked her why she was acting this way, why the drama? She had a slight *Jinn* but it was not serious. She told me that her husband was having an affair and would speak to the woman for hours on the phone. Because of this she behaved in this manner. I told her that her husband would stop but she had to stop behaving like that otherwise I would punish her. I had to warn her so that she would be too scared to behave like that. I then called the husband and approached this topic indirectly; I told him a story. Through this story the man learnt his lesson and realized that I knew what was happening.

Once upon a time there was a *sunaar* (jeweller). One day a very good-looking girl came to him and asked him to make bangles for her. He asked her to come the next day. When she returned he gave her the bangles and while doing that he caught her hand, put it on his chest and kissed it. She was embarrassed and went away. The same day when his wife was taking water from a man who had been coming to the house for many years, the man also did the same thing with his wife. His wife who was also very beautiful went inside the house and locked it. When the *sunaar* came back to his house in the evening, his wife refused to open the door, she asked him what he had done wrong. This was because a man who had been coming for many years and had never misbehaved had done something wrong. So the *sunaar* admitted his mistake. Even if you hide and make mistakes god sees you and it comes back to (affect) your sister, mother or someone.

The Maulana said that the man repented and promised never to repeat this again. It becomes evident that he uses different methods for different kinds of problems. For problems related to actual possession by *Jinn*, for instance, he does not perform exorcism as he is not so trained. But where problems are because of human or social causes he may take on different roles, of a counsellor or of a social worker wherein he accompanies people to hospitals, arranges their appointments or any other kind of help that they require.

(b) The 'private doctor'

'Private doctors' or the 'Bengali doctors' as many of them are called are an important part of the healthcare machinery in Jahangirpuri. Many of them are registered medical practitioners who have been trained in the clinics of qualified doctors and have set up their own clinics in areas like this where there is a lack of qualified personnel. They are in regular contact with qualified doctors and there is an informal referral system which works there. Some of them have done a short course in Ayurveda or Homeopathic medicine and started their practice. I was told to meet one particular practitioner as he practised allopathic, Ayurvedic and alternative healing simultaneously.

> I adapt my practice according to the patients and their problems. For normal cold or cough, it's allopathic; for chronic symptoms, Ayurvedic, in which in a different time, by examining the sweat and body constitution, doctors could make out what was wrong but now there are tests available for everything. Sometimes when women come in with headache, bodyache, I give them a painkiller and also press their head and read the 'aed' from the Koran. I have also studied in a madrassa when I was young; my brother is a maulvi and he deals with these things. I know that they benefit from medicine, but with a religious input they feel satisfied (*tasalli*); half the illness goes away because of this. I sometimes press certain points on the nose also and the headache becomes less. People usually believe that reading the Koran makes the difference. Mental health problems were present before also, now they have increased, because everyone has financial worries.

The accounts of both the healers illustrate that they use different and innovative ways to resolve the problems of the people who approach them. Their practice is usually tailored according to the needs of the person approaching them. The concept of *tasalli* or the satisfaction of the people is considered most important. They use different strategies to ensure that the person leaves them satisfied. This satisfaction with the interaction is often one of the most vital aspects of healing. Halliburtan (2003) found that among psychiatric patients in Kerala in southern India, people suffering from psychopathology and related problems had positive aesthetic reactions to Ayurvedic psychiatric treatments and some complained about the abrasive effects of allopathic medications and electroconvulsive therapy (ECT). In certain cases, this led patients to discontinue allopathic therapy and pursue other forms of treatment. Additionally, some people with intractable mental suffering have found a solution to their problems by living at religious healing centres which provide an aesthetically engaging process of therapy (ibid.: 161).

Another reason for the popularity of the healers could be because they rarely turn people away. This is not necessarily always a good thing as they might give wrong advice or harmful suggestions. The very fact that they would always provide solutions is what makes them attractive help-givers. It is also important to note that they both practise in areas where crime is high and they could get caught in the gang wars that go on.

(c) Doctors with degrees

The 'lady doctor' sits in a clinic run by the India Population Project which was initially started by the World Bank and was now being run by MCD. She said that she was looking to be transferred to a better area as she did not like this one. She was transferred from the area in a couple of months and for a long time there was no doctor available. The doctor did not like the area and the people living in it and wondered why researchers/social workers were so interested in people living there. According to her, unemployment of educated people in her own family was making her more frustrated and angry with the situations around her. She spoke about the work done by the ANMs and the ASHA workers and felt that the latter worked harder and better as they were on contract. She felt that even the doctors would work better if they had to be more accountable. She came regularly for work because of her own conscience as there was no one to really check on her. Many of the doctors never showed up for work on time which created more frustration in those who did. Doctors were the supreme authority in most of these clinics; this view was echoed by a lab technician as well who said that women's health issues are difficult to handle as nothing works without the doctor's permission. If he/she does not come in, then nothing moves forward because power is centralized. This centralization of work procedures creates problems for those trying to access the services as well, because people have to stand in long lines and wait for hours before they get a turn to see the doctor. This further pushes people towards private doctors. It is indeed ironic that the people (doctors) who are most powerful in the system are the ones who are also the most distant from the population that they are treating. This is evident from the views of both the gynaecologist and the homeopath.

(i) Gynaecologist

Women in the area usually came to her with problems related to RTIs (reproductive tract infections) and STIs (sexually transmitted infections). According to her, many of the women had STIs because of the 'sexual malpractices' that existed in the area; men and women were into partner-swapping with people who lived on different floors. STIs spread because women often don't know about their husbands' other relationships or they have multiple relationships of their own. She added that although people's engagement with sexual activities started at an early age, knowledge about safe sex practices was very poor. Women's understanding of their bodies was also minimal. She explained that there was great reluctance to use allopathic treatment and many women preferred home deliveries as their mothers delivered at home and mostly *dais* helped with the delivery. The difference in treatment could be one of the factors because of which women were reluctant to go to the hospital for deliveries. In a vulnerable situation, women are often more comfortable with the familiar as compared to the more distant world of a hospital.

> Women come to the health centre with cough cold, often with bruises. I can see they haven't got these because of a fall but because of some beating. They often talk about being slapped or hit but I am not interested in hearing these things and I discourage them from talking about this. People come here as a last resort; many of them go to homeopaths, Ayurvedic healers and learn myths from them. They often say *jhada karvaya tha phir aaye*. They never came on time and people have very little faith in allopathic medicine.

It appears that the inaccessibility of the doctor also prevents women from seeking help here. Most people tried everything; for the physical body they might take treatment under the allopathic system but for their mental and emotional needs they seek other systems.

(ii) Homeopath

The homeopath practised in the government dispensary. He was not a local person but had the proper credentials required for the job. The homeopath sits in the dispensary in the afternoon; in the morning the same room is occupied by the allopath. The homeopath walked in more than half an hour late to the clinic. He found it difficult to understand the nature of my research and said that there were no major mental health problems; it was only physical problems that he encountered. He appeared confused as to why his input was required in a mental health research. The mention of homeopathy as one of the holistic systems of healing decreased his reluctance to talk. He agreed with that and said that case histories always included mental issues.

> Why should allopathic doctors ask any psychological questions? They have many patients so they do not have the time. The psychological problems in women are usually husband-related: problems, fights, anxiety. These women come from bad places so they have problems. I see people with OCD and depression which are common here. 10 people live within 25 yards and then four people live within 100 yards; there are problems because of this. Any illness spreads and a dozen family members come; by the time the last one recovers the first one falls sick again. Chicken pox and colds get transmitted. Many ragpickers come with skin and respiratory diseases because of poor conditions of work. Bangladeshis arrive and the population increases, therefore the load on dispensaries is going up; there is no end to service provision unless things are resolved at the root.

According to him why people sought continuous treatment here is because it's all free, whether antibiotic or, consultations. He felt that for most people it was an outing and therefore they took advantage of the situation. He also felt that many problems occurred because the differences were very stark: one side of the road was better, cross the road and the living conditions deteriorated.

The homeopath talked in detail about the nature of the community but his focus remained on physical health aspects only. There were issues of family life which bothered women but it seemed from his descriptions that he ignored these problems and considered them out of his purview. Although in his case there was some recognition of the relationship between social conditions and the people's health, he considered himself an outsider and did not pay attention to these issues even when women brought them up. His views were in tune with those of the gynaecologist.

The position of both the allopath and homeopath appeared similar. They both spoke about the presence of violence in the lives of women who wanted to share it with them; both were disinterested and hence either ignored or discouraged patients from bringing these up. Their positions were very different from that of the RMP, who seemed to have at least some insight into the psychology of the people. It could either be a class issue or one of a sense of belonging: the homeopath and the allopath in the government dispensaries were outsiders whereas the RMP was a part and product of the community. Getting trained with doctors and being a part of the community had helped him to acquire two languages to express himself. He modified his language depending on the person he was interacting with. This was obviously lost to the doctors who came from other areas and carried the same language everywhere and had not learnt to be flexible. This in part could explain the attractiveness of the 'private doctors' or 'religious healers' to the people who also wanted to be involved in their own healing.

(iii) District Mental Health Programme (DMHP)

Jahangirpuri also had a psychiatry team coming to the local hospital twice a week. The team had been allotted two rooms in the hospital; usually one doctor and a social worker were present. During these two days the clinic would be very crowded and neither the doctor nor the social worker had much time to spend with any person. Most of the time, they ended up repeating the medication. The social worker also did not have any time or space for counselling. Lack of resources in terms of staff and space made quality input almost impossible. The mental health professionals in the programme shared that the DMHP did not have enough funds and therefore professionals were not interested in joining the programme. Provision of adequate services became difficult because of these reasons.

Dealing with mental health problems was more difficult because of a combination of lack of resources and the attitude of the people. This was apparent when one of the women from the organization's SHG groups approached the programme coordinator for help regarding any homes for people with mental disorders. She spoke about two children; one a girl who was kept tied up in the house. This was because she would frequently run out of the house and take off her clothes in the street. One day in anger her mother had put a burn mark on her. In another house, there was a boy who lived close to the road and he would run to the road and stand in the middle of the road and would keep sitting on the road. Because of which his mother tied him up at home because she did not have any other options.

The coordinators' immediate response to this was to instruct her to take some photographs and get a court order; only then would immediate action take place. The researcher raised questions about this and suggested that they be informed about other options like further assessment and medication if required. The coordinator just replied that these people did not understand anything till they got a court order. It seemed that to a certain extent this was an additional burden on the single mother who was probably trying her best to survive, instead of providing any support services. This was a knee-jerk response to the situation by someone who was relatively better informed. This new zeal for social action among NGOs seems to be a worrying trend. This example also clearly presents the difficulties of dealing with mental health issues in an urban slum community and highlights the absence of awareness as well as adequate institutional support services.

DISTRESS: A LIMINAL STATE

Madness is understood with the help of concepts related to supernatural forces or human and social factors. It is also seen as a state which can be long- or short-term. The features of long-term 'madness' described in terms of possession which leads to talking to self, laughing, inappropriate behaviour and which arises without apparent cause would be categorized under severe mental disorders in the language of psychiatry. Possession behaviour in this case would be seen as psychotic behaviour.

Possession which is episodic and is related to the social context of the person is categorized under the human and social realm by the community. The resolution of the problem would lead to an improvement in the possessed person's condition. ICD-10[8] refers to these as 'Trance and Possession Disorders' and calls them 'dissociative states'. Dissociative states along with somatoform and other anxiety disorders are represented under the category of 'common mental disorders'.

Within the community, women might be directed through informal sources to seek psychiatric help for conditions related to possession disorders (both the long- and short-term type). Psychiatric institutions are more likely to be approached in conditions that appear to resemble symptoms of severe mental disorders. When it comes to the expression of psychosocial distress through the body, aches, pains or 'tension', then general medical care is sought. Women often take medication for a long time without finding any improvement in their condition. This further increases their distress. They describe these problems as arising out of the difficult conditions in which they live. In spite of this insight into their problems, they explain them in bio-medical terms as this gives more legitimacy to their narrative of pain and distress. The way in which an illness is conceived by the wider culture will shape the way the agent feels throughout the illness and will likewise shape the narrative that is constructed about the experience of the same illness. McGuire (2010) explains that in her fieldwork among women with anxiety and depression, her informants were more prone to describing their symptoms through the lens of depression than anxiety. In

---

[8] International Classification of Diseases.

their understanding of their context, anxiety is accorded less medical legitimacy than depression. Strategizing to fit one's symptoms within legitimized categories of illness is indicative of how much culture works to shape how an illness is felt, experienced, and communicated (ibid.: 77).

The behavioural manifestations of common mental disorders are ambiguously defined even in psychiatric literature as they cover a vast range of states including anxiety, depression, somatoform disorders, somatization and so on. They have been found to be associated with economic difficulties, limited decision-making agency, and low levels of family support (Patel et al., 1999). According to Karlekar (2005), while a sizeable percentage of women's health problems lie rooted in familial dynamics and tension-ridden relationships, more often than not they get treated for physical disorders. This occurs because of the liminal state they occupy. Turner (1964: 97) notes that the liminality pertaining to states that have been ambiguously or contradictorily defined, differs from the liminality characterizing ritualized transitions between states. The status of many chronic pain sufferers cannot be accurately determined: they are 'not-quite-either' or 'some of both'. Women experiencing psychosocial distress usually 'fall' in these states thereby making the picture more complex. Women are in danger of being 'over-treated' because of being in this liminal state, as this has been appropriated by psychiatry into the realm of common mental disorders. These appear to provide a comfortable space within psychiatry for talking about distress that women faced rather than seeing their distress as 'illness behaviour'. This has led to some worrying outcomes which include the use of a 'social language' to prescribe medicine. This can be seen in the working of the DMHP where in spite of recognition of the social causes, the treatment consisted mainly of prescription of medicine. This is because constraints of resources and time made this most feasible. There was a de-recognition of traditional healing practices by the professional practitioners. There was no engagement with the question whether spirituality (defined here simplistically as access to the emotions of the sacred) had a role to play in self experience, healing and recovery (Seligman, 2005).

Although psychiatric drugs have been found to be beneficial in many of the severe mental disorders, their influence is increasing beyond requirement. The narratives of the women in this chapter show that they use multiple sources of help and move from one source to another. This ability to choose and utilize different systems together—allopathic, homeopathy, Ayurveda, voluntary work, spirituality and so on, in order to heal oneself, is empowering in itself. Since issues of illness and health remain embedded in social decisions and actions, it is important to understand the context in which they are being produced.

Women, Social Structure and Distress*

> Mental health cannot be defined in terms of the 'adjustment' of the individual to his society, but, on the contrary, it must be defined in terms of the adjustment of society to the needs of man, of its role in furthering or hindering the development of mental health. Whether or not an individual is healthy, is primarily not an individual matter, but depends on the structure of his society.
>
> —Fromm, 1956: 70

Physical and social structures of a community exert a great influence on the everyday lives of people. These structures either contribute to or protect the individual from development of psychosocial distress. There are times that they do both. The linkages between them and psychosocial distress are furthered through the use of Bourdieu's concepts of habitus and social space. Here the intersections between physical and social space, household organization and psychosocial distress are explored further.

STRUCTURAL CHANGES

Jahangirpuri: History

Jahangirpuri is a place of multiple realities and the view of the place presented here is based on the accounts of the people living there currently. It presents the way they viewed the place in the early days and the changes that they perceive in the present. The memories of origin begin around 30 years back. The settlement was established during

---

* Certain sections of this chapter have been published in *Social Action*, Vol. 84, No. 3, July–September 2014, pp. 254–67, *Psychology and Developing Societies*, Vol. 27, No. 1, March 2015, pp. 104–24 and *Indian Anthropologist*, 42(1), 27–38, 2012.

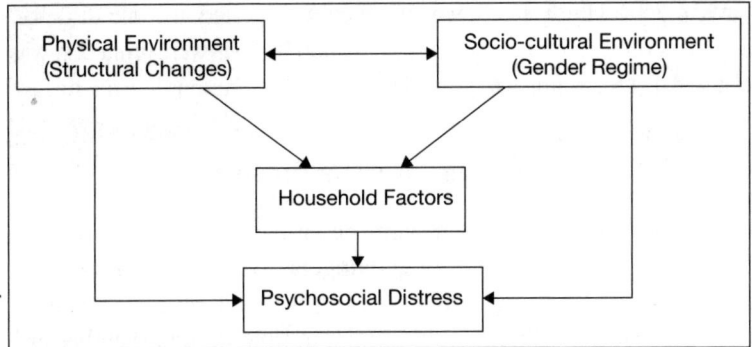

Figure 5.1 *Factors Affecting Psychosocial Distress*
Source: Author.

the time when Indira Gandhi was Prime Minister around 1976–77 (post-Emergency). Most inhabitants came from across the Yamuna. During that period each family was given small plots of land within large tracts of land which gradually evolved into colonies over the years during which various kinds of changes occurred. There was no drainage system, no latrines, and no potable water. The toilets were outside and everyone would go outside to relieve themselves. During the monsoon the problems would increase manifold as houses would get flooded. Many NGOs started working here during the floods of 1978 when many of the houses got submerged. The water had reached first floors of many houses. Even now the older houses get flooded frequently. At the time of its inception, Jahangirpuri was like a jungle with many open spaces.

The daily routine of women was tough as they cooked meals on the *chulha*. They were also responsible for fetching fresh water. For this they had to walk around three kilometres every day, as only saline water was available nearby. There were times that they would have to buy water from outsiders. When one tap became available everyone would have to stand in long queues waiting for their turn. Many conflicts took place near the water tap because of the long wait.

Electricity was erratic and there was only one dispensary where they took their children for vaccination. For anything more serious they would have to go to Hindu Rao hospital which was located at some distance. They had difficulties in travelling as transport options were limited. It was claimed that schooling was limited to religious institutions like madrassas.

Jahangirpuri: The Present

Women's lives became easier with the availability of water in every house and the introduction of cooking gas. The women I spoke to reminisced about being scared of using the cooking gas initially as they felt that the cylinder would burst; in time though they became habituated to it. Electricity became available to all subsequently and electric metres were installed in most houses.

There was a change from open toilets to community toilets for each block at some point. But these were inadequate as they would be damaged (missing doors, broken taps and so on) very quickly. Once Jahangirpuri was connected to the city level sewerage system around a decade ago, toilets were constructed in each household. This should have increased the level of security felt by the women as toilets outside the house made them vulnerable to sexual harassment. Presence of toilets inside the homes has reduced security concerns to a certain extent but many women said that they had felt safer in the past.

Medical and educational facilities also improved. There is one hospital located within the ward, Babu Jagjivan Ram Hospital with a capacity of 100 beds. According to the women this offers fewer services and the staff is rude and unfriendly, therefore, people prefer to go to Hindu Rao Hospital although it is further away. There are two Primary Health Centres and four dispensaries catering to a population of around 7,00,000. With the implementation of the National Rural Health Mission, skilled staff is also available. There is a government primary school for every 13 MCD primary schools as well as three 'big' schools (where secondary education is available) running in two shifts. Many private schools are also present in the area. The women felt that the teacher-student ratio was skewed and mid-day meals were not served properly. Data from the District Information System for Education reveal that all schools in India have on average of 41 pupils per teacher (rural 43 and urban 37 pupils per teacher). Government schools have a teacher-pupil ratio of 1:42 as against 1:30 in the case of privately managed schools (Sreekanth, 2009).

Transport options have grown manifold and the entire area looked different after the new flyovers were built and the Metro started running. One of the women in the group remarked:

'Metro *aur bypass ko dekh kar aisa lagta hai ki hum kisi picture ke beech main hain!!*' (After the coming of the metro and bypass, it seems we are living in the middle of some movie.)

All the women agreed with her statement and said that they had never seen something so 'fancy' and that too so close to their homes. The Metro also introduced the idea of air-conditioned (AC) travel to them: 'We can take rides in the AC throughout the day.' Many of them do not have the time or resources to do so but just the idea that they have an option like this available seems to give them a lot of joy. These were the early days when the Metro had just come to the area and it was a source of a lot of excitement.

There have been substantial physical changes in the area but with little real progress. In many of the inner lanes and by-lanes, things have remained unchanged. The lanes in certain blocks are narrow with open drains and garbage spilling out on the road. Some of the lanes have very little space to walk in as many houses have small shops in them selling items like biscuits, sweets, soaps and other sundry items of everyday living. The lanes and the houses differed according to the blocks. The differences that arose also led to another phenomenon which often occurs when there are vast socio-economic differences amongst people living in the immediate neighbourhood: increased crime.

Prisoners in our own house

Cases under the 'crime against women' category reported an increase of 2.9 per cent in 2016 over 2015.

—NCRB, 2016

Crime rates are increasing all over the country. Delhi has the dubious distinction of being one of most unsafe cities in the world for women. Statistics show that women in Delhi face more violence than in any other city in this country (Vishwanath and Mehrotra, 2007). In the discussions with the women in Jahangirpuri as well, the theme of insecurity emerged as an important marker of distress.

Member 1: Everyone has local pistols, also no one is safe

Member 2: People are always scared of their jewellery being snatched.

Member 3: *Ab sab kuch hai, chaen nahi hai. Bus woh chala gaya hai.*

(Now we have everything except peace. Only that is gone.)

—FGD

According to the women in the early days security had never been an issue. Their parents had never worried about them the way they worried about their daughters. They claimed that during the initial period no one had any doors, there were just curtains hung outside the houses and still everyone was safe. Now there were big locks on people's doors and yet no one felt safe. Kidnapping of young children and snatching were reported as being very common. Drugs and alcohol were seen as the main reasons for crime and had become a major source of worry.

Crime is so rampant and so little punished that there are many stories woven around it. Women narrate instances when the chain snatchers came back the next day and slapped women for not wearing real gold. Initially, these accounts appeared to be exaggerations. But later these claims were supported by the local health centre as well. It was one of the ANMs (Auxiliary Nursing Midwife) working there who had been treated like that. They were targets because they moved around in the community and were perceived to have more money as they held government jobs. Even when women stayed at home they were not safe from crime. They described many instances where they had to be alert within the house itself.

> Shakuntla (39 years): Things have become so bad that my mobile was stolen from my house. I had kept a good soap outside the house for a couple of minutes, when I went out it was gone. My neighbour is an addict; he steals everything. Others like him come to the house regularly and we hear them clearly so we cannot stand outside the house; sometimes it's suffocating.

Public places like parks were also not available to women. Men often gambled there and this would increase during Diwali. One of the women spoke about how she had been happy to move into a park-facing house without realizing its implications. Neither she nor her daughter could stand in the balcony for a long time because there were men sitting right in front of the house. Many women complained about being prisoners in their own homes.

> Shakuntla: I don't let my daughters or daughter-in-law move out of the house; I do all the household shopping. I go with them wherever they have to go. The environment here is bad (*yahaan ka mahol kharaab hai*). I sometimes feel like I have become a 'watchman'.

> We have daughters so we cannot go out of the house; they might be attacked. See how in the afternoon, they were trying to break in; we have been hoping that it would improve but we are still waiting.
>
> —FGD

Restrictions on the movement of women are evident from the examples given above. Both the working woman (ANM) and the women who stay at home are vulnerable when they move out. Even standing outside their house is problematic. The word 'suffocation' brings out the distress related to being trapped inside the house. Concerns related to safety are responsible for these feelings. For most women, these concerns increase manifold when it comes to their children.

The women frequently expressed fears for the safety of their children. With regard to their daughters they expressed concerns about them being followed, molested or sexually assaulted. As for their sons, they were worried that they would get into 'bad company'. 'Bad company' was explained as other boys who bunked school and experimented with drugs, sex and alcohol. Boys were introduced to drugs very early on and women described how in the evening seven to eight-year-old boys could be seen selling drugs in certain areas. Women spoke about many concerns regarding their children because of the high crime rates. Concerns regarding the children's education were also discussed. The informants related poor educational facilities with high dropout rates amongst boys. With regard to girls, poor facilities along with high levels of crime resulted in them dropping out of school. The connection between limited schooling and increased crime became apparent from the narratives of the informants.

'I made friends with bullies'

Lack of opportunities pushed many of the boys into gangs. The programme coordinator of an NGO shared that young men of the area came up to him frequently and complained that they had very few vocational programmes for them. Another issue that appeared to be present was the poor quality of education offered in the schools. In an informal conversation, some of the boys said, 'In junior classes children were there but teachers don't teach; whereas in class XI and XII, the teachers come but students don't. This is the story of every school in Jahangirpuri, schools outside might be better (*grinning*).'

This view of the educational facilities was often endorsed by other informants in the community:

> Schools keep refusing admission to children and parents have to pay for admission. Another major problem is that the water tank is usually open because of which the drinking water facility is full of germs. Teachers are always missing from school because they anyway get their salary from the government. There is never any electricity and teachers sit near the doors when there is no electricity while students have to sit inside the class in the heat and humidity.
>
> —KII_PC

The schools are in such a bad state that the boys just run away from them. The younger ones jump the walls whereas the older ones just walk out the gate and no one stops them. In junior classes (Class VI and lower), the boys are frequently bullied by their seniors. Their money and belongings are snatched by the older boys at the school entrance itself. Bullying affects children very intensely. Whether the bullying is direct or indirect, the key component is that the physical or psychological intimidation occurs repeatedly over time to create an ongoing pattern of harassment and abuse (Batsche and Knoff, 1994; Olweus, 1993). Being bullied leads to depression and low self-esteem, problems that can be carried into adulthood (Batsche and Knoff, 1994; Olweus, 1993).

The boys blamed the 'Bengalis' for the bullying. According to them, the Bengali boys of all age groups carried blades in their mouth; to survive, they had to befriend them. One of the boys said that when he was younger he had also been bullied but not anymore. He had made 'Bengali friends' who beat anyone in case they created a problem for him. When asked whether he was also called to participate in such fights, he denied it. His friend's response indicated otherwise. While he was talking, an effort had to be made to comprehend this particular boy's speech as he was chewing tobacco.

In order to survive in this tough environment, many boys befriended the tough crowd. If you were a member of the group, then you followed its code of conduct. This often involved smoking, drinking or drugs. The presence of drugs was visible if you spent some time in the community. During festivals, it was common to run into boys walking in the street who seemed to have no control over their bodies. One of the NGO workers remarked, 'This (alcohol or drugs) is an everyday problem in Jahangirpuri which is heightened during festival time.'

There were many stray incidents of violence that were narrated to me during my time visiting Jahangirpuri:

While walking back from a meeting, we overheard a group of adolescent boys planning a fight. This prompted the worker to describe her experience as a teacher. One of the younger boys in her class had been slapped by an older one. The next day he arrived with six-seven small boys and they threatened the older boy with a knife.

As we were crossing CD Park, the health worker was stopped by a woman. She looked very upset and the worker asked her the reason for this. She explained how her 23-year-old son had gone for a walk and never returned. He was kidnapped and killed. On hearing the story, the health worker added that two more bodies had been discovered in the area. She said, 'We have told our children that if someone insults you, you listen to them and ignore them. The world is not a place to pick fights now.'

It appeared that boys joined gangs at an early age in Jahangirpuri. Gang membership appeared to be a mode of survival for the young boys in this area. The description of life there was aptly summarized by one of the women who said, *'Mahol kharaab hai.'* The *'mahol'* or the atmosphere of the area was one of the main reasons which were turning the women I spoke to into constant 'worriers'.

'Give me your number'

While mothers worried about their sons getting into gangs and drugs, they worried about their daughters' safety from these gangs. There were many restrictions placed on the movement of girls. For the boys, poor educational and vocational facilities push them towards the streets whereas for girls the unsafe streets push them into their homes. Many girls spoke about how their education had been stopped because of these problems:

> Member 1: Our education is stopped because after a certain age it is not safe to go to school and many of our families feel that there is no use of studying after marriage.
>
> Member 2: We have to face comments as soon as we leave the house. There are certain streets where the ragpickers work and these are more unsafe. Often when we hear comments we have to look down and walk away which is very humiliating but the only thing we can do.
>
> —FGD (C Block)

Several studies related to the safety of women have come up with similar findings. Vishwanath and Mehrotra (2007) found that the harassment of girls in their neighbourhoods, on their way to the school, and in buses leads to them dropping out of school. A base line survey conducted by Jagori and UN Women in 2011 found that women of all classes contend with harassment as part of their daily lives. School and college students in the 15–19 age-group and women workers in the unorganized sectors are particularly vulnerable. The most common form of harassment reported was verbal (passing comments) and visual (staring and leering) and physical (touching/groping, leaning over, etc.). In addition to the fear of harassment outside the house, the girls also expressed concerns about the early marriages that were planned for them. They spoke about fears related to violence after marriage as they had witnessed many episodes of marital violence amongst their families and in their neighbourhoods.

In another group, girls belonging to families with slightly higher incomes felt that although there was harassment their lives were more secure as compared to the girls living in 'C' or 'D' block.

> Member 1: We have heard a lot about how girls were troubled but personally have never been troubled ourselves. Sometimes boys hang around in groups and pass comments if a group of girls walk by; they say things like 'give me your number' but it is best to ignore them. If they get no reply they stop on their own, it depends on the girl's attitude as well.
>
> Member 2: My mother has told me not to laugh, smile or sing when walking on the road so that I don't attract unnecessary attention but some girls often do that.
>
> Member 3: We hear that there are more problems for girls in C and D blocks, also in *jhuggis* behind the flats we live in. If they leave home for two-three days, then the house will most probably get robbed.
>
> —FGD (Double E block)

Even though the girls in the second group initially denied the presence of rampant sexual harassment, when probed further they described instances of difficulties when they went alone for some exams. These girls belonged to lower middle-class households. In their effort to differentiate themselves from the girls living in 'C' block, they wanted to show that they faced less crime. Their statements, in fact, give evidence of a greater aspect of social control in their lives. This is evident when they speak about the girl's attitude affecting the way she is treated. It is ultimately her behaviour, whether she laughs too much, sings and so on, which is responsible for her being safe or unsafe. The socialization is such that most of the women never question these norms and believe that this is the ultimate truth. The restrictions, enforced by the women of the family (mothers, grandmothers, aunts) are not presented to the girls as punitive measures but as the reality of the world in which they live. The curbs on their freedom are the way things 'naturally' are, and to which any 'good girl' must comply for her own protection and the good name of the family. She is made to understand, undermining a sense of female agency, that young women are weak and vulnerable, unable to resist determined male advances or the promptings of their own nature (Kakar and Kakar, 2007). Examples of harassment are used to restrict their mobility. One incident can lead to a spiral effect in which many safeguards are imposed on young women. These forms of violence structure the daily lives of women in ways that go far beyond acts of violence, controlling women's movements and behaviour through a constant and continuous sense of insecurity (Vishwanath and Mehrotra, 2007: 3). Although the sense of feeling unsafe is not confined to women, the fear that women feel in urban areas is quite particular. It is to do with physical and psychological honour. All women may not have been attacked or raped but the messages related to safety often make them feel uneasy. This feeling of uneasiness could range from discomfort to complete paralysis. The description of 'suffocation' by women and 'harassment' by girls emphasizes that this feeling of unease exists across age groups.

Ghettos of crime

In conversations with different people in the community (men, women, adolescent boys and girls), certain areas were mentioned frequently as 'bad areas'. People living in these areas were blamed for the proliferation of crime. These areas were often identified with the help of markers of caste, region and religion.

> Initially the Bengalis were nice and supportive, now they have become bad. At first, we used to leave everything outside, no one took anything. Now they even pick up utensils. They enter the house and steal things so I cannot go out of the house and leave the girls alone.
>
> *'Harijan' ki basti hai; wahan se talware lekar aate hain, yahan chori karenge to koi rok nahi sakta.* ('Harijans' have a basti; they come from there with swords, if they steal here, no one can stop them.)

—FGD

> Communities differ on the basis of the blocks that they live in, for example, K block (with people from UP and Bihar) is a clean and well-integrated one where all the children go to school. The Gujaratis (in H-block) are very poor and in these families everyone works: men, women and children. Among the Bengalis who usually do ragpicking, mostly the women and children work while the men do not. Male unemployment is on the rise as most people want to employ women as they can be hired at lower wage rates. Now people have started hiring adolescent girls as they can be given even lower wages. With increasing unemployment amongst men and boys, they tend to start drinking which often leads to an increase in violence at home.

—KII_PC

> I charge more so that certain people don't come. It's a very bad area, full of criminals; I was in the Bengali area, very bad area, they snatch women's earrings, chains. This area of *bhangis* is also very bad. They never want to pay; so many times they come to me after a fight; one group says if you treat them, we will kill you, and others say we will kill you if you don't. My Mrs comes and saves me, she stands in front of me and says, kill me before you kill him. They leave women alone to some extent. People come with cuts; if I call the police I find they are also involved. It's very bad; we are a few people who look after each other.

RMP[1]

There is a strong in-group out-group feeling that exists among people there. To conclude that communities are stereotyped on the basis of caste, region and religion by other communities is a simplistic assumption. People are often critical of their own community. The

---

[1] Registered Medical Practitioner.

RMP criticizing the Bengali area (C block) as being 'bad' and identifying Bengali-speaking Muslims as 'bad', is himself a Muslim who has worked for many years in C block. But in Jahangirpuri, Muslims tend to mention their place of origin especially if they are not Bengali because of negative connotations attached to the word 'Bengali'. Shakuntla, who talks about her neighbour stealing from her, lived in an area where others also belonged to the same community. Therefore, dismissing these statements as just stereotypes would be to dismiss the lived experiences of people. With respect to caste issues, not every area which was dominated by Dalits was considered crime-prone or unsafe. As compared to D block where the registered medical practitioner was located, Double E block which mainly housed Dalit (*Balmiki*) families was considered to be one of the 'good areas'. The roads were cleaner and broader and many houses had cars parked outside them. This indicated the community's better socio-economic status. In this block most of the people were in government service, men and women both worked, and tried to ensure that their children went to school regularly. One of the ASHA workers explained that in Double E block, people living in flats were considered to have better status as compared to the ones who lived in the smaller houses. The flats were considered safer and better places to live in. *Balmikis* are often envied by other castes. As sweeping is a stigmatized profession, the Indian state has introduced measures to improve the economic conditions of sweepers. Municipality jobs entitle *Balmikis* to salaries that are higher than those prevalent in most other informal sector jobs. This makes them one of the highest paid groups amongst the SCs (Searle-Chatterjee, 1981). The status of *Balmikis* has improved to a certain extent because of these benefits. One of the ways in which this has happened is through the flats that were allotted to *Balmikis*. Over a period of time, many of the *Balmiki* families sold their flats and went back to live in their *jhuggis*. Other studies also report similar phenomena where the original allottees sold their flats to higher-income households (Mehrotra, 1997; Tipple et al. 1996). This meant that people of different castes started living in close proximity. Currently, the flats house families from different castes: *Balmikis, Pandits, Baniyas* and so on. One of the informants living there reported that *Balmikis* were very clean (as opposed to the stereotypes associated with the 'sweeper caste' of being 'dirty' and 'unclean') and the area was well-maintained. She said, '*Sab theek hain, Muhamadan nahin hone chahiye*' (Everyone is okay, Muslims should not be there), exhibiting yet another bias.

These opinions can be contrasted with others who say that in spite of all the facilities given to them, the basic nature of the so called 'lower' castes was unlikely to change. One of the informants remarked, '*Aajkal toh harijan koh harijan kaho toh to bura maan jaate hain.*' (Nowadays if you call a harijan a harijan, they take offence). She worked with different Dalit groups and had a good relationship with the women there. But she seemed unaware of the derogatory nature of her statements and of her own underlying prejudices. Grover (2011) in her work in a Delhi slum points to the diminishing importance of caste discrimination in urban localities where resources need to be shared amicably. Residents socialize with each other during functions and occasions, and food is exchanged during neighbourly encounters and visits (ibid.: 26). But when one looks at the *Balmikis*, a different picture of caste relations emerges which is at odds with the liberal views currently being articulated (ibid.: 27). Most castes avoid commensal relations with *Balmikis*. Given their unique socio-political standing in Delhi, *Balmikis* are also resented on account of being perceived as an economically privileged group (ibid.: 93). Changing socio-economic factors have diluted the caste- and religion-based differences but strong latent biases continue to persist. These biases can be activated very quickly and are evident in many statements. Living next to people from 'lower' caste people may not be as stigmatizing as before but in inquiries related to marriages, the caste of the person is often the first question asked. In Jahangirpuri, religion-related stereotypes were more marked. Within religion also it was the Bengali-speaking Muslims who were blamed as compared to Muslims from other states.

Although crime was mentioned more in terms of certain blocks rather than religion or caste, these identified places usually consisted of certain stigmatized communities (for e.g., Bengali Muslims). These stereotypes were reinforced by incidents such as the following:

One afternoon while coming back from a SHG meeting, we ran into a big crowd outside the NGO's office in C block. On enquiry, we found that a man had tried to break open a lock in broad daylight in a street which is narrow and full of people. When he was stopped, he attacked someone with a knife and injured him. The crowd then managed to overpower him and called the police.

Incidents like this were frequent and cemented the position of C block as the hub of crime in Jahangirpuri. The existing stereotypes regarding certain places and communities need to be problematized and explored in detail to understand the reasons why certain areas and communities get earmarked as 'bad'. Menon-Sen and Bhan (2008) while describing newly resettled colonies in Bawana explain how the stereotypes about physical environment and crime there are grounded in truth. In Jahangirpuri as well, a similar phenomenon can be seen.

GENDER REGIME

Physical spaces impact men and women differently. Sociocultural norms of a community are an important factor in this differential experience. This section explores the relationship between ascribed social roles of women and the resulting stressors.

> Group leader: *Maine usko ek ghar main naukari deelaayi, par uske saas sasur chahate the ki woh maang maang kar khaye, is liye kaam nahi karne dete the.*
>
> (I got her a job as a maid where she was getting good money, but her in-laws would not let her work nor would they give her adequate money to take care of her children and herself. They wanted that she should beg and eat, that is why they would not let her work.)
>
> Member 1: *Kisi ko theek nahi rakhenge to woh kya kar sakte hain?*
>
> (If someone is not treated right, then what can they do?)
>
> Researcher: *Uske bachon ka kya hua?*
>
> (What about her children?)
>
> Member 2: *Unko toh le kar gayi hai, unhi ke liye to gayi hai, woh aadmi kamata hai, khyal rakhega, nahi to kyun jati?*
>
> (She has taken them with her, it was for them that she went, that man earns, will look after them. Otherwise why would she go?)

Group leader: *Agar akeli aurat ho to kisi na kisi tarah se guzara kar leti hai par bachon ke saath aadmi ki zaroorat padti hai.*

(If it's a woman on her own in one way or another she manages; but with children a man is needed.)

Members (amongst each other): *Usne galat rasata apnaya, par uske paas koi aur rasta bhi nahi tha.*

(She took the wrong way but she had no other choice.)

—FGD (Gujarati women)

This was a discussion about distressed women. The women in the group were talking about one of the women in their community who had run away with another man because she was troubled. The women explained that the woman's husband had been living with another woman and her in-laws treated her badly leaving her with very few options. As this was a group of women, without the presence of any man, these women were trying to defend the woman. In the presence of men this discussion might have gone differently. Here as well, the woman's decision to 'run away' with another man is defended not from the position of the woman who might want a companion but as that of a mother. If she had been on her own then she would have managed to stay even in these circumstances, but with children it was important for her to cross the '*lakshmanrekha*'.[2] Grover (2011) states that in an atmosphere of normalized violence, the sympathy factor amongst neighbours is more when women are denied *kharcha-pani*; hunger and disregard for children evoke greater public concern. In this case, the absence of the husband and the denial of basic rights to the woman and her children meant that women felt able to voice their support.

---

[2] *Lakshmanrekha*, the line that Lakshmana traces around Rama's hut, is the divide between nature and culture. Within the line Rama's law applies. Outside is the wilderness, the realm of Ravana. Within, there is regard for the law of marriage; without there isn't any. Inside it, Sita is Rama's wife; outside it, she is a woman for the taking. If Ravana enters Rama's hut and forces himself on Sita then he will be judged by the rules of society. But when he forces himself on Sita outside the *Lakshmanrekha* he will be judged by the laws of the jungle. Therefore, inside it, he would be a villain whereas outside he would merely be a trickster (Pattanaik, 2006: 100).

The discussion presented above brings out varying views on gender relations and roles that are ascribed to women. Internal structures, processes and beliefs ascribe different tasks and positions to men and women in the community. The women talk about how they are controlled and the roles they are expected to play. Many of them do not question this but merely state facts about their reality. It is important to understand the roles that this particular community assigns to the women in Jahangirpuri. The Figure 5.2 shows the relationship of gender regime with psychosocial distress.

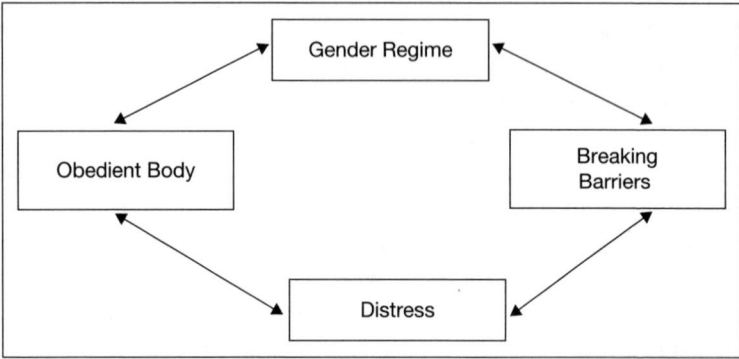

Figure 5.2 *Aspects of Gender Regime*

Source: Author.

Obedient Body

Guddo (37 years): Sometimes in our colony there are fights between men and women. If women speak badly, give replies then there is a problem, otherwise it remains okay.

Women are often assigned boundaries in which they are supposed to live out their lives. These boundaries are sometimes clearly spelt out but most of the times they exert a more subtle and powerful control as they are not mentioned frequently but just exist.

Haseena (19 years): Picnic; I can't go for any picnic; I don't have permission; ask my sister here. (Both sisters looked at each other and smile, a smile of shared understanding). Life was very different when my father was alive;

we had a lot more freedom, no one asked us how we were spending our money, now we have to account for every penny.

Being accountable for spending 'every penny' is obviously humiliating for Haseena who has now become answerable to her brother. She remembers with nostalgia the time when her father was alive and there was freedom. The death of the father has automatically conferred the status of 'the head of the household' to her brother who is only a year older than her. She finds it difficult to question his authority because of the organization of kinship structure in her community. Thapan (1995) argues that the possibilities of transformation are always bounded by the restricting nature of the dominant construction based on gender, class, caste and regional affiliations. It is not necessary that these constraints are located outside our embodied selves; in fact, more dangerously they have been accepted and internalized by women as being their defining characteristics (ibid.: 38). This internalization of norms does not mean that women never question them. They may not resist them actively but they do raise questions about them. Shilpa while narrating her story articulated this clearly:

> Shilpa: Please forgive me, I talk too much, you will think I am mad. Here people think that if a woman speaks then she is mad, but if men say them, the same things sound good.

Women expressing their opinions is not regarded as favourable which often leads to the silencing of women's voices in the community. The restricting nature of the habitus comes out starkly in women's narratives of not being allowed to work outside the house.

> Kunti: *Maine kabhi kaam nahi kiya, kyunki hamare main lugayi kaam nahi karti.*
>
> (I have never worked, because among us, the wife does not work).
>
> Neeta (35 years): I used to work sometimes but people here are very bad; if you dress up well they accuse you of doing sex work. I don't talk to many of the neighbours because they say things about me; what is wrong in being a sex worker; sometimes women need to do it. [She said this in a challenging manner as if waiting for the researcher to contradict her] One of my neighbours who talks to me, they say things to her so she keeps to herself.

> Sangeeta: We have no savings and he does not let me work also because in our family, no one (woman) works. I feel like working because at home I just sit and brood, but he keeps refusing to let me work.

Working outside the house and the kind of work that women can take up is regulated by caste considerations. Thapan (2009) explains that women from some communities are allowed to work in factories but not as domestic servants. Being a domestic help is associated with caste impurity, cleaning other people's floors or dishes. The space of the factory appears as a more neutral space where no major caste factors are visible (ibid.: 144). Therefore, women from higher castes like Kunti (*Rajput*) are not allowed to take any work whereas others might be 'allowed' to work in neutral spaces. Apart from caste, women such as Sangeeta are restricted from working because of issues related to control and suspicion. Sangeeta's husband is dependent on alcohol and is frequently violent after drinking. Studies have shown that men who are dependent on alcohol become increasingly suspicious of their wives' movements. Men become completely focused on drinking, and women often have to fulfil both the masculine and feminine roles in the household which reduces the power of the husband. Usually violence is the consequence of a crisis in representation, both individual and social. The inability to maintain the fantasy of power triggers a crisis in the fantasy of identity, and violence is a means of resolving this crisis because it acts to reconfirm the nature of masculinity otherwise denied (Moore, 1994: 69). Violence obviously becomes a way of exerting their authority as financial control shifts from the husband to the wife. If the wife starts working, then the power equations would tilt further in favour of the wife. The imposed powerlessness leads to the sadness expressed by Sangeeta who is unable to supplement her household income. The curtailment of her agency gives rise to psychosocial distress. Psychosocial distress is often a result of the societal restrictions on women's movements preventing them from exercising their agency. This is brought out by Neeta's statement as well. Neeta's husband is dependent on alcohol and contributes very little to the household income. For Neeta, exercising her agency (looking presentable in spite of the frequent absences of her husband and going for work) means facing malicious comments. Neeta voices her anger at the fact that people are unhelpful and judgemental about the kind of work women might have to undertake in order to survive.

'Passing comments' appears to be an effective way to influence the actions of women in Jahangirpuri. This strategy is effective in a variety of circumstances: (a) when women want to work; (b) if in times of need they use different methods to generate money; (c) if they wish to be different; or (d) even if they just want to look clean and presentable. The regulation of women's actions and movements is also a result of the responsibility placed on the women to maintain the honour of the family. Das (1995) in her accounts of women during the partition era describes how they were expected to accept violent death rather than submit to sexual violence by men of other communities in order to save the 'family honour'. Many of the women looked upon these burdens placed upon them not only as a form of violence from men of other communities but also as a form of violence emanating from their own men (ibid.: 63).

Within Jahangirpuri as well, the accounts of women depict their ambivalence towards the controls that are imposed on their movements, actions and appearances. This emphasizes how social space delineates a person's sphere of social interactions and aspirations. The notion of gender is stereotyped, contained and transmitted through multiple channels, oral and written traditions, folklore, morals and myths (Deckard, 1979; Quinn, 1977; Reiter, 1975). Social space remains a place for contestation and conflict. Therefore, the nature of the social space and the restrictions it imposes on women often gives rise to psychosocial distress.

Breaking Barriers (Breadwinners vs Homemakers: Dichotomy or Continuum)

Traditional notions about the gendered division of labour consist of men as 'breadwinners' and women as 'homemakers'. The accounts of women in Jahangirpuri challenge this traditional notion. In cases of abandonment, out-of-marriage relationships, or death of a spouse, women have taken over as the main providers. Other reasons included alcoholism and ill-health of the husband. In some cases, even when the husband was working, women needed to start work to meet the household's financial requirements.

Many studies on paid work and mental health of women have concluded that having a job outside the home protects women's mental health (Bartley et al., 1992; Brown and Harris, 1978; Kandel et al., 1985; Warr and Parry, 1982). However, it has been noted that combining paid work with family and home responsibilities may reduce the well-being benefits from employment (Lundberg and Frankenhauser, 1999). Important issues to consider are women's role in the formal labour market or the informal sector such as market- and home-based work, and how work roles are integrated with household labour (Arber, 1991; Nathanson, 1980), the division of labour within the household, and other family and household members for whom the woman may be responsible (Matthews and Power, 2001).

Many of the women in Jahangirpuri had to start working because of financial conditions at home. Usually, at the time of starting work they did not have much education, training or confidence and hence their work options were limited. Often, they expressed a dislike for the kind of work that they had to do. A crisis at home was one of the main factors for pushing women into work.

> Rubina (works as a ragpicker): I work long hours from 4 AM, in the dark, till noon or even till 2 PM the next day in order to get the work finished. I go for work in the dark so I have to be careful; sometimes I go with other women, sometimes alone in a rickshaw. Now no one helps each other; now many Bangladeshis have come, and at night the police beat people and take them away, I feel very bad when someone is being beaten, all the time it keeps going on in the head. On the way, the mechanic boys who know me tell me if there are boys near the park hanging around after drinking, so that I can take a different route. I once saw boys from a good home being taken by the police; a girl (who looked like you) was also there. I felt very

bad that people from good homes are also stealing now; now there are thieves everywhere.

Shahbano: Once during Ramzan my daughter got dizzy and fell down. I took her to the local hospital; there was no doctor there so we took her to Azadpur. She had a broken hand that took two or three months to recover. Then her left side kept hurting; I thought that some injury had happened about which she had never told us. After X-rays we found that she had TB; I had to stop working on some days. I make an excuse that I have to go and talk to someone and go ragpicking instead. I don't tell my daughter; she says that she will have bland food but does not want me to do this work.

The shame related to a certain kind of work is very evident in Shahbano's narrative which forces her to hide her work from her children. Medical emergencies can also push a family quickly from a state of stability to chaos leaving the resources of the family severely taxed. This is true in the case of Rubina as well who had to start working after her husband fell ill. Rubina's work requires her to exercise caution as she needs to leave home in the dark. Her experiences in the dark are often unpleasant. What she sees is upsetting for her and therefore 'it keeps going on in her head'. Ludermir and Lewis (2005) found that informal work was associated with high prevalence of common mental disorders among females. They suggest that working outside the protection of employment legislation and with limited opportunity for skill use may be a risk for women's mental health.

A study on the impact of work and environment on women's morbidity in a sample population in Mumbai found that cohabiting women with children engaged in paid work had the highest morbidity rates (Madhiwalla and Jesani, 1997), higher than that of either single women or housewives. The types of morbidity experienced by the women included reproductive problems, aches, pain and injuries; weakness, fever, respiratory problems; problems in the gastrointestinal tract; skin, eye and ear problems and a residual category of 'other' problems. The study also found, quite significantly, that degraded living environment, as in a slum, has deleterious effects on people's health and that the morbidity rates were highest for those adult women with children who were living in slums and were engaged in paid work (ibid.). Most of the women in Jahangirpuri were engaged in informal work (either outside the house or within it) and lived in conditions similar to those of women in Mumbai slums. This exposed them to higher levels of psychosocial distress. Rubina and Shahbano were forced into work which they did not like. They seem to be caught in difficult circumstances. But not all women respond to these social situations in a similar manner. An ethnographic study by Channa (1997) in a Haryana village shows how there are some women who are able to manage their existing social environment so that they are granted the space that they want. This 'space' need not take the individuals outside the sphere of social interaction. In fact, there is space for individuals to exert their individualism, often in a manner which goes against normative patterns and yet allows them to retain their social identity (ibid.: 29). Padma's narrative follows this kind of a trajectory.

I was introduced to Padma by the nurse at the local health centre. She was working as the ANM at that time. Padma is a 39-year-old dynamic woman; she has seven children, five girls and two boys. She is a tall woman with broad shoulders which makes her stand out. She described how she had been working in the area of HIV and sex education, and the kind of difficulties that presented in her work and personal life.

> I worked with several NGOs, even distributed condoms on the road. In the early days I had no confidence but now I can talk to everyone. Women have many problems. Men drink, and then they are violent, they go out with other women outside the house, because of this women fall ill. If they go out for work, they are again harassed. When they are in trouble they catch me, if they are beaten or there are problems related to dowry, I take them to Kiran Bedi's organization 'Navjyoti' or get help from some other organization. I take them to the hospitals also. I can't sit at home, they come there as well. My husband jokes that you take an umbrella and start off in the night as well. But this is my identity now (*par yeh toh ab meri pehchan hai*).

> When I started working in the field of HIV, I was confused and I didn't understand. When we train adolescent girls we tell them that when you have relationships use condoms to make yourself safe. Then I feel that we

are teaching some kids who are innocent about sex. NGOs and us, we give lectures but if the condom fails and girl gets pregnant then the NGO will not come; that is why it is both right and wrong. At least we talk to each other; TV, Internet do not do that.

When this NGO Sahara opened, they came looking for me. They had been told by someone that I had worked in the area, so they came to my house. They had tea and asked me to start working. They had no office here and I had no fixed salary; I used to sometimes get ₹1000, 1500 or 2000. When the office started I did a lot of work and their NGO did better and better; work spread like anything. I used to have good relationships with all the coordinators. When the third coordinator joined, he was no good. I caught him with two sex workers who also used to work there. People used to call me a sex worker because I worked with them; this man also thought the same. But I ignored him. So he started finding faults in my work. I told him to see my diary and that it was filled properly but he still kept troubling me. So, I had a fight with the two women when they also lied about my work. When I do my work with sincerity how can I take their lying? I beat them up, slammed her heads against the wall. They complained about me but the coordinator was the one who was shifted out [says this *with pride*].

The next coordinator was also no good; he was only concerned about targets. If I get one person than I get one person, I can't get 20 people so finally I decided to confront him. I would never stand any nonsense but he kept abusing me so I also gave it back. I would have hit him too but another man intervened and calmed me down. I told him that the organization could not survive too long after I leave and it did not. I do not like such people who are not concerned. I have worked a long time here and there is not a single person who does not recognize me. I have been left behind only because I don't know English.

When I started working I used to tell my husband everything; in fact I told him about a lot of new things. Others used to see me giving lectures about AIDS, condoms and go and tell my husband about how I was talking like this. My husband would say, she is just talking not doing anything. It was because I would tell my husband everything in detail so that he could trust me. Otherwise people tried their best to create trouble between us.

My husband used to work in a *mandi* (vegetable and fruit market). We had losses of about six to seven lakhs because of which I have been under a lot of pressure. I had to pull my boys out of a good school and my daughter was sick so where would I get money from? People kept coming to our house demanding money. Finally, I said you take the money from me not from him. I stood with a sword in front of them: *main jhansi ki rani ki tarah ladi aur sabko bhaga diya* (I fought like Rani of Jhansi and made everyone run away). My husband is simple so everyone tries to fool him. Recently, I got a cycle repair shop opened for him.

I have lost a lot of weight in the past two years; I used to look much better. I was much healthier and fairer [important markers of beauty. Good health implied one was able to eat well and hence signified prosperity]. Now in the last two years because of tension.... My children tell me I should stop worrying; it's spoiling my health.

Padma in her narration makes evident her concerns about creating awareness about HIV/AIDS. She is a part of a community where talking about sexual issues is taboo. Often mothers of young girls refrain from educating them about sexual changes in the body. Girls usually get answers through their friends or learn by experience. By talking about sexual issues in public spaces, Padma is violating many taboos. This not only has an impact on her public image (at least at the beginning) but also creates dilemmas within her about whether she is doing the right thing or not. Gradually though, her faith in her work increased and she acquired an identity because of it; she described how she had managed to survive whereas many of the NGOs that had not valued her as a worker had shut down. This also showed the changing nature of the place as many people and institutions passed through there.

Padma's experience brings out the issue of sexuality and harassment. She worked in the field of sex-education and HIV, and gave lectures on safe sexual practices. This created rumours about her; that she could speak about such issues with ease only because she herself had been involved in prostitution. Because of this there was a constant effort by the people in the community to 'inform' her husband about her activities. The perception of Padma's work is extended to her personal life as well and she is often defined by it. In spite of this, she is able to maintain good relationships within her household. Channa (1997) describes how a woman can manage accountability by adhering to the norms of the most important status for women in most societies, namely motherhood. Padma fulfilled her duties by ensuring the best education for her children and looking after her daughter. By keeping her husband informed, by protecting him from adversities and also helping him to start a new business, she had fulfilled her wifely duties as well.

Padma's ability to create a niche for herself both in the public and private spheres shows her agency. Whatever people might say about her, they also seek her out for help. Work creates difficulties but also provides her with a sense of identity which helps her to carry on; therefore, in spite of the rumours and doubts she wants to continue with the work that she is doing. Although she has managed to create an identity this has not been easy. Now she feels tired and anxious most of the time. Fighting all the battles within and outside her household has led to a deterioration in her physical and mental health.

Padma's narrative also shows how individuals are not completely structured by their environment; their actions also transform the environment. Therefore, in spite of the 'structuring structure' of the habitus, there are many women who exercise their agency to bring about changes in their 'structuring environment'. This structuring environment is present not just outside the household but also within it and has an important impact on the level of psychosocial distress faced by women.

HOUSEHOLDS AND DISTRESS

Women often describe themselves in terms of their relationships and therefore these have a significant impact on their psychosocial health. Inability to perform roles and responsibilities as well as performing these roles can lead to distress. In the first scenario, the distress usually arises from guilt; in the second, it can arise from a feeling of exhaustion and burnout because of performing these roles continuously and with poor support.

There are various studies which indicate that fulfilling the routine tasks can also be extremely stressful if the they are multiple and difficult. Feminist scholars have characterized the family/household as the site of women's oppression and as the locus of conflict of interest between men and women (as cited in Deshmukh-Ranadive, 2008).

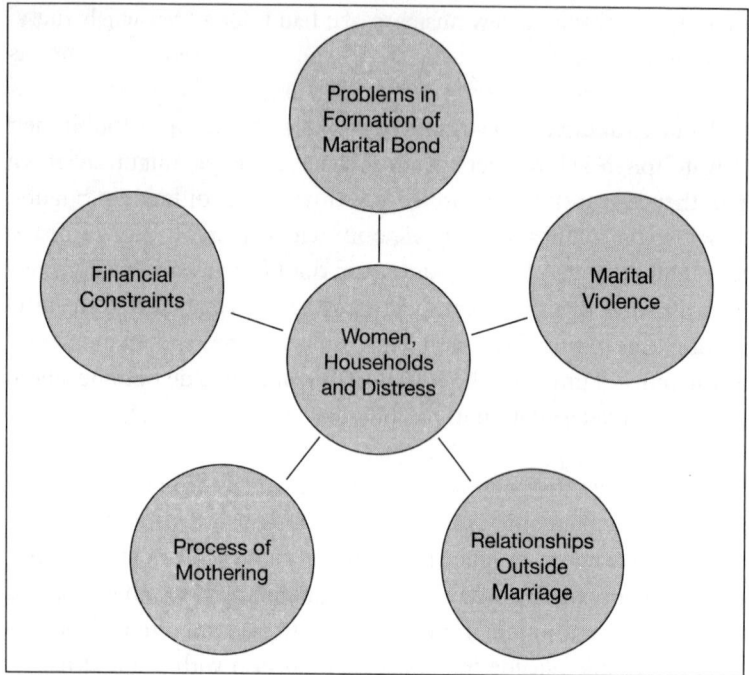

Figure 5.3 *Households and Psychosocial Distress*

Source: Author.

Women face multiple problems. They are the ones who are employed, take care of their homes and children and also have to give money to their husbands for alcohol.

—KII_PC

Padma: *Shaadi ke baad, cheezeyen badal jati hain, aurat bandhi ban kar reh jati hai, independence nahi rehti, par shaadi bhi zaroori hai kyunki akeli auraton ki apni hi problems hain.*

(After getting married it is not the same; you are answerable and the woman becomes a prisoner, with no independence. But marriage is also necessary; because single women have their own problems.)

Marriage was considered a necessity by most women. This was considered to be a stage in the life cycle which all women had to undergo.

Among Hindus, marriage sacralizes and sanctifies female sexuality, while Islam wholly disapproves of sex outside marriage. Since sex is viewed as the natural craving of human beings, marriage is visualized as an event that is a necessary part of life, particularly for women (Dube, 1997: 109). However, marriage, even though considered to be a natural transition in life, is viewed with a lot of anxiety by girls. In our conversations, girls in Jahangirpuri expressed concerns about how their lives would change after marriage. They were worried about being burdened with responsibilities after marriage. Many of the girls (C block) in an FGD expressed fears about violence as they frequently witnessed it in relationships around them. Most girls entered the marital household with these fears in mind.

Problems in Formation of Marital Bond

Kakar and Kakar (1997) describe a bride's feelings of heightened anxiety and feeling of loss when she enters the husband's family. There is a wariness bordering on antagonism toward her mother-in-law who has usurped the place of her own sorely missed and needed mother. And then there are the ambivalent feelings of hope and fear towards the usually unknown man who is now her husband and claims her intimacy (ibid.: 57). The extent of violence that they see around them makes women in Jahangirpuri more apprehensive about marriage. Studies show that in the case of poor women in traditional India, the expectations from a potential husband are pretty basic 'He should not drink or beat me, and support me and the family'. Yet, in-depth interviews with women from the poorest slums reveal that their dream of love, of integrating tenderness with eroticism, mutual respect with caring, has not disappeared (Kakar, 1995). In reality however, marriage often entails severe social and psychological costs for the woman (Addlakha, 2008: 245). These costs are evident in the case of Neeta and Rama (mother and daughter) who both described difficult marriages.

Neeta's parents died when she was very young and her brother who was dependent on alcohol would frequently send her to stay with their *chacha-chachi* (father's younger brother and his wife). They were very abusive and would often shut her in a room or beat her, so she did not want to stay with them. Her brother arranged her marriage when she was around 13–14 years with a Dalit man (they were Baniyas and hence it would be considered that she was marrying into a 'lower' caste household). After marriage she moved from Kanpur to Delhi. Soon after getting married, she found that her husband was also dependent on alcohol. After drinking he would become very hungry and keep demanding food. She usually had no money as it had all been spent on alcohol. When Neeta was unable to provide food, he would beat her. She describes that he would start hitting her with whatever he had in his hand and she would scream so much that all the neighbours were aware of their fights. Her husband's family in the village was also unwilling to keep him for long as he would hit them as well. In one of his drunken stupors, he mortgaged the house that they were living in and they had to spend two days on the road before they could get the money to recover it. She complained that her husband was extremely suspicious and would get upset even if he saw her talking to me. She felt scared that he would kill her when she was asleep as he slept with a knife in his hand. She says, 'I stay awake when he is around; if I have to be killed it should be when I am awake, not when I am sleeping.'

Neeta was also worried about her daughter (Rama). Rama's marriage had not worked out because of trouble with her in-laws. According to Rama, her husband was fine but her father-in-law was not. She said that soon after marriage, Rama found out that her husband's brother's wife was forced to have sexual relations with their father-in-law. Her sister-in-law was from a village so she did not complain but when she (Rama) resisted there were fights. Her husband did not believe her and one day when he was away Rama was thrown out of the house in the middle of the night. Rama was pregnant at that time; she had a son in her natal home but her husband did not come to see her. She explained that her husband was in a relationship with another woman and hence did not care about her or their son. Her husband did not come even when the son was unwell; after the son died he blamed her for neglecting the child. Rama says, 'After our son died he did not visit but said that I had killed him which made me feel very bad. I had named our son Sachin after consulting the astrologer. Since his death, I cannot sleep at night. I sit and think about him; often I do not feel like eating any food.'

Rama's marital family was willing to accept her only if she went to the village with her father-in-law. This was not agreeable to Rama or her family. Neeta laments the fact that they gave so much dowry but Rama's in-laws were not satisfied and in addition to that, they had abandoned her daughter.

Conflictual relationships were a major source of concern and distress amongst the women of Jahangirpuri. Ayesha, a 20-year-old described how since her husband did not work, she was frequently taunted by her in-laws. Lack of privacy for the married couple was another issue. She described how a refrigerator was deliberately kept in her room, because of which her mother-in-law would enter the room frequently under the pretext of using it. This was also used as a method to prevent any intimacy between the couple. In addition to the lack of material and ideological entitlements in the marital home, the absence of intimacy between the spouses (Nandy, 1980) and the close involvement of the conjugal kin, especially the mother-in-law, in the everyday life of the couple (Sriram, 1991) render the wife more vulnerable to violence and abuse.

Marital Violence

Khushboo (34 years): By 14, I had one son; by 16, when my second son was two months old my husband left. He used to beat and abuse me and I used to cry all the time. Then he started having an affair with another woman and left. My husband used to earn ₹10,000; he used to earn a lot so he had a big ego.

Mariam: My husband was a big man; he would often get angry. He would keep beating me. In those days we used to get water from far away; if I was late he would beat me. From my chest to back, it hurts. I take medicines from a private clinic. The doctor says it is weakness (*kamzori*).

Mumtaz (15 years): I have been thrown out by my husband. From the beginning of the marriage he used to hit me a lot; he once hung me from the ceiling with a cloth and pulled the chair away; my devar (younger

> brother-in-law) saved me. I live with my in-laws and brother-in-law. All of them hit me whenever they get angry over small matters; I was beaten even when I was with a baby. On Eid too, I was bleeding from the mouth; they have even tried to burn me. My husband earns and gives all the money to his mother. We stayed on the first floor, he would not give me any money for food. He would eat at his mother's. There was no food even for my child. He refuses to separate from his parents. I don't know what to do, I cannot sleep [starts crying]. I can't sleep ever since I got married because I am not allowed to. My husband drinks every day, smokes, has tobacco and my mother-in-law tells him to beat me.
>
> Shahbano: I was married at 13, my husband was around five years older and he used to beat me after drinking. I would hide because at night he would throw me out on the road. I broke my hand once, got it treated, then again it was broken.

Violence against women in India cuts across caste, class and other divides. Nationally it is estimated that 21 per cent of women have experienced beatings or physical mistreatment 'by husband, in-laws, or other persons' since the age of 15 (IIPS and ORC Macro, 2000). Although women have difficult relationships, there are various reasons why they stay on. Deshmukh-Ranadive (2008) talks about the emotive nature of relationships within the family. The emotional content within kin relationships and those that develop due to co-habitation are a strong force to 'fight' when decisions to exit have to be taken. The matter is further complicated by the fact that sociocultural norms condition people into feeling certain appropriate emotions. Not only are behaviour patterns charted out but the accompanying mental and emotional patterns are also determined (ibid.: 7).

Relationships outside Marriage

Relationships outside marriage were another reason for conflicts in marriages and a frequent cause of distress for the women. In many such cases, wives were often abandoned.

> Babita: I am a Bengali married to a Punjabi man. He was a good-looking man so I had agreed to marry him readily but he left me after some time; at that time I was pregnant.

Zayeeda: My husband is having another relationship [this was said abruptly in a soft voice]. After he started having a relationship with another woman my husband stopped giving money at home. I feel very bad because he stays with another woman.

Abandonment by husbands increased the vulnerability of women as they were left with poor support. This was especially true for women who had chosen their partners (love marriages). Women who have love marriages endure greater vulnerability as compared to women in arranged marriages as they are hesitant in bringing their grievances to the natal kin (Grover, 2011: 110). The dominant discourse in Delhi's low-income neighbourhoods is that women should accept responsibility for their violent and unhappy love marriages as they have chosen their partners (ibid.: 117). Leela's case shows the ways in which she made changes in her life to ensure the fidelity of her husband.

Leela is around 35 years old and lives with her husband and three children. Leela had a 'love' marriage; she says that her husband was very attractive and therefore she had fallen in love with him and married him against the wishes of her parents. She said that her husband was 'useless'; although he did some work, most of his time was spent on having affairs with women from within the colony itself. According to her, he had relationships with women who were like his daughters-in-law (kinship networks within the block) and this made it even more shameful; when she protested he would beat her on the street in front of everyone, even the children. If anyone came to help her, he would insult them as well. To supplement the household income, Leela started working. During this time when she was away for the whole day, her husband would call whomever he wanted to their home. Because of this she stopped working, 'I have to keep an eye on him. I keep worrying all the time where he is, because of this I can't sleep or eat.'

Leela's decision to quit work in order to 'keep an eye' on her husband is another example of how through different ways the mobility of women gets restricted. Her concern about sustaining the marriage is obviously leading to psychosocial distress as she 'constantly worries' and is losing her sleep and appetite. Marriage and family have been noted as necessary stressors in the lives of Indian women by psychiatrists. Mental disorders in general, and common mental disorders in particular, correlate with marital status, implying that housewives have a very high rate of psychiatric morbidity (Sethi et al., 1972, 1974). The highest rates of distress are observed in the reproductive years, a period in the life cycle that coincides with marriage and child-rearing (Addlakha, 2008: 245).

Process of Mothering[3]

In the ancient as well as later Sanskrit texts, the main purpose of marriage was seen to be the creation of offspring, with a distinct emphasis on male progeny (Dube, 2001: 121). Female sexuality has always been discussed by linking it with motherhood and sons (Pande, 2003). Menon and Shweder (1998) describe how the newlywed bride in Orissa has to face the pressures and responsibilities of having children and at least one male offspring. Indian women often go through multiple pregnancies in an effort to have a son. Ginsberg and Rapp (1991) highlight the importance of understanding reproduction not as a single event, but as a process which includes pregnancy, birth and motherhood. It is these stages that we keep in mind while looking at the experience of reproduction for women in Jahangirpuri. What becomes evident is that decisions in each stage frequently lead to distress among women.

(a) Pregnancy

For women in Jahangirpuri the issues related to mothering start from the very step of conception; the responsibility for which is usually

---

[3] Walks and McPherson (2011) prefer the use of the word 'mothering' as it includes behaviour, practices and engagement. Motherhood, on the other hand is seen as an identity and an institution. Although I use Ginsberg and Rapp's terms for dividing the stages, the word 'motherhood' is replaced with 'mothering'.

placed on women. Female sterilization is the most widely known method of contraception in India followed by male sterilization (Dutta et al., 2004). Reproductive years are fraught with difficulties as many decisions have to be made related to pregnancies, children, their education and upbringing. Many studies have shown that women in the age group of 18–50 years (childbearing years) face a greater risk for common mental disorders (Blehar, 2003; Patel et al., 2006; Paykel, 1991). Accounts of women in Jahangirpuri show that with growing poverty and difficulty in managing large families, couples in urban slums do have problems with multiple children.

> Reena: We don't use any method, even though there are so many now to control children. In the village they can grow up, here every mouth has to be fed with money. For water also we have to pay bills.

Reena talks about not using any method, but other women spoke about poverty as being important in the regulation of reproduction. However, the onus of this regulation usually falls on the woman. One of the lab technicians in a dispensary spoke about the changes that have been occurring in the community. There have been changes, and according to him, more and more Muslim women are coming in. He added, 'we can't tell them much; they often start fighting so we back off because it is seen as attacking their religion. They believe that they will not receive *"jannat"* if they use any contraception. Now slowly there is a change; one woman who benefited must have passed on the information so other women also came. Initially they used to be scared of *fatwas* against them.'

Although the emphasis has been on female sterilization, when women get over their fear and speak up about contraception choices they opt mostly for Copper T as it is reversible and invisible when set in place (Pande, 2003). Since IUDs are cheaper and more convenient, their availability seems to increase the choices of women. This does not always translate into empowerment. In one of the dispensaries (previously the India Population Project) one woman came in for removal of the IUD (Copper T). Since she was in a lot of pain and was bleeding excessively, she wanted it removed soon. The nurse told her that removal of IUD in the middle of her cycle could result in a pregnancy. The woman was asked whether her husband would be ready to use a condom. She replied negatively; she also became unsure about the removal of the IUD when she realized this could lead to a pregnancy. She said that she would wait but since she was in pain and bleeding, the nurse requested her to bring her husband to speak to them. The staff there would try and reason with him. The nurse was not very hopeful of intervening successfully. She said: 'Few men are ready to use condoms. Men primarily don't use condoms because they don't feel satisfied; we tell them to use RV jelly but that's expensive.' (KII_N)[4]

Many women consider regulation of fertility as their responsibility and try and encourage other women to do the same. But multiple views exist with regard to this. It became evident in one SHG meeting which was held at Rubina's home as the original room was unavailable. Her house consisted of a two-room set. The first room where we sat had the kitchen as well. The second room had a bed, trunks and other household goods. When the other members realized that 10 people lived in this much space, they asked Rubina the reasons for not using birth control. To which, she replied: 'Rubina: Bache allah ki marzi hai, woh apne aap kha lete hain, who allah ka tohffah hain(Children are Allah's will, they eat on their own, they are Allah's gifts).'

The worker questioned her stand and said that poorly planned pregnancies and lack of nourishing food were making her health deteriorate. Other women in the group told her, *aapki kaum main bhi brake lagate hain, brake lagao* (even in your sect people step on the brakes, so step on them!) Many of the women appeared shocked that a family of 10 was surviving on ₹150 per day but the woman herself remained unfazed and held on strongly to her beliefs. Although in front of other women she portrayed an image of unconcern, on her own she spoke about her many struggles related to her children. This brings out another aspect of how much control women actually have over their bodies. The discourse on regulation of pregnancy is

---

[4] Nurse from the dispensary.

complicated. It appears that women are able to exercise their agency and exert control over their body through contraception. But the question arises, what kind of options are available to them. Lopez (1993) studied the experience of sterilization among Puerto Rican women in New York City. She found that Puerto Rican women make decisions about sterilization that are limited by their socio-political conditions. Their reproductive decisions are based on a lack of options circumscribed by myriad personal, social and historical forces that operate simultaneously to shape and constrain their fertility options. Their oral histories revealed that women actively seek to transform and improve their lives, and controlling their reproduction is one of the primary ways they try to do so. Yet, as their oral histories also show, the constraints of their lives play an equally significant role in shaping their reproductive decisions and experience (ibid.: 300). Women in Jahangirpuri face similar complexities. In India, the decision to have a child is further complicated by a strong son-preference which leads to frequent cases of female foeticide.

(b) Birth

> A young woman walked in and all the women there started asking her about her health as she had recently given birth. She gave monosyllabic answers; then the women asked her about the sex of the child. When she replied that she had given birth to a girl, the news was received in silence and everyone went back to work. No one expressed any happiness nor did they wish the new mother and she also did not show any emotion.
>
> —Observation in an SHG Meeting

The birth of a daughter usually goes unheralded and anthropologists have documented the unconcealed disappointment in families which already have a daughter or two (Aggarwal, 1971: 114; Lewis 1965: 49; Madan, 1965: 63). The distinct son-preference and the pressure on the woman to have a male child are evident from the following statements:

Bela: Three years my daughter stayed with us, then a good proposal came and we had to marry her off so we did but her new family was not so good. Now she has a son so her status has improved; when I hear about other people I think her position is better than others.

Lata: Things changed after my son was born; my husband became much better, my mother-in-law too became nice. Before that my husband would always taunt me and threaten me that he would send me to my mother; he would leave me there too.

Manu (19 years): After I had my son, who is three now, my mother-in-law became much better; now she looks after me.

From these statements, it is evident that women find their life circumstances much improved after giving birth to a son. Deshmukh-Ranadive (2008), while describing the hierarchy amongst women in a domestic unit, attests that women who have produced male children have a higher status than those who do not. Therefore, it is not surprising that women pray continuously for the birth of a son and are often very unhappy when they give birth to girls. Time and again when women were asked about the number of children they spoke about the number of sons. It was only when they were asked again that they would mention the number of daughters as well. It is also the wish for a boy that leads to them having multiple children. One of the women while talking about her children outlined that she had had her last two sons on the behest of her mother-in-law. Also, that they were 'god's' gifts and hence had to be treasured. The same premise does not apply to the girls as is evident from a case study given below:

> Ayesha was living with her parents and brother because of conflicts with her husband and his family. Although her in-laws were ready to take her back, she was waiting for her husband to get some work. If she went back without that, she would again have to live with the taunts of her in-laws. Her family was worried that if she went back and things did not change, she might come back to them with another child and there would be more mouths to feed. While talking about this they laughed and said that luckily the first child, a girl, had died soon, Ayesha also supported this. She voiced her support in a soft voice and did not appear to share the relief that her family was expressing. But in this situation where she was also considered

a burden on the family there was no way that she could express a view that was contrary to those being expressed by the people supporting her.

In a study on depression among women attending an antenatal clinic in Goa, Rodrigues et al. (2003) found that son-preference was most marked for mothers who had living girl children and was often expressed through lack of support and hostility from the husband and mother-in-law. The girl child was cited as a heavy economic drain on the family. This was partly due to the perception that most girls would ultimately be married and would not contribute economically to the family. Dowry payments at the time of marriage were another major reason for not wanting a girl child. The male, on the other hand would one day be an earning member of the family and also eventually gain a dowry. A poor marital relationship may act as a vulnerability factor, which in the light of a provoking element such as the birth of a girl child, triggers a depressive episode. On the other hand, the birth of a boy may act as a protective factor even for mothers who are living in an unhappy marital situation (ibid.: 1802). Lata's and Manu's accounts show a similar trajectory wherein the birth of their sons improved their relationships with their husband and mother-in-law respectively.

(c) Mothering

Bela (55 years): My husband is good; we were poor but that can be managed, our problems started with children. Everyone used to say your children are very good, they speak nicely and are attractive but all of them are in trouble. I lost one girl to jaundice when she was 1.5 years old. My other daughter had a good marriage, they were very nice people, but her husband died suddenly.

The main difficulty in our life is our son. He started drinking; we don't even know what he drinks. He used to work as a driver and used to live separately, he had a love marriage. They used to be very happy; he was always buying things for her. Then suddenly they had a fight and separated. After that he got into trouble, took something expensive, lost his job. So, he came to live with us and then started stealing things from the house, watches. I felt very bad that my son had turned out like this. He was once beaten up and left to die because he tried to steal someone's wallet. My son used to be handsome and earned well, now he is skin and bones. We kept him in a home in Sonipat, he became okay for some time. But his wife stays nearby, he watches her go by; she looks very nice, wears jeans. I don't know what he feels but he becomes very quiet.

My younger son wears clothes this length [pointing to her knee], cut jeans. When I say anything, he says, 'you are old fashioned' (*aap purane zamaane ke ho*). He wants a bike but left work at the factory saying that the pay was less and work is more. Instead of thinking of a bike he should work; they want things fast without working these days. I tell him earn at least ₹2000, that will help but they want to be like big people: new clothes, things without working hard for it.

When my daughter was unwell and in the nursing home, they did all the tests and told us that she had TB; her stomach was swollen but she improved in a year. That was a tough time for me. We felt we had done something wrong with our children [keeps her hand on the stomach and said it was hurting]. When I have pain, I have a medicine which is for one or two rupees. While talking about this I feel sad, that is why it hurts (*yeh baat karte hue gam hota hai, isliye dard hota hai*) [with tears in her eyes] I always have problems with the stomach now.

Chanda (60 years): My elder son lives upstairs, he works but contributes nothing to the family income. He comes home drunk and spends all his money on that. I have been taking care of both his daughters since his wife died. She died when the younger daughter was six years old. If he gave one rupee for them he would expect more in return so we don't ask anything from him. I have pains and aches in my body but I don't worry about them; I had an eye operation after which I could not get out of the house in the sun. My younger son and brother-in-law now manage the vegetable shop which I have managed since the time my husband died around 25 years ago. My mother asked me to marry again but with five kids my family was too big. Mother used to sell vegetables, she lived nearby, she taught me this work and I ran my family through this. I have brought up all the children on my own. 25 years of bringing up the kids alone (three girls and two boys), my health is affected. I have pains and aches in my body but I don't worry about them. I am just tired now. My worries are almost never-ending with four women in the house. My sons were the ones who wanted to pressurize me to put the property in their name but I believe that I would be on the road if I did that. Till I die I will keep the property because this might ultimately help in the granddaughters' marriages. I have to worry about that as well. My boys are useless, but my elder daughter earns. When I die what will happen to the granddaughters, in two years they will start looking very grown-up. There is one regret; two of my daughters did not get married. The older one was engaged but suddenly her back started hurting, she herself refused to get married because her back used to ache so much. At that time, she used to scream with pain and after that her back became bent.

Studies have shown that older women are twice as likely to be living in poverty as older men (Choudhury and Leonesio, 1997). The life trajectories of Bela and Chanda bring out the financial constraints that both have faced. They are the main providers within their households as Chanda is a widow and Bela's husband is very unwell.

In their narratives both Bela and Chanda focused mainly on their children and relationships. Bela sometimes blames herself for the way things have turned out for her children and at other times wonders what exactly went wrong. In some ways she had lost two children, one to death and the other to drinking. Chanda on the other hand talks about being a single parent, she does not elaborate on the difficulties but focuses on the way she has managed. In spite of her efforts she finds that her sons have not been helpful, and she is still responsible for the household even though now she is aging and suffers from various aches and pains. In addition to her existing responsibilities, she now finds herself with the additional responsibility of her two granddaughters. With two of her own daughters still unmarried, their impending marriage weighs heavily on her. Vartanian and McNamara (2002) described women's economic vulnerability in old age as a product of longstanding life characteristics combined with the effects of later life events. Both Bela and Chanda talk about pains, aches and incessant worries. Cohen (2003) describes how it is significant to understand the various manifestations of 'weakness' in understanding the poor aging body. The language of weakness brings out the themes of hard labour by aged persons, of under-nutrition and of other forms of deprivation that might have informed a different understanding of aging (ibid.: 108). Chanda's narrative brings this out when she says 'I am just tired now'—this brief sentence brings out her exhaustion related to long years of labour in bringing up her children after the loss of her husband at a young age. In addition to that she still continues to be responsible for the future of her granddaughters.

With the existence of sadness and unhappiness there is also a clear account of agency in the narratives of both women. They have dealt with difficulties in their life and moved on. Dealing with continuous difficulties with poor support has been a stressful experience for them. Their bodies appear to be breaking down under the pressures of *'mamta'* or mother love. *Mamta* is constructed as indestructible, continuous, natural, involving self-sacrifice, devotion, forgiveness and self-realization through unity with one's child (Chaudhary and Bhargava, 2006). *Mamta* also involves ensuring the well-being of the family. To do that, women describe carrying out certain rituals that are taxing but necessary for the 'good' future of the children.

> Shama Devi: I also have to fast on *Chhat*[5] (festival usually celebrated in Bihar) because when my daughter was born I observed it for her well-being; I made a big mistake when my son was in my womb, forgot to observe it and things went wrong. Then I promised *Chhat Devi* I would always observe the fast. I go and stand in the lake for almost an hour with all the women till the sun sets completely. We are immersed in water till our shoulders until the sun sets completely; I get very tired but it has to be done now, you have to have baths all the time. Before you do the *puja*, then after it is done, because the water is dirty. Some women change there but I come back wet and have a bath here.

Shama Devi describes the process as tedious since she lives in a one-room house, where space has to be cleared for bathing. But not performing these rituals is not an option as she feels that her children's well-being is related to that. Her narrative brings out the self-sacrificing, devoted aspect of *mamta*. The concept of *mamta* transcends

---

[5] Chhath is an ancient Hindu festival dedicated to the Sun God, Surya. It is practised most elaborately in Bihar, Jharkhand and the Terai regions of Nepal but is not exclusive to them.

all bonds. These bonds are more pronounced if a woman has a child with a disability. Vaidya (2011) talks about the over-determined conceptions of the centrality of the mother's role in shaping the child's development that become magnified in the case of a disabled child. She states that women often talked about being frustrated, anxious and irritated; some mothers felt so burdened by the demands of constant care that they felt like escaping or even committing suicide (ibid.: 236). Women in this study also expressed their anxieties about their disabled children and the multiple responsibilities they had with regard to them.

> Rubina: One of my sons is not well; I realized that he was unwell because he did not want to study, also he would talk to himself, become quiet and weep while sitting alone. We were confused so we took him to a healer because he was affected by something supernatural. The healer sent us to a doctor (*Hum hafi ke pass le gaye kyunki upar ki hawa lag gayi thi, unhone doctor ke pass bheja*).

> Salma Khatoon: My son was not awake for two hours after he was born, he was born at home. He was different from other children, slower, less intellect (*kam dimag hai*). I took him to the hospital; they sent me to Shahadra; I have gone there so many times. I teach him about money, he forgets; I have made him sit at many small shops, after a few days they say that he cannot manage. He keeps sitting at home or roaming around. I am very anxious (*pareshaan*). I have not told this to anyone [she looked around, dragged her chair next to mine and whispered]: My elder son had TB so he also cannot do any work. Sometimes my daughter tells me that he sits alone and weeps; he forgets things. I have to collect money for my daughter's wedding. I am not educated so filling all the forms is difficult; someone told me to pay a lady and she will fill it; I did not understand so I came back.

> Satwanti: After the medication stopped things have become worse; she has gone completely mad, keeps running away. She has not eaten in a week. I shifted just one month back; how many houses can I change? Everyone has come to know she is mad; every wrong thing is then blamed on her. My neighbour said that the dust on her roof had been thrown by my daughter. I want a medicine so that she can die; then I can live in peace. My eldest daughter says that she cannot live with her. She says, Mummy how can you live with her? The second one came with her son to live with me for

a month in his holidays; she had to leave in a day; she would not let her stay. She has become completely mad, I want her to die.

Rubina, Salma Khatoon and Satwanti bring out multiple responsibilities in their narratives. Along with managing domestic work, they are also involved in seeking external help. Salma Khatoon's husband also suffers from a major mental illness and Satwanti is a widow. Therefore, they both function as single parents managing domestic as well as public worlds. Satwanti's daughter suffers from a major mental illness and therefore has to be taken to the hospital for regular follow-ups. In case there is a relapse, it is difficult for Satwanti to manage alone. Frustrated and burnt out, the only solution that seems to exist for her is the death of her daughter. When I met Satwanti next, she was more hopeful as with proper medication, her daughter had settled down. Salma Khatoon, in addition to care-giving, also performs a quasi-therapeutic role by using behavioural techniques to teach her son activities of daily living (managing money, making him sit in shops).

Bourdieu (2001: 77) writes that 'it has often been observed that women fulfil a cathartic, quasi-therapeutic function in regulating men's emotional life, calming their anger and helping them to accept the injustices and difficulties of life.' In this study, it can be seen how women seem to perform this role for all members of their family. According to Reay (2004: 59) women engage in emotional labour far more than most men, taking the responsibility for maintaining the emotional aspects of family relationships, responding to other's emotional states and also acting to alleviate distress. While women are fulfilling all these functions, there seems to be an emotional void in their life. In Salma Khatoon's case, this void is being filled by anti-anxiety drugs. She explained that on visits to a psychiatric hospital with her son, when she talked about her problems, she was given drugs. She has been on medication for some time but finds it unhelpful as she continues to have sleepless nights worrying about the present as well as the future. Prescribing medication for much larger problems highlights the biological reductionism that is taking place in psychiatry. Objects for study are selectively determined. Thus, brain neurochemistry may be a legitimate object whereas excessive responsibilities, poor support systems, poverty may not be. Bourdieu (cited in Thompson, 1984) has termed this phenomenon 'Symbolic Violence', when attention is directed to some information while other sources are ignored. Often, certain sources of knowledge, certain kinds of logic, and various types of information such as context and meaning are discredited. Information that does not meet a specific requirement is excluded because it is 'soft' or 'subjective', and hence, a variety of options are undermined.

In most of the narratives, concerns about daughters were prominent. Concerns related to crime were also there, as we have seen in the previous chapter. Other concerns were related to finding suitable grooms (of the same caste) and making financial arrangements for the daughter's marriage. Another responsibility that falls on women is the management of the household budget. Keeping in mind the variable nature of monthly income of most households, this makes it more difficult for women as they have to deal with daily routines and emergencies through various strategies.

Financial Constraints

In the previous chapter, the RMP speaks about how mental health difficulties have always been there but they have increased because everyone has financial problems. Within the household, most of the decisions are taken depending upon the financial situation of the family. With an increase in the prices of basic commodities, the families find it difficult to meet even their most necessary expenses. Most of the families had incomes which helped them to survive but they had very little savings; any emergency could push them from a position of stability to instability. Risk types associated with the life cycle and social events can be either covariate or idiosyncratic depending on the actual event. Many of them are quite severe in some contexts (marriage, dowry), while others may be less severe individually, but are repeated and therefore can be a drain over time (religious festivals)

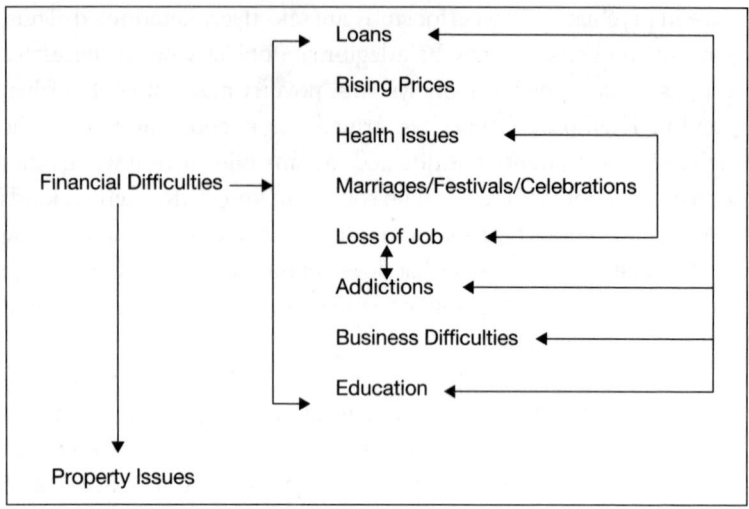

Figure 5.4 *Factors Leading to Financial Constraints*
Source: Author.

(Kantor and Nair, 2003: 959). The main factors which lead to financial constraints are:

(a) Health issues

Health issues can often take a family from a position of stability to instability. Illness in the main earning member of the house creates many difficulties and often leads to lifestyle changes for the rest of the household members. Medical expenses are an important reason why households fall into the debt trap, with nearly 16 per cent of households reporting that their largest loan in the preceding five years was taken for medical expenses (IHDS,[6] 2010). Abruptly stopping work because of health issues has an impact not just on finances but also on the mental health of the person who might become depressed because of ill-health as well as loss of work and the inability to provide for the household.

---

[6] India Human Development Survey.

Kamala: Honestly there are problems in everyone's life; who does not have any problems? I have had no problems; my family is very nice, except my husband's health has deteriorated with time. He worked in a steel factory, in Accounts for 25 years, but when he left, he got no compensation. It was a private job, what to do. But he felt very bad because of that.

Neera: My husband is nice, he does not want me to work so I have not worked for so many years but expenses are going up. I had to take leave because my daughter fell ill; I could not sleep for so many days. I went to the Mullah, Bengali doctor but the medicines did not work so I went to another doctor at the corner. I had to purchase medicines worth ₹700. Then I went to Babu Jagjivan Hospital; they said that my daughter had some injury because of which she had fever. I had to take leave from work; madam said to me, why was I making her run around? But I also wanted to go back. I feel better when I go for work, there is something new to do. My head feels heavy when I don't go.

Health issues often lead to frequent visits to the doctor/clinic/hospital, multiple tests as well as loss of work days. In such a scenario, when women want to take some responsibility, social norms might prevent them from sharing the financial burden although it provides them solace as seen in Neera's narrative. Das and Das (2005) in their work on mental and reproductive health among poor urban women in Delhi describe cases of women who suffered from headaches, debilitating aches and pains. The women in their study described themselves as being overwhelmed by illness. It is not simply the presence of chronic illness as such but severe treatment failures due to poor training of practitioners, lack of economic resources, and familial dependencies that increase the burden on families and thus result in converting treatable disorders into fatal events for the health and well-being of women (ibid.: 32).

(b) Marriages in the family

Marriage is another major life event which can cause increased levels of anxiety in most members of the family. The SHG workers said the maximum number of loans taken by women was related to marriages. IHDS (2010) data reveals that more than 15 per cent of the loans that households acquired are directly related to marriage expenses. This included loans to travel to their villages or city of origin for a relative's marriage. The IHDS found that even among households in the lowest income quintile, the expenditure for the groom's family is about ₹43,000, while that for the bride's family is about ₹64,000. The data also revealed that in addition to the wedding expenses, gifts of large consumer durables (car, motorcycle, refrigerator or TV) in dowry were also prevalent. Nearly, 16 per cent of the households in the lowest income quintile also reported that these items were frequently given (ibid.: 151–52).

Although travelling and attending marriages was an expensive affair, these were occasions where people met their kin and kinship ties were strengthened. This was especially important for families who had been living away from the extended kin from a long time. Marriages which were to take place in one's immediate family were the main reason for worry. Concerns about gathering money to provide for the daughter's dowry is one of the main sources of anxiety among many women (see Table 5.1). Dube (1997) states that dowry has assumed enormous proportions and has spread even to groups such as peasants, artisans and lower castes who earlier practised bride-price. This further leads to the devaluation of daughters who become distinct liabilities. Although dowry does not have religious sanction among Muslims, even here violence and torture are reported to accompany demands for dowry (ibid.: 135). The findings in this study support this statement as many Muslim women expressed anxieties related to arranging for dowry.

(c) Festivals/Celebrations/Religious rituals

Festivals and celebrations increased the expenditure of households as these are times when it is considered auspicious to buy new things. Some of the festivals which had previously not involved so much expenditure had become more about buying and selling. The older women considered this to be an impact of television. This was evident

Table 5.1 *Descriptions of Financial Difficulties*

Health Issues	'He used to earn the most money in the house. The other two sons sell fish but they only give ₹600–700, their employer does not pay them on time. My husband is also not well so he can't work anymore.'
	'My husband has Polio and is unable to do any heavy work so I also started working; breaking stones is what I do at a construction site.'
	'He goes for work regularly but he has been unwell for some time, he has gone for work even in fever.'
	'I started working after my husband fell ill, he used to work as a coolie near the bus stand and his income was good, I had no worries then.'
Marriage	'My father died suddenly just before my two sisters were to be married. It was a very tough time; we took loans and managed to get them married.'
	'What to do, I have to get my daughters married, we are looking for a boy in the city, we have to spend minimum one lakh. When I got married *'dahej'* (dowry) was not there.'
	'When I got married there was money in the house so I got everything, bike and things, now there is a problem. Anyway at a girl's wedding whatever you give is less, that's why mother gets worried.'
	'We are unable to save anything; my husband used to earn more than all three sons put together, he used to sell fruits in a standard area. If we can't save how will I get my daughters married? This worries me constantly.'
Children's Education	'I have so many worries, all day long I keep thinking about things. I wanted to send the children to a private school but they don't go because they have to study; in the government school they don't have to bother.'
	'My husband is the only earning member; for the children there are school fees, tuition fees, the elder one also wants tuition in English but we can't afford it. My husband wants me to work but I told him I can't; my health is not good.'

(Continued)

Table 5.1 (Continued)

Unforeseen circumstances	'We have many financial problems, many people have taken advantage of us. My husband never got money from his work; we had saved money through a committee, but people stole that money and ran away.'
	'Everything is very expensive; now daily living has become a problem. Rich people can manage food but what will the poor do? They used to have *dal-roti*, now *dal* is unaffordable, even onions are expensive. We are middle level, not too rich not too poor; we manage.'
	'Few years back we had suffered losses in the mandi and had to take a loan of ₹60,000–70,000. People started coming to the house to ask for money, we borrowed from different groups and returned the money but every month I have to pay interest to different groups (SHG).'
	'My daughter-in-law goes for work but there is little income. Every time life becomes okay something happens and now this little help (old age pension) also that I could have got from here, it appears will not remain for long.'

during the festival of *Karva Chauth*[7] when we went to the *Som bazaar* (Monday market) after an SHG meeting. The market was extremely crowded and women kept pushing each other to get to the roadside stalls. Some of the women wanted to buy new things, and an older woman commented, *'Nayi cheezen kharidna aaj kal ke ideas hain'* (Buying new things is a modern idea).

She said that she did not allow her daughter or daughters-in-law to buy new things, 'what would happen to the old ones'? But now with all the TV shows the festival has become more important, she added. The bazaar was full of fake jewellery, clothes and cosmetics. This new aspiration to buy new things usually taxed the household budget but the wish to acquire things had gone up considerably. Many of the vendors complained of women stealing from their stalls in the crowd as well.

---

[7] Fast kept by many Hindu women for the long life of their husbands.

The increase in acquisition of new wares would also create similar pressures for others and it could often lead to discontentment amongst others who could not. Although the spending during festivals is a pleasant form of spending, the loans add to the already existing financial burdens. This is also the time when the lack of money affects women more when they are unable to participate in festivities to the full extent. As expressed aptly by one of the informants, 'Diwali is fun for those who have money.'

Money was required during festivals not just to buy new things but also for charity. During Eid, women described how everyone was short of cash: 'We have to give a certain percentage of what we have to the poor. All the people who come begging have to be fed, given new clothes for the festival. All that we save is for now, what else do we save for?'

Festivals were a time when many of the women asked for loans which they would spend months repaying but their importance is apparent from the statement 'what else do we save for'. The correct behaviour during various festivals involving fasting, donating and so on, forms a part of the social norms of the community and hence women ensure that they abide by them. Religious festivals and rituals may be considered non-obligatory, but they are often vital in terms of building and maintaining social assets that can be drawn upon in times of crisis (Lund and Srinivas, 2000). Giving them up is a potential response strategy related to allowing social assets to decline. Following these rituals and customs are important as they are seen as ensuring people's well-being in the present as well as the future. Festivals and rituals also provide a 'space for forgetting' where bothersome problems of the mundane world are banished (Scheper-Hughes, 1992: 480). Things which must be forgotten can be forgotten if the celebration is to be experienced as a social utopia (da Matta, 1984: 232). Scheper-Hughes (1992) further discusses how the importance of festivals is increasing with the rise in problems as there are many more things to forget.

(d) Unforeseen circumstances

Life cycle and social events are economic stresses for which families can plan (Sebstad and Cohen, 2001). Examples include childbirth, education costs, religious festivals and rituals and, to some extent, even widowhood. There are many instances, however, where unexpected developments create difficulties. These unexpected or unforeseen circumstances include sudden illnesses (minor or chronic), accidents, financial losses in business or other enterprises, rise in prices, and reduction in welfare programmes.

The impact of these emergencies on the household is determined by the characteristics of the household. The risk of households being pushed to an unstable position is influenced by occupation, education levels, household size and composition, gender of the household head, race and caste. Within the household women and children are often those most exposed to risky events (ibid.). The most common responses to chronic and non-chronic illnesses, religious festivals and social expenditures were reducing consumption, using savings, taking loans, and in some cases, doing nothing (Kantor and Nair 2003: 965). This is evident from the narrations of informants in Table 5.1.

(e) Children's education

As a result of lifestyle changes there are many new demands which have come up especially in terms of educational facilities. Although education is subsidized, many parents aspire to send their children to private schools rather than government schools. The policy of national and state governments to ensure that all children of school age receive an elementary education through Universalization of Elementary Education has also led to growing numbers of children in schools. The teacher-pupil ratio is very high in government-run schools in comparison to public schools. This has an impact on the quality of education: teachers' care and concern diminishes as the classroom becomes ever more unmanageable and chaotic (Sreekanth, 2009:

237). It has been reported that more instances of violence occur in MCD and KV schools than in public schools or international schools (*Times of India*, 2005, cited in Sreekanth, 2009). As we have seen in the previous chapter, bullying is another factor because of which parents aspire to send their children to private schools. Private schools have higher fees and therefore are usually inaccessible to most children. Poor quality of education in school also means that students require tuitions to ensure good performance in examinations. All these factors increase the financial burden on parents.

(f) Addiction

Drugs and alcohol often disrupt the normal functioning of the household. This in turn creates pressure on the women who try to maintain the stability of the household. Several studies have shown that spouses of persons with alcohol dependence (PAD) may find themselves with significant rates of mental and physical problems including communication problems, low social activity and poor marital satisfaction (Halford et al., 2001; Moos et al., 1990). Addiction in one member of the family depletes the already scarce financial resources and leads to many other kinds of problems.

> Neena: My husband has just come back from the village; he creates many problems. From the beginning he would drink a lot and spend all his money on drink; he works as a *mistri* (carpenter) and earns well but spends it all in drinking. So there is no money at home.
>
> Sangeeta: My husband drinks a lot, after he drinks he starts fighting and hitting. He gives money for the household expenses but not much which worries me a lot, how to manage the house?
>
> Sanjeeda: My son whom I am taking to the hospital used to earn well, he was working in the private sector; then he started taking something (*kuch khane lag gaya*). He was very good but after that his mind did not work. He fell into bad company and then problems started; now he wants to leave but it is not easy.
>
> Satwanti: My son is useless, he is in jail, he was an addict (*woh nasheti tha*), did all kinds of drugs, gambled. He sold off all the rooms that we had, we used to have so many. His wife and two children are with her parents. How

can I keep them here? She will not keep my daughter (who is a person with mental illness). I will get them back once I have a settled place; we keep shifting houses because of my daughter. Now the landlord has increased the rent further, I did not know that they will do that.

Grover (2011: 49) describes that, women and higher scheduled castes in her research area identified MCD male employees indulging in group drinking throughout the day whilst abstaining from work. They were able to do so as they paid a sum of around ₹1000 to others who did their job for them. She observed that apart from them, men from all castes and professions gathered to drink regularly. This was observed in Jahangirpuri as well when men gathered in groups on roadsides and parks with bottles of alcohol and gambled; these games usually went on throughout the day. Women often describe how the drinking behaviour of men can at any given opportunity plunge their families into debt (Magar, 2000). The women point out that they are forced to find wage work as a response to male unemployment, and they often end up providing for their families for several years while their husbands neglect paid work (Grover, 2011: 48).

There is an angle with regard to the aspect of drinking, that is, of male distress. Jasinski et al. (1997: 828) described how ethnic groups facing poverty, unemployment, and economic instability use alcohol to relieve stress. MacAndrew and Edgerton (1969) drew from examples of indigenous cultures and argued that drinking behaviour is culturally constructed in each society, and they introduced the 'time out' hypothesis as a framework for understanding alcohol-related behaviour. The 'time out' theory suggests that certain rules exist for drinking behaviour that allow the individual who is perceived as 'being drunk' to ignore the normal social rules of a society. This 'time out' confers upon the drinker a special status that frees the drinker from responsibility for any actions committed when drunk.

This abdication of responsibility and way of dealing with stress is available to men only. These avenues are usually not available to the women who live with similar uncertainties and who do not have these options of reliving stress. The strategies that women use for reducing stress are influenced by their habitus. The cultural values and family norms influence women's choices, prescribing a range of coping strategies that are available or acceptable to them. In some cultures, leaving the relationship might not be viable for many women because of religious or socio-economic constraints. A pressure to comply with collective welfare and family harmony over one's individual needs and rights, and to save the family's face may be stronger in some cultures than others. Thus, some women may appear 'passive' in their victimization because of such cultural prescriptions (Yoshihama, 2002).

(g) Property issues

In an area where space is a valued resource, conflicts over space create many differences and fights. It creates the 'us' and 'them' feeling within households as well as outside them. The conflicts related to space are related to financial difficulties but often go beyond that to issues of power as well. Property came up often in the narratives when women were talking about distress and the reasons behind it.

> Chanda: The house is in my name, the children tried to make me give it to them but I refused. They will throw me out of the house. If we could have saved money and built several floors, we would have lived comfortably on rent but now we can't.
>
> Rajwanti: I have fallen from the sky to the ground; I used to be very well-off when my husband was alive; he was in service. After he died my sister-in-law duped me. She got some guests at home for tea and I entertained them; how was I to know that they were there to buy my house. For a few months they gave me some rent. Then all that also stopped and I was thrown out of my own house.

Cohen (1998) in his study on aging in India has found that the ownership of property was considered a safeguard in ensuring filial obedience. Chanda and Rajwanti highlight the power that comes with the ownership of property and the increased vulnerability without that power. Rajwanti clearly described her fall from a higher position after the loss of property. Not having control of the entire property and sharing it with others bring other stressors:

> Sita Devi: Expenses are a huge issue, my sister-in-law keeps fighting; we use to have a single meter in my mother-in-law's house on the ground floor but they use it more so why divide it half and half? Every day there were fights. My brother-in-law does the same work as my husband but his daughters also work. At home, they make things and watch TV; we don't use electricity so much. We put on one fan and they put on two, so my mother-in-law told us to have separate meters. Even then there are fights every day. They accuse us of putting our lines on their meter. I am tired; they also complained that we have taken two houses, we had the second floor, but we were staying with my mother-in-law on the ground floor. This was because I gave my mother-in-law food, and also because of poor health it was difficult to climb up every day. But they kept fighting so we stay upstairs now.

Sita Devi brings out the difficulties of living in a 'shared space' wherein there are multiple conflicts. The conflicts among family members regarding property were reported to be frequent. Women talked about the continuous harassment they faced from their family members regarding this. Along with the harassment women talked about a feeling of continuous anxiety arising out of a fear of being displaced from their households.

(h) Loans

Initially there had been fewer avenues for savings; with the emergence of SHGs women had wider options for saving money and taking loans when required. The loans are usually for family requirements such as marriages, festivals, education, business (often of the husband); the repayment usually falls on women who are the members. Various studies outlined in Chapter 2 (in the section called households and distress) highlight the increasing burden on women related to repayment of loans. The importance of SHGs has grown in the area not only because women benefitted but largely because men benefitted as well. The programme coordinator explained the process to me. According to him it was difficult for him to start the SHGs in C block which is a Muslim-dominated area as giving and taking loans is usually against the norms of the community. In the beginning he faced a lot of criticism for this initiative. He countered this by hiring Hindu women as workers who handled the groups, even though he is Muslim. With the passage of time several Muslim men became involved in the group and therefore it acquired some acceptability.

In the course of field work, I observed that several Muslim men would accompany their wives for demanding loans, they negotiated loans with the workers either because they were prominent members in the community or because of their relationship with the coordinator. These loans were of course taken in their wives' names. Usually women repay loans but festivals and other circumstances (illnesses, other loans, marriages) do sometimes lead to non-repayment of loans.

Another reason for the acceptance of SHGs was the need to save money and a place wherein money could be availed of during times of need. Financial difficulties are frequent as most families survive on basic incomes and they have meagre savings. In such a scenario, different strategies are adopted by the household to deal with the crises that might emerge. Gandhi (2008) describes three main ways in which families deal with financial crises: expenditure reduction, income enhancement and tapping social networks. These three strategies work in financial as well as other crises that arise in the lives of women living in low income neighbourhoods.

SOCIAL SUFFERING

While reading the narratives of women, a pattern emerges which helps in understanding some of the reasons for psychosocial distress. The everyday lives of women in the field site are marked by problems created by living in a certain social situation and there are many similarities in the women's experiences. Distress appears to be arising out of similar reasons and leading to similar outcomes (pains, tensions, worries). This indicates the presence of social suffering. Bourdieu's conceptualization of social suffering draws attention to social misery:

not just the unequal distribution of material goods in society, as welfare policy has tended to emphasize, but also people's lived experience of domination and repression, including feelings—humiliation, anger, despair, resentment—that may accompany, for example poverty, class or race. The notion of 'suffering' denotes the intermeshed components of thinking, feeling, responding, and acting. Suffering is both a reflexive and non-reflexive phenomenon: it is something which at times can be thought about, critically and creatively, and at times is embodied, enacted or projected precisely because it cannot be thought about (Bourdieu, 1993). This becomes clear by listening to the women speaking. At times they clearly related their social position to distress, at other times they talked about life crises and bodily distress in an unrelated manner.

Expressions of bodily distress are often agential strategies to voice protests against the existing unequal structures. Symptoms of sleeplessness, restlessness, tiredness represent the power struggle among the individuals and institutions. Ware and Kleinman (1992: 556) explain how as idioms of dissent, symptoms form part of a 'hidden transcript', a covert, unofficial discourse that takes place out of sight of the wielders of power. The hidden transcript comments on, and often challenges or contradicts, publicly agreed-upon versions of relations between dominant powers and their subordinates. Suffering, as hidden transcript, becomes a way of addressing the desire for change in one's social life (ibid.: 556).

The section on structural changes brings out how the presence of crime in the form of bullying, sexual harassment, drinking, drugs and so on leads to restriction on movement resulting in feelings of suffocation, uncertainty and insecurity. The structure of physical space influences the existing gender regime. The structures created by this regime often lead to role strain, violence as well as power struggles within and outside the household. Another aspect of social suffering is that certain mental and social health problems have social roots. Illicit drug and alcohol abuse, related violence, sexually transmitted diseases, many neuropsychiatric disorders, and suicide are on the increase in many areas of the world, rich and poor alike. A leading hypothesis is that these conditions are more adequately configured as forms of social suffering that result from the massive political, economic, and cultural changes of our era of triumphal global capitalism (Bowker, 1998). Social suffering is a marker of disadvantage, relative powerlessness, and the devastating effects of social change, and in this sense is a moral indicator of cultural or societal disorder.

The suffering and distress that women undergo as a result of the physical and social structures often becomes individualized and internalized. Social suffering is inscribed on the body: the low self-esteem, low status, lack of social capital and lack of power to direct one's life (ibid.). Women become ill usually because of diminishing self-worth, isolation as well as role strain. Although many women follow this trajectory, examples in the text show the ways in which women exercise their agency and challenge the existing role prescriptions. This boosts their self-esteem but also taxes their resources. This is explained by a study conducted by Yoshihama in 2002 who investigated the types of coping strategies used by women of Japanese descent (both Japan-born and US-born) and their perceived effectiveness in dealing with their partner's violence. Japan-born respondents were significantly less likely to use 'active' strategies and perceived them to be less effective as compared to the US-born respondents. For the Japan-born respondents, the more effective they perceived 'active' strategies, the higher was their psychological distress, whereas the more effective they considered 'passive' strategies, the lower was their psychological distress. The opposite was true for US-born respondents. These findings indicate that a match between cultural prescriptions and coping factors might serve as a protective factor for psychological distress. This implies that the very factor of exercising agency can also cause psychosocial distress in the short term. An individual might present and motivate certain behaviour, as a matter of personal 'free choice', but the choice can in fact be a result of restricted circumstances dependent on culture, or on class or political legislation (Johansson et al., 1999: 1792).

In spite of the distress that they faced, some women in Jahangirpuri were challenging the existing gender regime through their actions. In this way they were creating spaces for other women in the community. This often led to them being labelled in various ways (mad, prostitute) but they remained proud of the fact that they had managed to carve out spaces for themselves. The next chapter presents the life story of one such woman in Jahangirpuri.

Learning to Live Alone
Paisa, Bimari aur Jinn

Histories or documents of life are not there waiting to be taken. They have to be composed; they are partial views. Life histories are accounts of how individuals independently shaped their destinies or had them shaped in relation to opportunities and constraints. Life histories enable us to understand the implications of structural change at the individual level. They prevent false assumptions that the individual experience is represented by aggregate change. Life stories are an effective method for identifying various multi-discourse layers (Jacobs et al., 1995). Thus, the reading and interpretation of women's life stories must include paying attention to the complexity of voices and to those narrative elements in personal accounts in which self-image and experiences find themselves in conflict with dominant cultural models.

Organizing a life history to present it in a coherent form is a seemingly impossible task. It is hard for us to talk about our own lives in a consistent manner. To undertake the presentation of another person's life and ensuring that the narrative reflects the informant's voice rather than that of the researcher complicates the task even further. Keeping all this in mind, an attempt has been made by me to explore psychosocial distress and its manifestations through the life of Radha. Radha's life history has been organized around themes of psychosocial distress. It has been constructed not through formal interviews but through the gathering of testimony offered in the context of other everyday activities (Das 2000). The stages in which I have presented her life history is the result of the way Radha presented the different stages of her life.

INITIAL INTERACTIONS

Radha has been living in Jahangirpuri for more than 20 years. She is an attractive woman of about 40 years and is always dressed well with a little make up (*bindi, kajal* and lipstick). Radha is very confident and immediately took me under her tutelage, telling me about the area and the programmes in a detailed manner and the kind of problems that they faced while running these. I was asked to accompany Radha as she managed the local community-based rehabilitation (CBR) programme. In addition to giving me an overview of the CBR programme, Radha also introduced me to other women in the community through SHGs. Having observed some of my interactions with the women, Radha asked me to record her story as she had had a tough life.

Radha was a single parent bringing up her two sons on her own. Her husband had had an extramarital relationship outside marriage after which she refused to take him back. I chose to present her life history here because of several reasons. First, she wanted to talk about her life and wanted it to be recorded; second, her life history is representative of the women in the community and illustrates broader social processes and themes. At the same time, even though her life circumstances mirror those of other women in the community, her method of dealing with them makes her unique. Her life history was not the norm, yet she represented the stereotypes, attitudes and wishful figures among the community (her ability to take initiative and voice her thoughts were often spoken about by other women). Often in a life history narrative, the anthropologist does not seek out the narrator but vice-versa. Behar (1993) describes how her informant sought her out: 'Her manner of persuasion was to feed more words into my tape recorder than the other women, to plunge into levels of complexity and contradiction, and to refuse, simply, to tell her story too quickly' (ibid.: 6). I had a similar experience with Radha. On listening to my queries and the stories of other women, she felt that I should just talk to her as her life story was full of distress. Later when I tried to talk to her in detail, she would brush me aside saying, *'mere baare mein to bahut si case studies ho chuki hain'* (there have been many case studies on me). When I continued to accompany her as she went about her work, she started confiding in me.

CHILDHOOD YEARS

Radha's years before her marriage were strongly influenced by her relationship with her father who played a pivotal role in her life decisions. Whenever she spoke about him, her face would light up.

> I come from a land-owning family. I had a happy childhood; we used to eat fresh food off the land and enjoy ourselves. I have three brothers and five sisters. I studied in a government school and we would go to school by bus. In case we missed the bus, we would take a short cut through the fields to reach the school.
>
> After I grew up, I began facing difficulties (*maine to jabse hosh sambhala hai, pareshania dekhin hain*). My mother was diagnosed with cancer and she died when I was 16. My two elder sisters were married by then so I had to take over the responsibility of running the household and looking after the other brothers and sisters, especially the youngest one who was only six months old at that time. I was very fond of my father and I was his favourite too. He supervised my studies and I used to enjoy studying with him. He also made many decisions for me and he was mostly right. I had got through the police exam, written and physical, but my father refused to pay the customary bribe. At that time, you needed to give ₹20,000 to get through the interview stage. But someone told him that women were misused, transferred to bad postings, and then senior officers took advantage of them or dismissed them. I had a friend who was forced to drink alcohol with the police officers she worked with and when she refused further things, they suspended her for drinking on duty. She had to leave. My father prevented me from getting into a bad situation. He was a just and fair man who was willing to listen to people.

After the death of her father, Radha's siblings stepped in to help her. They represented an anchor in her life, which provided her with both instrumental and emotional support. Radha was always confident that her sisters would help her out when required. Her family's support enabled her to move out of the city for trainings. In spite of their help, the loss of her father left a big gap in her life.

The social context of Radha's life ensured that she became the 'mother figure' after the death of her own mother. In addition to that, her compliance with the wishes of her father ('my father took decisions for me and he was mostly right') and her dependence on him are indicative of dispositions that arise from a habitus. Her habitus was one wherein the male figure is the main authority and the female plays a supportive role. Therefore, even though she took on a care-giving role at an early age, the decision-maker was always the father.

MARRIAGE AND SEPARATION

My marriage was arranged by my father but it was as per my preference. I used to stay with my *mama* (mother's brother) here and my future husband lived in the same house as a tenant. After seeing me, he followed me; he was good to look at so I was flattered. He approached my father; my father thought the boy was suitable and he [her future husband] exaggerated his good background and so after asking me, my father made the wedding arrangements. Soon after getting married I realized that all that my husband had said about his background was not true, there were many exaggerations. Immediately after the wedding, we started having fights, there used to be a lot of violence and I was sick of him. Every day I used to taunt and question him. When he left us, my sister-in-law was worried about us and sent her husband to see if I was alright. I was actually quite happy that day; a bad omen had gone from my house (*shanichar chala gaya mere ghar se*). My sister-in-law said that I was unaware of the society (*duniyadari se bekhabar hai*). But it's only because of society it is important; I felt free that day, released from jail.

I am lucky; he had never been able to hold down a job. Many women have to suffer with such husbands because they create more trouble by drinking non-stop, hitting them, stealing from them and so on. I thought that my husband would come back in three months; he would have had his fun and be back; actually he did come back but I refused to take him in; told him never to come back.

Sometimes I miss him because he used to do half my work, he would clean and I would cook. We lived in harmony, he still figures in my life. It's because of circumstances, he had his own shop and we used to earn ₹15,000 in a month. Someone bought a sample of ghee which turned out to be adulterated so he had to go. My husband calls (in between he did not call), he has a problem, he misses his sons at night, but by the next morning he has forgotten us. That woman, whom he is living with, has done something to him (*Kuch kar rakha hai us aurat ne jiske ke saath reh raha hai*). Things also went wrong because I have a *jinn* which does not let anything work for me. That's why my husband cannot stay with me. It should have been removed before my marriage, now when I die the *jinn* will go with me; it is attached to my soul for 1000 years. That's why I cannot live with another man too. Sometimes when I get angry it's because of the *jinn*. I used to become very stubborn, my husband had to have sexual relations with me after hitting me (*zid pakad leti thi, sambandh bhi aadmi maar kar rakhta tha*). I did not feel like it because of the *jinn*.

Two years ago, when my husband came back, he brought this purse [pointed to the purse that she was carrying], he also got clothes for Rakesh [their older son] and left ₹1000 for the younger one and did not come back after that. My elder son is very angry with him. I have seen 10 years of this and I know that he is not coming back but sometimes my sons still hope. He called me on *karva chauth* and asked me to eat, I had not kept the fast but if I told him that he would have been angry; why should I tell him everything? He does not tell me everything...he called because he could not send me a *mangalsutra* and sari; what is the use of that if he does not come to visit? My husband is aware of what I am doing, there is a big CID on me all the time [laughs]. I had gone to an astrologer to seek advice and to know about my future. He told me that my husband would come back to me as all men were attached to their children.

Sometimes, I think it is good that he has gone; all that I have achieved today would have never been possible if he were here. There are two kinds of addictions—alcohol and women. He went after a woman, spent all the money on her and her children. The money should have been spent on our children; he has arranged the marriages of her children also. He called when I was in the hospital and told my son that your mother did not even tell me (that I was ill). My son responded in anger; they don't want him in the house. I tell them if you let him enter the house, he will destroy your household also, they will never keep him with them even in his old age. After my husband left, I was supported by my father, brothers and sisters. They would gift me clothes for my children, they paid for my sons' education. I only had to manage the daily expenses and some small things. They also helped so that I could go for work; when I travelled outside the city for trainings my brothers would take care of my sons.

Radha's description of her marital relationship is marked by ambivalence. She lives in a culture wherein she is expected to tolerate the structural violence in order to preserve the norms of the family. A number of researchers (Acharya, 1993; Chowdhary, 1994; Geetha, 1998; Karlekar, 1998; Thapan, 1995) have explored the themes of sexual and mental violence and commented on the primacy of considerations of family image and family security that define women's constructions of femininity and that make women compromise and/or internalize cultural violence and abuse. This is evident in the narratives of women in Jahangirpuri as well wherein they talk about their husband's frequent relationships outside marriage. These narratives bring out the fact that women's anxieties related to cheating and abandonment are based on real experiences. Radha's experience of being abandoned by her husband mirrors the experiences of other women. The difference lies in her response to the situation: the initial indifference to his leaving and ultimately refusing to take him back in spite of his efforts to apologize. Although she misses the companionship, she is not ready to give up an independent life (which she has built with a lot of effort over the years) for a man who remains inconsistent in his attentions.

STARTING WORK

I have been working here for more than nine years. How did I start? When my husband left for three months, I rested at home thinking he would come back in some time; I sold my earrings, then my *payal*. My younger one was small and so it was not much of a problem. When he did not come back I started looking for work. For a month I roamed around the industrial area looking for jobs. Finally, someone told me to meet a Punjabi woman who used to do sales. She asked me if I could sell Tide [a detergent brand]; I said why not if the money was good. It was ₹75 and we got two green suits…no orange colour suits, like the box (of Tide). We went from door to door. Once when we went to a new area called Shalimar Bagh, I rang the bell in a house a couple of times. An old man, he must have been sleeping, came out and saw us; he abused us badly. I just handed over the bag to the other woman and told her that I was not going to do sales anymore. After some time, I went with her again when Ariel [another detergent brand] came out, then with sanitary napkins; there used to be a Bihari woman with us. She was very smart and earned a lot of profit. She told me, 'Radha you are useless, you don't know how to lie and earn money.' She taught me how to earn profit, on the MRP and the price we paid; the margin was huge. Then someone told me to contact a man who ran a typing school; he asked me whether I could take tuitions, I said yes. So, from 1 to 4 in the afternoon, I used to take classes for ₹1200. I did a survey, started teaching many kids and made good money. Then I heard that there was a vacancy in the Balwadi. I asked sir, and he felt I would not be able to manage. But he let me take the class saying I had the required qualifications. Then my elder son fell ill, had high fever. I took him to Bhatia hospital; the fever did not come down for a day and they gave me a bill for ₹4000. I questioned them on the amount; after all they had only given him glucose and a few injections. They said that the injections were expensive. But my son's condition had not improved. They refused to release him without money, so I said, 'fine keep him'. I sat outside and started telling all the new patients about the goings-ons in the hospital. Some time later, a nurse came to me saying that the doctor was calling me. They must have told him what I was doing [smiling]; he asked me whether I could pay and I said no. He said that I needed to pay at least ₹2000. I took out ₹1500 and gave it to him, and told him again, 'I am telling you I have no money' [laughed as she reminisced]. He said, okay you can go.

When I came back I was sure that I had lost the class to another teacher but then someone advised me to pay the teacher for the days of work and take the class back. I went to her and she said okay. Then another project came by and the officer asked me if I could manage English; I said I would since I used to teach it. Then I became a CBR worker; I kept hoping to get ₹2500–3000; I got 3500 which was more than what I expected. Now my salary has not been increased for a long time whereas others keep getting raises so why should I work?

I have surveyed this area on my own, the whole place, I know this place better than anyone else. I have got a lot of experience from working, travelled to many places for work, met many people, it has made me who I am.

Working gave Radha a lot of exposure; she travelled to different places for trainings, met different kinds of people and developed new skills. Radha was also chosen for a training programme by a mental health organization which was working to spread awareness about mental illness in the different communities. They were being trained in care and guidance, information about mental retardation and mental illness. She said that their plan was to introduce the topic of mental illness in SHGs. This training also influenced her understanding of her own life.

Another area of support came from the women with whom she started working. She learnt a lot about surviving on her own and ways to make more money. Women working together who are united in the effort to stretch the scarce resources at home, as it typically becomes their responsibility to ensure that all needs are met, often swap ways and means to make money, save money and also hide money for emergencies. The women whom Radha worked with provided her with both emotional and instrumental support. Her friends from the office also helped her during her illness.

INTIMATE RELATIONS

> I have a friend; he has helped me a lot. He is my partner as he helped me buy a house. He has been a lot of help to me, never refused when I had to go to the hospital. He would always take me on his bike. It is more than what others have done for me... look at my husband who has run away.

I first met Radha's friend (whose name she never mentioned, he was always addressed as her 'friend' in all conversations) when we were going for some work outside of Jahangirpuri. While we were waiting for the bus, two men came to see her; one of them went to buy some tobacco and she started talking to the other man. This man was tall and heavy built and smiled at me when Radha introduced me. After this when Radha went back to talking to him, her body language and tone underwent a change and suddenly I felt a little out of place and tried to move away because I was obviously witnessing an intimate conversation. Later when we were walking to the office, she called up the man she had met earlier and started talking to him; again the conversation was intimate and she made no effort to lower her voice. I felt a little uncomfortable because it was almost like eavesdropping on someone and tried to walk a little ahead but I could still hear her. In the course of the conversation, she would call out to me and ask about the way as well. She then told the man that she met new people every day unlike him who was stuck with meeting the same people. Here she was obviously making a point to him about her social capital as compared to his. Then a sort of 'flirtatious teasing' continued between the two of them for some time. She castigated him for not calling her in the morning, and accused him of having found someone else because of which he had been neglecting her for the last couple of days. The conversations and talk of early morning calls led me to assume that there was a sexual relationship between Radha and her 'friend', but it soon emerged that I was wrong.

One day while we were sitting for some work in the rehabilitation centre, Radha took out a newspaper and said with a laugh, '*Mujhe bimari iss wajah se to nahi hai?*' (Am I unwell because of this reason?). It was an article on how sex helps in regulating BP, preventing heart diseases and so on. She said, '*Par sex kiske saath karen?*' (But whom to have sex with?). After this she started talking about her 'friend' who had brought her some bangles. According to her, all men were untrustworthy; she quoted a proverb popular among the women in the area, '*Aadmi ki baat, kutte ki jaat aur ghode ki laat par kabhi vishwas nahi karna chahiye*' (A man's word, a dog's caste and the horse's foot should never be trusted). She was voicing the lack of faith among women in Jahangirpuri as far as men were concerned. It appeared that she was hinting at the presence of an offer for a sexual relationship. This was a period that marked a slight change in her relationship with her friend and she frequently spoke about having fights with him.

> He did not wish me; I went to his house, took food for his wife and children but he never came so I was angry. Today when he came in the morning I sent him away. His wife called me, he was angry with me because he says I insult him sometimes. His wife says that he always gets angry but I told her, *tum uski kamai khaati ho to suno, main kyun sunun?* (You live on his earnings so you listen, why should I listen?) The woman who is financially

supported has to listen; she takes the beatings also if she gets the money. I am very clear, I never take any money, and I also return the money that I get. He says that sometimes I am very particular; I am like that.

Her insistence on paying back the money was an effort to reinstate some boundaries with her friend so that the relationship would continue on her terms. Her effort to become friendlier with his wife seemed in line with this as well. She did not want to lose his support, and in order to do that she became a friend of the family rather than remain his exclusive friend. Although Radha might have been attracted to her friend, the effort to rearrange the nature of the relationship would be the result of both societal and personal factors. Societal norms and mores would look down upon such a relationship; more importantly, her 'self' which over the years had imbibed the same social norms would prevent her from getting into such a relationship. This would be in keeping with the behaviour prescribed by her caste (she was a Rajput) wherein sexuality of women is regulated strictly. Kapadia (1996: 169) notes: 'With the lower castes the stress is on norms controlling fertility, but with the upper caste norms controlling sexuality are emphasized.'

With further changes in their relationship, Radha became even closer to her friend's wife and started addressing her as her sister. The 'friend' then changed to 'jijaji' (sister's husband). In describing the relationships of women living in a slum in Delhi, Grover (2011: 133) observes that women in a quest for emotionally fulfilling relationships often develop multiple attachments and do not talk about companionship in a unitary voice. Vatuk (1969) describes how in urban areas relations between unrelated men and women are somewhat distant and formal but newly developed patterns of fictive kinships modify the form and strength of these patterns. Building a kinship relationship with her friend's wife ensured that Radha continued to have the support of her friend in a socially accepted manner. This also helped her in laying down boundaries in the relationship. Her behaviour, which enabled her to sustain her social capital, highlights her agency in dealing with the social structures around her.

BODY AND MIND

Radha suffered from several ailments and often spoke about her health issues when we went for work. One of her main problems was the blockages in her arteries. She needed a surgery to remedy this condition. The planned surgery was a topic of discussion for several months; initially she was unsure whether she wanted to go in for it or not. Therefore, she was trying many other alternatives. She had more faith in the capacity of ayurvedic medicine in removing the blockages without any operation.

> I have pain in the eyes and yellowness now, although my heart is better. I take both allopathic and ayurvedic medicine and my monthly costs exceed 1500 rupees. I had also gone to Jammu for my treatment but have not been able to go again; I often go for acupressure as well. Someone told me to take ayurvedic treatment and have aspirin once in a while, and then I will not need a heart operation. I think that I should go for open heart surgery which is cheaper but requires more rest. I have a sister working in AIIMS who has arranged for my treatment. All my treatment money has been arranged because of the BPL card. I have not told my doctors that I earn 4000 rupees a month so that I can get treatment with a BPL card.
>
> I have been having chronic headaches for a long time; I keep thinking the doctor asked me whether I sleep well but I don't. I told A (employer) to talk to me nicely; I will even clean waste but if someone scolds me, I keep thinking about it. I will get a scan done for the headaches otherwise the doctor will give me medicines to cover the wound, not to cure the problem. I will get an MRI done, it's better than a CT scan, it diagnoses properly; looks at all the nerves.
>
> I postponed the operation for after Diwali. When I was in the hospital, a 75-year-old woman died after getting stents, then an 80-year-old man also died...I was scared. I had to go and get water for myself and the nurse asked me who the patient with me was? I said I was the patient [laughs]. I asked the nurse to sit down but she asked me when I was going to sit?

While she was narrating this, one of her tenants came to pay her rent and Radha immediately started screaming at her, threw the money that had been handed to her saying 'I will come to CD Park and do a drama then you will know.' Public humiliation was a method which was used frequently and effectively in many situations in Jahangirpuri. The other woman insisted that she had been paying the bills as per her ability and that with the Diwali bonus she might be able to pay more. But Radha kept screaming at her and banging the table after which she got up and started showing the rent records to all the women in the room. Then she said that she wanted to go to CD Park with the woman and settle this thing. The woman kept insisting that she was not running away with the money. Radha told her to empty the house, if she did so, she would not have to pay the rent. The sudden shift from talking about her own life jokingly to a flaring fight occurred often with Radha. Although she was talking to me in a light-hearted manner, the incident highlighted her struggle and her loneliness, the fact that her husband would not visiting and she had to go all alone to the hospital. At this point the tenant's arrival gave her a legitimate reason to vent her frustration and anger.

Radha had a successful operation and her heart problems reduced, but she frequently complained of other problems citing different reasons for them. 'I have a bad cold. There is *reetha* breaking in my street, they pay ₹1 per kilo. I told my neighbours that they would suffer because they are being greedy and no one should do it when I am walking down the street.' These are the sort of things she attributed her niggling health problems to.

While studying for her exam after the training that she had received from the mental health organization she started discussing her behaviour more. She called me to help her understand the material that had been distributed.

> I have learnt a lot from this course. Earlier if anyone said anything about me, I would be angry, keep thinking about it. Now I feel that let them say anything; what does it matter? Sleep disturbances, frequent headaches, stomach upsets, pain; I have everything. I don't have addictions, suicidal wishes and I have always had self-confidence; it's only on the basis of that that I did everything. I always looked for a way to solve the problem; if I had started crying that my husband left me, I would have never done anything. I did whatever work I got, sold detergents, etc.,

Ariel, Tide. Today if I am out of work I will work as a labourer; after all I have to get money.

I asked her whether she felt that her heart condition had been worsened by stress. She replied, 'No my condition was not physical or mental, it was because of accidents. I hurt my back a couple of times very badly. Once I fell down from a swing, it must have blocked some artery. My main nerve was okay, the one going into the back was blocked.'

After reading a bit more of the material, she read out a section which spoke about how distress affects the heart and stomach. She thought for a while and said that maybe her tension had increased her problems. She said, 'My father died a year before I had my heart problem, I was his favourite.' While saying this Radha looked pensive; the loss of her father who was a big support in her life would have triggered feelings of abandonment, as after her husband left, her father was the main male support for her. Losing him therefore would have further increased her distress. Even though her brothers have been helpful, the presence of her 'friend' (who is well-connected in the community) and her relationship with him signifies that both psychologically and practically she finds the need to have at least one powerful male figure in her life.

In addition to the heart problem, Radha described other bodily complaints and the ways in which she tried to overcome these problems.

> Even now, I frequently urinate, get dizzy, sleep very little or sleep a lot; the last two days I just did not want to come to office because I was feeling low; this is very frequent nowadays. I will wash my hair, become totally clean and then go to the Pandit (the one who sits in the temple). He will tell me what to do; give some alms so that things improve, *parcha padwa ke dekhti hun* (let's see after I get my horoscope read). I even asked the Maulana about my problems. He told me that some great misfortune was going to affect me and that he would give me a powerful *taweez*. When I asked Sir (who is also a Muslim) whether I should take it or not, he told

me that if I did, I could become the Maulana's third wife, which is why he was giving it for free.

This highlighted her vulnerability as a single attractive woman in the community. Radha had the ability to ward off unwanted attention but still had to be extra careful in her interactions. Radha was curious about my interaction with the Maulana and wanted to know what explanations he had given me about women having outbursts and their erratic behaviour. When I told her that the Maulana had mentioned extramarital relationships as being the main reason, she retorted that the Maulanas always give reasons related to that: either the husband or the wife is having an affair. On asking what she thought happened and where should people go, she replied that they should go to the doctors. She added as an afterthought, 'That is what we have to tell them, but there are times when people don't get well after going to the doctors and they have to go these people and they cure them.'

This belief was further reinforced for her when a year after her operation, Radha had some problems with the vents that had been put into her body.

> They told me that another operation would have to be done. My sister who works in the hospital wondered why there was a problem as the best vents had been used. So we approached a *Pandit* who said that someone had done something. He came to the house, did the *Puja* and I became better; my medicine dosage reduced from 40 to 10 mg. This, when a few days before the doctors had said that I would have to be operated on. If you believe, there is everything, if you don't, then there is nothing.

Radha believed that it was best to try everything. Approaching multiple systems with contrasting ideologies is also a way of looking for answers. Most systems are not able to provide adequate answers regarding different problems that arise in life. Charms, amulets and giving alms seem to offer concrete solutions and also require the participation of individuals. They involve long discussions with the healer who listens to the person and therefore appears to provide more satisfaction.

Radha constantly spoke about her physical problems within the frame of emotionality, her relationships, and the way people were behaving with her (this is evident in the last section when she raised a concern that her heart problem was related to the fact that she had no avenues available for sex). Although there is recognition that taking medicines is only about addressing the surface issues, medical language has seeped into the community to an extent and there is more belief in technology rather than the doctor. MRIs seem to be a status symbol as well and getting one done meant that you are trying your best to ensure good health. These seem to have become acceptable terms co-existing with traditional ways of thinking.

Radha hid her anxieties under the garb of laughter and cynicism; she often narrated her experiences in a humorous manner. This was one way in which she coped with the reality of her circumstances as well, her anecdotes sometimes revealed her loneliness in spite of the support system she had.

ASPIRATIONS

Radha liked to talk about the future, the plans that she had made and what she wanted to do. These plans were centred on having a house and her children. She described various ways in which she had made efforts to raise money for her house failing which she had other plans.

> I had gone to the office again, a woman was sitting there, she refused to give me the BPL card.... if a man was there he would have given it. I want to buy a house of my own, a complete proper house. But I don't want to take a loan, why should I take a loan? I will pick a committee;[1] one lakh from there, 60,000 from a partner, I will give it back to him later.

---

[1] A group of women contribute a fixed amount every month, run a potluck and the winner gets to use the entire collection for that month.

Radha kept talking about moving jobs as she was not satisfied with her salary. After a while she decided to stay on as this workplace was nearer her house, and because the job helped her financially with the household. One day when I went back to meet her after a break, she happily told me that her house was ready: she had got ₹20,000 from the office and now they were giving her ₹1000 for her medication as well. She described how she fought for it; she said, '*Main father ke paas gayi aur boli, father paanch saal mein agar mujhe 4000 mil raha hai to kya fayeda, main kaam chhod dungi, phir unhone socha aur unhe bhi laga, ab aakhir mera ghar to ban gaya*' (I went to Father (director) and said that in five years if I am getting ₹4000, what's the use? I will leave work; then he also thought about it and realized my position; now at least my house is made).

Radha's description of '*unhe bhi laga*' is difficult to translate as this does not describe any emotion per se but implies that her statement made her employer think and feel. This also highlights the fact that there are many situations where the plight of the person is obvious but others do not stop to think about it. When they do, they are often moved to take some action. Bringing up problems and making them visible illustrates Radha's agency in solving the problems that she faces in her life.

The future of her children was another thing on her mind. She wanted both her sons to get a good education. Being a single parent, she faced many day-to-day issues and had to deal with the emotional upheavals of living with two adolescent boys largely on her own. There were issues related to their education, daily negotiations on how they spent their time, finances, and so on. The changing infrastructure of Jahangirpuri had brought about new challenges. Radha and her elder son often argued on how he travelled. After the Metro started running, everyone wanted to travel in air-conditioned comfort; the Metro was also a faster means of transport. Radha and her colleagues were paid by the office and therefore the travel cost of taking the Metro which was higher did not affect them directly. For Radha's son this was a sign that even he should be allowed to do that. Overall this greatly increased the monthly household expenditure and she was finding it difficult to manage the budget and keep her son happy. While showing me photos of a trip to Manali sponsored by the office, she talked about her younger son's anger with her as she had taken her older son while leaving the younger one behind. She explained that it was important for the older son to feel privileged as well because he was the older one. She would try to take the younger one with her some other time. Radha had to manage with the meagre resources that were available to her and therefore she had to prioritize things. Prioritization was an important way of coping with inadequate resources. Radha had to take many other decisions regarding the children on her own which included decisions related to their education. For instance, she wanted to move her younger son to another hostel as his previous school was only till class eight.

> I have been looking to put my son in a Bal Sanstha, children without a father are taken there. Poor women's children are taken there and educated. I have tried the Arya Samaj home; they said that they don't admit children who have parents. They give religious teachings also, how to do a havan; we are just interested that he completes his education. He can become a temple priest and they have good education. I don't want to bring him to Jahangirpuri because the atmosphere here (*mahol*) is bad.

She was concerned about the future of her elder son as well as she wanted him to finish his education before he considered job options. Radha often discussed her plans regarding her son's marriage. She needed to make jewellery to give his wife at the time of marriage. This would be an expensive affair and therefore she needed to save for a few years to be able to do that.

> I will make only two things, bangles and mangalsutra, and if he has a love marriage then I will not give him anything; if I didn't get anything, why should I give anything? [*Laughs*] My son knows me; he said that you did not let father stay, why would you let me stay? With arranged marriage you get things, most of all, respect; with love marriage you get nothing.

While talking about the plans for her children Radha often expressed loneliness as both parents are usually involved in making these plans. Talking about the future frequently brought out her anger and resentment against her absent husband who had abdicated any responsibility towards their children. The resentment also came from the fact that he had been fulfilling these responsibilities for the children of the 'other' woman. The experience of being a single parent was stressful for Radha but it also provided benefits. One of the reasons she was able to carve out a space for herself was because like Padma (see Chapter 5) she also adhered to the norms of 'motherhood' prevalent in the community.

SEARCH FOR IDENTITY: FINDING MEANING

Gender regime in a particular community reveals the intersections between structures, processes and practices which shape the lives of women there. Radha's life history also needs to be understood through the social context in which it is situated. Her life has been influenced by the macro-level changes that were occurring in the social space. In Bourdieu's (1993) terms her 'practice' is influenced by the relationship between the physical and social space that she occupies.

The predominant theme that emerges on reading Radha's narrative is a struggle for self-respect and her search for an identity. Her behaviour is shaped by her habitus but that in itself is not an immutable concept. Her negotiations with her surroundings bring out her agency in influencing the habitus. The gender regime of the community ensured that Radha took on the care-giving role after the death of her mother at a young age. Since the feminine role was internalized early on by her, when the trajectory of her life turned out to be different from what was envisaged, it was disconcerting for her to take on the masculine role as well. This is because the strongest elements of habitus are those that occur in early childhood because the habitus requires a long period of inculcation for practices to unfold (Bourdieu, 1990). Radha's narrative brings out the continuous conflict between prescribed roles and her own changing aspirations.

When her husband first left her, she assumed that he would be back in a month and she would then take him back. Three months later on his return, she surprised herself by refusing to take him back. She found that she was unable to forgive his transgressions so easily or quickly. There were times when she regretted her decision because of the subsequent periods of loneliness and struggle. In spite of this, she remained proud of the fact that she refused to 'swallow her rage' about her husband having an extramarital relationship. She expressed her dissent by remaining unforgiving in a culture which usually allowed men a few transgressions. A part of Radha wishes that her husband would abandon ties with the 'other woman' and come back to her. This wish is reinforced as her husband continues to keep ties with her and their kids which raise their hopes. Radha explains this belief through the use of witchcraft. She alleges that the 'other woman' in her husband's life is the one who has done something to him. Nabokov (2000: 152) states that sorcery suspicions were initially formulated on the basis of known resentments or jealousies. Generally, the initial suspects were familiar personal enemies. Since Radha, being the mother of two sons and the legal wife represented a threat for 'the other woman', she felt that her husband's 'other woman' had done something to her. This kind of reasoning was important in protecting the self, as acknowledging the fact that the husband might have left on his own account would be too emotionally painful.

Radha uses sorcery to try and find answers in her life. Nabokov (2000) explains that it is a private logic; a psychology of painful revelations that is at the heart of the sorcery discourse. One was forced to see what one suspected but could not accept or internalize. This state of blindness conforms with what readers have now learned about the key condition of sorcery victimization; these commands grip people, causing them to feel fear, the emotion that tricks them. This emotion (fear) prevents them from seeing the negative forces heading their way: from discerning, for example, that they no longer existed for the father of their children and from acknowledging that a person took deliberate measures to eliminate them from the world. Their inability to face such a personal repudiation becomes the cause of their suffering with such symptoms as paralysis, mutism, frantic trances, convulsions, nightmares, violent head or stomach aches, and infertility. What human beings do not or cannot see, what remains hidden from people, ends up stalking and commanding them. To arrest this degenerative process and regain the capacity for independent action, victims must be empowered to see what is blocking them. This is precisely what séances and other encounters with the healers begin to do (ibid.: 153). For Radha as well, these consultations provided a space for examining the past and its influence on her present and future.

Radha continues to hope for the return of her husband for several reasons. One of the reasons given by her is that her husband continues to keep track of her movements. She sees this surveillance as continuing love for her. Also, she is told by several astrologers that husbands always come back to their wives especially if they have sons. The astrologer's explanation for why the husband would come back appeared to be a culturally sanctioned statement of support. This supportive statement also carried within it the low status allotted to the woman who just appears to be a vehicle for reproduction or a link between the man and his children without having any identity of her own. This explanation did not make Radha very happy. She also challenged his act of sending gifts during *Karva Chauth,* as this implies that she was expected to remain hungry and thirsty for an absent husband who is also indulging in infidelity. She refrains from telling him that she never kept the fast in the first place, not just to deflect his anger but also because she refuses to be accountable to him.

Her ambivalence towards her husband is reflected in her discourse of *jinn*. She explained that she had a *jinn* attached to her which prevented her from having a healthy relationship with her husband and will ensure that she will not have one with any other man as well. The *jinn* is representative of two forces within her: the voice of self (ego) and the voice of community (superego). In its 'ego' functions it explains her refusal to be subjugated and assertion of her rights. Seen from the 'superego' point of view it prevents her from developing a relationship with any other man. The *jinn* therefore is a personification of forbidden sexual and aggressive wishes. Kakar (1982) describes the wide prevalence of the traditional idiom of possession (by the ghosts of forbidden sexual and aggressive wishes) among Indian women. According to him, the use of this particular cultural myth of passivity is a reflection of certain social conditions prevailing in society. In other words, there is no individual anxiety that does not reflect a latent concern to the group (ibid.: 76).

These explanations are given by Radha more often in public whereas privately she often reflects on the positives of being independent of her husband. The *jinn* explanation also unconsciously helps her to leave a path open for reconciliation without compromising on her principles or her self-respect. Radha's attempts at self-assertion are not restricted to interactions with her husband. These are evident in the work place as well. Even in a difficult situation she leaves a job when she is screamed at and emphasizes that she requires to be treated with respect in her current workplace.

Her assertiveness is respected and feared because of her ability to create and maintain social capital. She would go out of her way and help women in getting ration cards, contact the local leaders, and explain different ways in which to get work done. If the coordinator sought her help she would feel happy and ensure that the work got done. She was known to be someone who was resourceful and could ensure the completion of work. But other colleagues also spoke about her as someone who could become angry quickly and was jealous of other people's success. This view prevailed primarily amongst her administrative colleagues. It could be because Radha was confident enough to articulate if she felt that there was some injustice being done and was not scared to fight for her rights. Fighting for rights brings out another attribute of Radha's which was 'survival'. In the years after her husband left her with two small children, she had learnt to modulate her reactions according to the situation at hand. There were times when getting her work done meant transcending the acceptable. She learnt different ways of getting the work done: by acting helpless, through anger, reacting dramatically, and by forming good relationships. She often tried all the strategies till she got the desired result. Examples of this included her managing to get both a BPL and an APL card, and managing to get her son out of the hospital without paying the full fees. According to her, as a single mother she had to find different ways to ensure the survival of herself and her children. Since the world itself was not an easy place, she would bend the rules whenever required.

In everyday life, her position as a separated 'visible' woman in the community led to many comments about her activities. Her effort to look good and always be well-dressed was in itself a confrontative stance to take in a society which considered simple dressing appropriate for a single mother:

> People talk all the time, if I wash my face and put cream; they say where is she going? I screamed and abused that day. It's hot and what is wrong in being clean; what is wrong in looking after yourself? Why can't I look good for myself, why always for a man?

Many of the comments on her appearance were centred on her friendship with a powerful male in the community. Radha's friendship with this man helped her in many ways: emotionally, financially and instrumentally. Initially, it appeared to be sexual as well, but further interaction revealed that though there was a flirtatious aspect to the relationship, Radha ensured that it did not go beyond that. This interpretation leads us back towards Simmel's (1984) understanding of flirting as a game whose instrument is reality, a play in which status differences are suspended and erotic offers and refusals are made. He understands flirting as a game in which hierarchy is far from clear. Indeed, power is often in the hands of the female player: 'In saying no and saying yes, in surrendering and refusing to surrender themselves, women are the masters...woman is the chooser' (ibid.: 140). But the point of the game is decidedly not erotic consummation: 'There is no real sequence in which what is gained... guarantees... that the decisive terminal value will be obtained... this also results in an increase in value... as a result of the fascination of risk, especially if the element of fate... heightens its mysterious attraction' (ibid.: 143). In Radha's relationship some of these aspects are present as her association with an influential high-status man in the community has also increased her social capital. Osella and Osella (2000: 201) explain how if this kind of relationship remains, as it usually does, within conventional confines, it remains characterized by flirting, with features of deferred or deflected desire. Whenever couples flirt, they evoke indeterminacy and ambiguity, and arouse those diffuse powers, which are the enemies of fixity and of the stability necessary for the maintenance of hierarchy (Osella and Osella, 1998: 201). Radha's increased intimacy with the wife and the formation of a fictive kinship with her helped her to create boundaries without breaking the bond. This again brings out her ability to challenge hierarchies in everyday life and emphasizes her agency in structuring her life and of those around her.

Radha's narrative has two pictures; one in which there are themes of helplessness, abandonment, illness, discrimination, and difficulties as a single mother, and another in which aspects of strength and survival are revealed. She sometimes presented the first picture in order to evoke sympathy and get some help. Initially that was the picture presented to me as well, but this changed quickly when she realized that I did not have the means to provide concrete help. As the trust grew there was an establishment of equality in terms of sharing money when we spent it on travelling and so on. The frames of vulnerability and strength coexisted in the same person; the switching from one frame to another was not always a conscious process. This was evident from the fact that very often she chose to do things independently even though she could have got help if she asked for it. People with difficult life experiences frequently shy away from taking help as this might give the impression that they are weak and dependent. Radha's efforts to ensure equality between us at every stage emphasized this.

It is easy to dismiss the problems of deprivation if we see shades of opportunistic behaviour. In that we forget that helplessness and manipulative behaviour are both a result of the struggle for survival. Both are true; the distress and the struggle are real. Accounts of abilities are also exaggerated when people wish to believe in and present their power over their external reality. But for individuals there is also the aspect of shifts in power which can give rise to distress. Continuous struggle and the need to fight, and to find out new things without much help can be translated into aches and illnesses through which they are able to get a break. In Radha's life as well, there was a repression of many natural desires in terms of the relationships. Her wavering attitude towards her husband also reflected the confusion in her mind. The times when she wished for her husband's return signalled the presence of a loneliness which she refused to talk about. Her narrative of the hospital stay and the consequent anger at another apparently unrelated incident reveals how repressed emotions can come out in behaviour. The wish to have a 'normal' family life is activated as a result of her habitus. Bourdieu sees family as a fiction and a social artefact, a well-founded illusion because it is produced and reproduced with the guarantee of the State and operates as a central site of normalization and naturalization (cited in Skeggs, 2004: 21). The difference between this normalized 'illusion' and her actual family life often led to frustration and conflict in Radha's everyday life. Her struggle for an identity independent of that of her family (natal or marital) had taken its toll on her. The effort to stand out while conforming to some of the norms in the community had led to sleep disturbances, frequent illnesses and sudden mood shifts. The constant rebellion against feminine role structures and her continuing sense of unease with them led to psychosocial distress. This ambivalence is manifested largely through bodily distress.

Even though Radha has lived in difficult circumstances, her social capital (actual and fictive kinship network) has helped her to fulfil her aspirations to a certain extent. Her ability to find different kinds of work was also possible because of the changes happening around her (opening up of the economy and introduction of new products). Eventually she was able to start her own organization in partnership with another person. The organization was named after her, which made her very proud. She says that the dream for a name came when she saw someone being felicitated at a function in the organization where she worked. She thought that some day she also wanted to be in that place and looking at her name on the cheque book meant that this was not far away from that aspiration being realized.

'Twelve years is a long time; my vision has changed—from wanting to be a wife to having a name. Now even if I die my name will live on.'

Conclusion
Pathways to Health and Healing*

I began the book by asking the question: So what is abnormality? In all the interactions with women and men in Jahangirpuri, I found that there are multiple answers reflecting multiple realities. Psychosocial distress is embodied and expressed through the categories of possession and illness experiences. Any behaviour which is considered away from the norm (talking and laughing to self, abandoning the household, excessive aggression, shouting, singing songs or becoming excessively quiet) is usually categorized under possession. This behaviour is commonly recognized as madness or mental disorder. Presence of such behaviour is attributed to supernatural as well as human or social causes. Possession experiences are seen as powerful negotiating tools as they provide a means of communication to those who have been silenced (for example, *Dukhyari* women). In addition to possession, psychosocial distress is expressed through the 'tired body' (pains, aches, sleeplessness and disinterest). Stressful daily routines, negative life events and worries about the future are related to bodily distress. Caste, class and religion may shape and change the terms used for description of psychosocial distress/madness but the experiences appear to be on a similar continuum. This is evident from the growing use of bio-medical idioms to describe conditions of distress amongst women from different backgrounds in Jahangirpuri.

---

*Certain sections of this chapter have been published in the book *Disability, Gender and State Policy* by Nilika Mehrotra, Jaipur 2013 and as part of a chapter in *Disability, Gender and Trajectories of Power*, Asha Hans (ed.), SAGE Publications, 2015.

Psychosocial distress was also related to the substantial changes in the physical structures in Jahangirpuri, but this has not translated into a better subjective quality of life. Crime rates continue to be high. Constant and continuous sense of insecurity prevails among the women of the area and leads to restrictions (internal and external) of their movements. This internalization of restrictions often leads to feelings of suffocation. Along with a high rate of crime, increased costs form the main macro-issue of concern for women. The everyday lives of women living in the site are marked by problems created by living in a certain social situation and there are many similarities in the experiences of these women. Distress appears to be arising out of similar reasons and leading to similar outcomes (pains, tensions, worries). Women face frequent emotional, economic and physical violence within the household. They are the ones responsible for maintaining the emotional aspects of family relationships.

This task is complicated by the extent of macro-level changes occurring around them which accelerates the aspirations of people and leads to financial strain. Performance of multiple roles within the household with very little time for leisure or relaxation is increasing women's psychosocial distress.

Women's explanatory models of distress determine the kind of help they seek. Instead of viewing possession and illness experiences as being purely bio-medical or supernatural, in most instances, women view them as being symbolic of distress. Through their narratives, they explained that family and societal relationships were instrumental in determining the health of women. Although there was some recognition and verbalization of the power dynamics involved, only some women were able to question and challenge societal norms. The presence of civil society organizations working for women has helped bring about some changes. But these organizations are not seen as 'legitimate' sources of help by everyone in the community. Therefore, women seek help mostly from culturally sanctioned spaces. These include traditional or folk healers as well as bio-medical doctors.

The causal attributions to psychosocial distress determined who was approached first for a 'cure'. Help was usually sought first from the traditional or folk healers who initiated the cure regime and this could include a referral to the bio-medical practitioners as well. Women usually sought multiple sources of help simultaneously. The traditional or folk healers appeared to pay more attention to the psychosocial context of the women. When distress was expressed through aches, pains and tension, women sought general medical care. This often led to women being on medication for long periods of time without much change in their situation. Chronic sufferers were in danger of being over-treated as their problems have been appropriated as common mental disorders by psychiatry. Since these are 'common' and 'chronic', a large pool of individuals require 'treatment'.

WEAVING IT ALL TOGETHER

The narrative of psychosocial distress or madness is in fact a description of the social reality of the person. It brings out the ways in which intersections between macro (social, cultural, economic and political) and micro factors (household, neighbourhood, relationships) influence the behaviour of the person. The social position of the person impacts the health of the person. Linkages between poverty and ill-health have been well-established through various studies (Das Gupta and Chen, 1996; Judge and Patterson, 2001; Wagstaff, 2001). It has been found that people living in poverty are at increased risk of developing common mental disorders, through social exclusion, high stressors, reduced social capital, malnutrition, obstetric risks and increased risk of violence and trauma, all of which increase the risk for higher prevalence of mental disorders, inadequate care and a more severe course of the condition (Saraceno and Barbui, 1997).

In the everyday life of the person any behaviour away from the defined norms of the society may be explained in terms of madness: *pagal, gumsum, bawali*. These behaviours although different still fall within the repertoire of emotional reactions in the community. This is because deviant behaviour also forms a part of the social dramas of community life. Deviant behaviour has become 'pathological' with the introduction of the bio-medical system. The increasing reach of bio-medicine has led to the formation of a new language of distress. This has happened through misrecognition of behaviour. Embodied distress arising out of the social position of women is misrecognized as a disease of the body requiring 'treatment'.

Bourdieu's concept of *doxa* is useful in understanding this phenomenon. *Doxa* broadly refers to the misrecognition of forms of social arbitrariness that engender the unformulated, non-discursive but internalized and practical recognition of that same social arbitrariness. It contributes to its reproduction in social institutions, structures and relations as well in minds, bodies, expectations and behaviours. In modern societies, *doxa* refers to pre-reflexive, shared but unquestioned opinions and perceptions mediated by relatively autonomous social microcosms (field) which determine 'natural' practice and attitudes *via* the internalized 'sense of limits' and habitus of the social agents of the fields. *Doxa* is 'a set of fundamental beliefs which does not even need to be asserted in the form of an explicit, self-conscious dogma' (Bourdieu 2000: 16). *Doxa* allows the social arbitrary nature of power relations (e.g., classifications, values, categorizations and so on) that have produced the *doxa* itself to continue to be misrecognized and as such to be reproduced in a self-reinforcing manner.

The power of *doxa* is seen in the way problems related to gender, caste, religion and ethnicity factors are simplified and seen as psychiatric problems. Not only are they envisaged as primarily problems of the 'body' in the bio-medical paradigm, they are also accepted as such by those who are suffering. These symbolic fields (gender, caste, religion) on the basis of their specific principles, establish hierarchies of discrimination. This process of misrecognition is a type of 'symbolic violence'. The legitimations of the system of social domination and subordination constituted within and through these symbolic relations are ultimately based on 'interest' (Moore, 2003: 104).

Political struggle is found in efforts to legitimize those systems of classifications and categorizations, and violence occurs when we misrecognize as natural those systems of classification that are actually arbitrary and historical. Symbolic violence is thus a generally unperceived form of violence and, in contrast to systems in which force is needed to maintain social hierarchy, is an efficient and effective form of domination in that members of the dominant classes need exert little energy to maintain their dominance. They need only to 'let the system they dominate take its own course in order to exercise their domination' (Bourdieu 1977: 190). Hierarchies and systems of domination are then reproduced to the extent that the dominant and the dominated perceive these systems to be legitimate, and thus think and act in their own best interests within the context of the system itself.

The social origins of suffering are often misrecognized and internalized by members of society, a fact that exacerbates suffering and perpetuates symbolic systems of domination. Symbolic violence tends to be a 'more effective, and (in some instances) more brutal, means of oppression' (Bourdieu, cited in Bourdieu and Eagleton, 1992: 115). This can be understood in the increasing usage of the term 'common mental disorders' (CMDs). Davar (2008) traced how in order to find a language to locate women's miseries in the realm of 'distress' rather than 'illness', the concept of CMDs was used. It was thought to normalize the experience of women by bringing psychological suffering within the spectrum of everyday experiences. A continuum from well-being to ill-health, intersected by social structural vulnerability, was offered by the CMD discourse (ibid.: 278). The creation of a cadre of NGOs providing psychiatric services were initiated (Pathare, 2005). There was no engagement with the question whether spirituality (defined here simplistically as access to the emotions of the sacred) had a role to play in self-experience, healing and recovery (Seligman, 2005). Eventually Davar (2008) opines that this rationalist approach created a market for the psychiatric/psycho-pharmaceutical industry. Citing improved clinical and economic outcomes, doctors have advocated the use of antidepressants such as fluoxetine (Prozac) in general healthcare (Patel, 2003). It has been said (ibid.) that in poor countries such as India counselling is not as effective an alternative as medication. There is a colonial flavour in this view, that 'natives' somatize (Davar, 1999b), and this view is much to the benefit of the pharmaceutical companies. Views such as this led to the liminal state of psychosocial distress or disability (between mental health and madness) being categorized as 'mental illness' and treated as such.

This medicalization of oppressive social conditions falls under the rubric of symbolic violence. Social suffering is misrecognised as 'individual' suffering and efforts are made to 'cure' or 'treat' it. The narratives in this research clearly bring out the social nature of suffering. For example, Suraiya's (Chapter 4) account brings out her vulnerability as a Bengali-speaking Muslim woman in her community. Her narrative is reflective of other women in the community and outlines some of the factors which are related to the increasing vulnerability of women. Robinson (2008) argues that increasing ethnic violence over recent decades resulting in the further ghettoization of Muslims has impacted the lives of women and their families in specific ways. In the situation of threat that Muslims feel, women are affected the most. At the very time they are called upon to acquire economic independence and support their families, they find themselves bound by both community norms and fears of attack from outside. Restricted mobility, within-kin marriages and relatively larger families ensure that women are burdened with household cares and are rarely free of the dependence on or control of older men in the family (ibid.: 190). Suffering, therefore, becomes ever present and is usually experienced by most of the women living in similar contexts.

Bourdieu's conceptualization of social suffering draws attention to social misery: not just the unequal distribution of material goods in society, as welfare policy has tended to emphasize, but also people's lived experience of domination and repression, including feelings—humiliation, anger, despair, resentment—that may accompany, for example poverty, class or race (Frost and Hoggett, 2008: 439). Social suffering lies at the heart of this subjective experience (of distress), the lived experience of the social damage inflicted in late capitalist societies on the least powerful and the intra-psychic and relational wounds that are a result of it. In other words, both inner worlds of psychic suffering and outer worlds of social structural oppression are constitutive of such subjects, their capacity for agency, and the forms of agency that are possible. Traditionally, social policy has understood the well-being of citizens in terms of the distribution of material goods and services rather than in terms of the lived experience of domination and exclusion and the feelings this produces. In other words, social suffering draws attention to the lived experience of inhabiting social structures of oppression, and the pain that arises from this (ibid.: 440).

Social suffering arising from the experience of domination and exclusion is often not understood as such and therefore not experienced consciously. Therefore, this suffering which is not thought about or voiced becomes embodied. It is most often expressed through the 'possessed body' or the 'body in pain'. The body performs or lives out unspoken distress. Butler (1997) recasts the concept of performativity in this way, de-rationalizing and de-intentionalizing it so that the act contains a thought which is nevertheless unrecognizable to the one who acts. As Butler puts it 'a thought that is unthought to itself and thus opaque, but nevertheless alive and persistent' (Butler, 2003: 408) and therefore the source of what she terms a 'melancholic agency', an agency haunted by a past (experience) that cannot be represented. Stress and coping literature uses stress as a bio-psychosocial category, in which the psychological aspects of suffering undergo conversion into a physical symptomatology. Stress then refers to the realm of the psychosomatic or, more properly, the social psychosomatic. To the extent that shame and grief can only be thought about in individualized terms, as further proof of inadequacy, or cannot be thought about at all, then these effects become embodied in psychosomatic illnesses or become carved onto the body in terms of posture, facial gestures, pallor and so on (Frost and Hoggett, 2008: 451).

Psychosocial distress is thus 'misrecognized' by the very individuals undergoing it. This misrecognition is further legitimized by the 'dominant groups'. Forms of non- or mis-recognition and disrespect can inflict harm and be personally damaging, undermining people's sense of selfhood and self-worth; they can thus be a form of oppression (Lister, 2004; Lovell, 2007; Taylor, 1992). A politics of recognition is thus concerned with both personal and social identities and the interaction between the two, and with the intersubjective shaping of subjectivity, or sense of self (Honneth, 1995). In the process of articulating their life-worlds, women traverse untrodden paths of revelation, strength and surprise as well as the more frequented ones of abuse, dishonour, shame and rejection. In these, they revert to memory, narrative, and voice as tools for reconstructing their emotions, thoughts and experiences in making sense of their own constitution as embodied gendered beings (Thapan, 2006: 203). Habitus clearly constructs their experiences in many important and non-subversive ways but their voices also reflect the call for challenging the structuring structures of the habitus through negotiation, contestation and transformation (ibid.). Jahangirpuri, like any other place, is a space for contestation. Hence, it is important to discuss the two main pathways (apart from bio-medicine) to healing that have been available to women which help them to reduce their distress: the women's movement and cultural ways of healing.

Women's Movements

Chapter 1 describes how the women's movement in India itself was seen as a mental health movement (Shatrughna, 1999; Uberoi et al., 1995). The open-ended non-hierarchical structures of autonomous women's groups provided an outlet to women in distress who could share their anguish with those having similar experiences. However, its approach towards de-medicalization of mental healthcare was not without problems. Davar (2008) argued this route was more accessible to educated and middle-class women and therefore many women were left out of its ambit. In its engagement with psychiatry to find different ways of looking at psychosocial disability, it inadvertently created more spaces for it. The collaboration of psychiatry with movements of women and persons with disability had some worrying outcomes which included the use of a 'social language' to prescribe medicine. Although there was recognition of the social causes, the treatment consisted mainly of prescription of medicine because constraints of resources and time made this most feasible. There was the de-recognition of traditional healing practices; women who were visiting traditional healing centres were seen as superstitious, backward and forcibly driven by cultural norms into acceptable spaces defined by a patriarchal society. In its discourse of strength therefore, the women's movement sometimes failed to acknowledge the individual woman's agency. This had been brought out by Dube and Dube (1986) who while describing the Hindu rituals and practices, argued that although these practices set certain limits in terms of the dispositions they inculcate among women and the varying statuses that they assign to them in the family, it is also within these limits that women question their situation, express resentment, use manipulative strategies, utilize their skills, turn deprivation and self-denial into sources of power, and attempt to carve a living space. In many ways, women's movements have provided secular spaces for women, spaces which have enabled them to seek the support of other women, to help themselves and others, and to explore ways of coping which have enabled them to feel empowered.

Cultural Ways of Healing

Cultural ways of healing have usually been indiscriminately branded as inappropriate by mainstream psychiatry without acknowledging that a certain kind of psychiatry is in itself a cultural practice. Minkowitz (2011) argued that practices of involuntary diagnosis, involuntary institutionalization and involuntary treatment in psychiatry needed to be recognized as harmful cultural practices. These practices, by claiming to be scientific, erased the world views of individuals who rejected their objectification. These harmful cultural practices of psychiatry were affecting both individuals from countries in the west (where psychiatry originated) and the countries where psychiatry was extending its sphere of influence.

Davar and Lokohare (2009) also talk about how western psychiatric practices are replacing indigenous psycho-spiritual practices such as mantra, prayer, song, use of percussion instruments, song-making, storytelling, meditations, yoga, trancing, mediumship and accessing alternative states of consciousness. This erasure of indigenous practices is leading many, especially women, to depend on psychiatric drugs for longer periods of time. There is a need to focus on the fact that certain global hegemonic practices that claim to be based on scientific method and evidence are not above or outside of culture and are open to challenge as being harmful (Minkowitz, 2011). This also makes it important to look at how 'madness' has been viewed from other lenses which explore it in terms of local understandings.

Therefore, spirit possession and local explanations of mental illness can be seen as women organizing their agency to make spaces for themselves within existing structures. This is evident when women spoke about resorting to 'madness' as a way of expressing their anguish. When they were asked about their understanding of the relationship between the problems women faced and madness, they replied, '*Jab pareshanian had se bad jati hain toh auratain chandi ban jati hain*' (When problems cross a threshold, women take on the role of '*chandi*'). Becoming '*chandi*' here implies taking on the characteristics of goddess Kali which are considered negative, like excessive anger and aggression (seen as being possessed by the goddess). They said that women become '*chandi*' and scream because of the problems that they are facing, but others just consider them mad. No one realizes what they are going through except other women who might be undergoing similar experiences.

Rapid social change is another reason for increasing levels of distress. Witchcraft articulates with the wider discourse of modernity, 'addressing the mysteries of the modern market economy: the vagaries of prices and employment possibilities, the staggering enrichment of the few and the misery of the many' (Geschiere, 1998: 822). As well as being associated with the accumulation of wealth, sorcery is also seen as a levelling force, opposing new inequalities and relations of domination (Geschiere, 1997). Witchcraft has successfully adapted to a transnational capitalist economy, and the consumerist ethos embraces both the spiritual and material (Romberg, 2003). Anthropologists have observed that sorcery accusations thrive in times of rapid social change; they proposed another positive function: sorcery (and this applied to witchcraft as well) served to index the forces of disorder and chaos deployed by colonial and postcolonial political economies (Comaroff and Comaroff, 1993; Douglas, 1970; Marwick, 1982; Redfield, 1941).

Spirit possession phenomena have generally linked them to culturally specific forms of conflict management that disguise and yet resolve social tensions within indigenous societies (Firth, 1967; Lewis, 1971). In contrast, policymakers and professionals see spirit possession episodes as an intrusion of archaic beliefs on the modern setting (Chew, 1978; Phoon, 1982; Teoh, Soewondo, and Sidharta, 1975). This kind of de-legitimization of alternative routes to healing mirrors the early stages of medicalization, when the work of traditional birth attendants, healers was de-recognized and 'doctors' became the last word on health and sickness.

Psychosocial disability or distress cannot be explained just as physiological illness or a reaction against patriarchy. The use of 'medical' as well as 'social' can be seen as different mediums through which women exercise their agency and voice their distress. Across the world, women's health has come into prominence along with the broader women's movements (Leeson and Gray, 1978). Self-help movements which involve self-examination and self-education; original research into health issues; group support for specific problems;

and attempts to analyse and change aspects of the healthcare system locally are most effective. Leeson and Gray describe how women's groups studied herbal medicines, yoga and massage and used them as alternatives (1978: 196). Chiu et al. (2005) conducted research on spirituality and treatment choices of Southeast Asian women with mental illness. They found that many women were using conventional medicine: they went for astrological readings, and tried various traditional healing practices like acupressure, acupuncture, diets, praying and worshipping God. They also experienced spirituality by helping others. Examples included showing compassion for those who were suffering and being willing to help, learning that by helping others, one helped oneself, and by getting involved in volunteer work and so on. These studies show how the cultural ways of healing that have been used by women over the ages are being incorporated within the women's movement as well.

The influence of both the women's movement and cultural ways of healing is evident in the findings of this research study as well. For example, the narratives of both Padma (Chapter 5) and Radha (Chapter 6) bring out how they have managed to carve a space for themselves in the community. They have been able to form a distinct identity for themselves by being involved in work related to helping other women. Being a part of NGOs has increased their exposure and helped them to articulate the discomfort that they have felt with the structures around them. Radha's narrative also brings out how along with medical treatment she regularly accesses folk healing practitioners. This is because folk healing explanations have helped her to find meaning in the difficult circumstances that she has often faced. The coexistence of different ideologies and systems of healing do not seem to create dissonance in the people living in Jahangirpuri, the dissonance appears to be more etic than emic.

Through this study, it has been reconfirmed that the social position of women affects the level of psychosocial distress they face. The multiple roles that women have and their ascribed caring roles make their position more vulnerable. Questioning certain societal prescriptions often leads to them being labelled as 'mad'. It is the support of other women that has enabled women to change the homeostasis and bring about a change in power relations. In many ways, it is the women's movements that have provided secular spaces for women, spaces which have enabled them to seek the support of other women, to help themselves and others, and to explore ways of coping which have enabled them to feel empowered. It is important to recognize the role of both the women's movement and the cultural ways of healing as they complement each other. On their own, the cultural ways of healing provided a space for expression and negotiation but did not challenge existing gender hierarchies. Whereas, the women's movement while focusing on systems of equality created a new discourse on normality. With its emphasis on strength and empowerment, it ignored the spaces required for vulnerability and healing. These spaces were termed as mere superstitions or worse were viewed as communal practices. The fact that they are much more than that is evident from the fact that they continue to hold an important place in people's lives and are continuously accessed in the hope of being healed.

Women's movements and medical pluralism both seem to provide choices for people who are suffering. This research does not negate the importance of psychiatric drugs and treatments. There are many instances wherein these have helped women and their families. But there is a need to exercise caution in their usage and prevent their rampant misuse. Issues of illness and health remain embedded in social decisions and actions, not only in medical decisions about transmission and cure. The complex nature of 'madness' or 'psychosocial distress' has to be addressed from a variety of perspectives as multiple factors influence it. More data is required on the linkages between poverty and psychosocial distress. Poverty underlies the poor health status of developing world populations, and women represent a disproportionate share of the poor. Furthermore, the cultural and socio-economic environment affects women's exposure to disease and injury, their diet, their access to and use of health services, and the manifestations and consequences of disease.

Women's disadvantaged social position, which is often related to the economic value placed on familial roles, helps perpetuate poor health, inadequate diet, early and frequent pregnancy, and a continued cycle of poverty (Tinker, 2000: 151). These factors are important in increasing the level of psychosocial distress faced by women. Over (1991) argues that poor health outcomes, manifested in high fertility, mortality and morbidity rates, affect both quality and quantity of labour, and reduce the number of hours worked, which affects national income adversely. Taking this argument further, ill-health of the population, if sustained over time, is bound to affect the rate of growth of national income. Poor growth, on the other hand, squeezes the resources of the government, forcing it to reduce its expenditure on education, health, food and other developmental fronts. This further exacerbates the vicious circle of ill-health and lower well-being.

In order to reduce the levels of psychosocial distress and disability faced by women, it is important to incorporate the health issues within other programmes for development of women. Enacted policies on transportation, housing, energy, education, and agriculture have both direct and indirect consequences for health; yet in most governments or administrations, health policies are only haphazardly integrated with those of other departments (Bowker, 1997). This shows that there is an effort to take attention away from the real issues and that problems are given names that can be referred for a cure instead of addressing the larger systemic problem.

Meaning-making needs to be critically evaluated as a political tool that reworks experience so that it conforms to the demands of power. In order to improve the health of women, policies aiming to improve the social status of women are needed along with 'health policies' targeting the entire spectrum of women's health needs (Desjarlais et al., 1995). Gupta and Mitra (2004) state better health will also lead to lower poverty. Accompanied by improved investment in education and growth-promoting areas like industry, an increased investment in health might be a necessary condition for putting countries on a path of accelerated growth with better levels of living and health status. Reduction of psychosocial distress of women thus implies not only a better quality of life for them but also better governance.

There is a need for more ethnographic research on the intersections between sociocultural conditions of different societies and the psychosocial distress faced by people living in these societies. It is evident that cultural ways of healing serve a function in society and hence there is a need to examine their role further. Douglas (1970) explains how it may well be possible that a therapeutic tradition in which the patient and doctor construct their own world of fantasy for comprehending the illness may work in a particular kind of social structure and not in another. Therefore, it is important to understand the social structures and their relationship to healing. This also becomes important because of the mushrooming of many nefarious kinds of healing practices, centres and cult figures as a result of increased suffering.

Another important area of research is the linkages between women's movements and their role in alleviating the psychosocial distress faced by women. This would also give us the connections between a theoretical understanding of madness and women's life practices. There is a need to involve women whom the programmes are being designed to serve at all stages of planning, development and management (Desjarlais et al., 1995: 201). District and National Mental health programmes have till now not taken into account all the stakeholders involved in the alleviation of distress (women's movements, civil society organizations as well as cultural healing practices). Focusing on the medical model has led to ineffective functioning of these programmes which have failed to live up to their promise. Effectiveness of programmes designed with the help of all stakeholders has to be investigated and if successful, these practices need to be replicated or modified accordingly.

Almeida-Filho (1998) outlines that the general hypothesis about 'modernization' resulting in the breakdown of coherent cultures and communities and leading to mental health problems has not stood up well to empirical investigation. The impact of development (which is not a linear or progressive process) on the mental health status of the population of a place needs to be understood and explored further as 'development' seems to be the new '*mantra*' to cure all evils. This needs to be examined critically as development, without taking into account its consequences, is leading to increased chaos in the long term. In order to understand psychosocial distress in this context, there is need to develop newer models which take into account intersections between the cultural, social and economic realities faced by women.

BIBLIOGRAPHY

Acker, J. (1989). The Problem of Patriarchy. *Sociology*, 235–40.
Aday, L. (2001). *At Risk in America*. San Francisco: Jossey-Bass Publishers.
Addlakha, R. (2001). The Lay and Medical Diagnosis of Psychiatric Disorder and the Normative Construction of Femininity. In B. Davar (Ed.), *Mental Health from a Gender Perspective* (pp. 313–33). New Delhi: SAGE Publications.
———. (2008). *Deconstructing Mental Illness: An Ethnography of Psychiatry, Women and the Family*. New Delhi: Zubaan Books.
Aggarwal, P. (1971). *Caste, Religion and Power: An Indian Case Study*. New Delhi: Shri Ram Centre for Industrial Relations.
Al-Krenawi, A., & Graham, J. (1997). Spirit Possession and Exorcism in the Treatment of a Bedouin Psychiatric Patient. *Clinical Journal of Social Work*, 25(2), 211–22.
Almeida-Filho, N. (1998). Becoming Modern After All these Years: Social Change and Mental Health in Latin America. *Culture, Medicine and Psychiatry*, 22, 285–316.
Appadurai, A. (2004). The Capacity to Aspire: Culture and the Terms of Recognition. In V. Rao, & M. Walton (Eds), *Culture and Public Action* (pp. 59–84). Delhi: Permanent Black.
Arber, S. (1991). Class, Paid Employment and Family Roles: Making Sense of Structural. *Social Science and Medicine*, 32, 425–36.
Arun, S. (1999). Does Land Ownership Make a Difference? Women's Roles in Agriculture in Kerala, India. *Gender and Development*, 7(3), 19–27.
Bargen, D. (1988). Spirit Possession in the Context of Dramatic Expressions of Gender Conflict: The Aoi Episo of the Genji Monogatari. *Harvard Journal of Asiatic Studies*, 48(1), 95–130.
Bartley, M., Popay, J., & Plewis, I. (1992). Domestic Conditions, Paid Employment and Women's Experience of Ill-health. *Sociology of Health and Illness*, 14(3), 313–43.

Basu, K., & Basu. (2000). Urban Poor Women: Coping with Poverty and Ill-health in Slums of Delhi. *Social Change, 30*(1&2), 179–91.

Batliwala, S., & Dhanraj, D. (2007). Gender Myths That Instrumentalize Women: A View from the Indian Frontline. In A. Cornwall, E. Harrison, & A. Whitehead (Eds), *Feminisms in Development* (pp. 21–34). London: Zed Books.

Batsche, G., & Knoff, H. (1994). Bullies and their Victims: Understanding a Pervasive Problem in the Schools. *School Psychology Review, 23*(2), 165–74.

Behar, R. (1993). *Translated Woman: Crossing the Border with Esperanza's Story.* Boston: Beacon Press.

———. (1996). *The Vulnerable Observer: Anthropology that Breaks the Heart.* Boston: Beacon Press.

Ben-Ezer, G. (1992). *Migration and Absorption of Ethiopian Jews in Israel.* Jerusalem: Mass Press (in Hebrew).

Benedict, R. (1934). *Patterns of Culture.* Boston: Houghton Mifflin Company.

Bergin, A., & Payne, I. (1993). Proposed Agenda for a Spiritual Strategy in Personality and Psychotherapy. In E. J. Wothington (Ed.), *Psychotherapy and Religious Values* (pp. 243–60). Grand Rapids, MI: Baker.

Bhardwaj, R. (2010). Medical Pluralism in India: The Interface of Complementary and Alternative Therapies with Allopathy. In A. Mishra (Ed.), *Health, Illness and Medicine: Ethnographic Readings* (pp. 30–60). Delhi: Orient Blackswan.

Bhore, J. (1946). *Health Survey and Development Committee Report.* New Delhi: Government of India.

Bibeau, G. (1997). Cultural Psychiatry in a Creolizing World: Questions for a New Research Agenda. *Transcultural Psychiatry, 34*(1), 9–41.

Bilu, Y., & Witztum, E. (1995). Between Sacred and Medical Realities: Culturally Sensitive Therapy with Jewish Ultra-Orthodox Patients. *Science in Context, 8*(1), 159–73.

Blehar, M. (2003). Public Health Context of Women's Mental Health Research. *Psychiatric Clinics in North America, 26,* 781–99.

Blue, I. (2001). Urban Inequalities in Mental Health: The Case of Sao Paulo, Brazil. In D. Matcha (Ed.), *Readings in Medical Sociology* (pp. 217–24). Boston: Allyn and Bacon.

Blue, I., Ducci, M., Jaswal, S., Ludermir, A., & Harpham, T. (1995). The Mental Health of Low Income Urban Women: Case Studies from Bombay, India, Olinda, Brazil, and Santiago, Chile. In T. Harpham, & I. Blue (Eds), *Urbanization and Mental Health in Developing Countries* (pp. 75–102). Brookefield: Ashgate.

Bondi, L. (1993). Gender and Geography: Crossing Boundaries. *Progress in Human Geography, 17,* 241–46.

Bourdieu, P. (1977[1972]). *Outline of a Theory of Practice.* Cambridge: Cambridge University Press.

Bourdieu, P. (1984). *Distinctions*. London: Routledge and Keegan Paul.

———. (1986). The Forms of Capital. In J. Richardson (Ed.), *The Handbook of Theory: Research for the Sociology of Education*. New York: Greenwood Press.

———. (1988[1984]). *Homo Academicus*. Cambridge: Polity Press.

———. (1989). Social Space and Symbolic Power. *Sociological Theory, 7*, 14–25.

———. (1990). *The Logic of Practice*. Cambridge: Polity Press.

———. (1999[1993]). *The Weight of the World: Social Suffering in Contemporary Society*. (P. Parkhurst Ferguson, S. Emanuel, J. Johnson, & S. Waryn, Trans.) Cambridge: Polity.

———. (2000[1997]). *Pascalian Meditations*. Stanford: Stanford University Press.

Bourdieu, P., & Eagleton, T. (1992). In Conversation: Doxa and Common Life. *New Left Review, 191*, 111–22.

Bourdieu, P., & Wacquant, L. (1992). *An Invitation to Reflexive Sociology*. Cambridge: Polity Press.

Bourgeault, I. (2006). Sociological Perspectives on Health and Healthcare. In D. Raphael, T. Bryant, & M. Riox (Eds), *Staying Alive: Critical Perspectives on Health, Illness and Healthcare* (pp. 35–57). Toronto: Canadian Scholars Press.

Bowker, J. (1997). Religions, Society and Suffering. In A. Kleinman, V. Das, & M. Lock (Eds), *Social Suffering* (pp. 359–82). California: California University Press Ltd.

Brown, G., & Harris, T. (1978). *Social Origins of Depression: A Study of Psychiatric Disorder in Women*. London: Tavistock.

Budman, C., Lipson, J., & Meleis, A. (1992). The Cultural Consultant in Mental Healthcare: The Case of an Arab Adolescent. *American Journal of Orthopsychiatry, 62*(3), 359–70.

Butler, J. (1997). *Excitable Speech*. London: Routledge.

———. (2003). Afterword: After Loss, What Then? In D. Eng, & D. Kazanjian (Eds), *Loss: The Politics of Mourning*. Berkeley, CA: University of California Press.

Campbell, M. (1998). Institutional Ethnography and Experience as Data. *Qualitative Sociology, 21*(1), 55–73.

Castillo, R. (1997). *Culture and Mental Illness*. Pacific Grove, CA: ITP.

Chakraborthy, A. (2001). Mental Health of Indian Women: A Field Experience. In B. Davar (Ed.), *Mental Health from a Gender Perspective* (pp. 34–60). New Delhi: SAGE Publications.

Channa, S. (1997). Gender and Social Space in a Haryana Village. *Indian Journal of Gender Studies, 1*, 21–34.

Chaudhary, N., & Bhargava, P. (2006). Mamta: The Transformation of Meaning in Everyday Usage. *Contributions to Indian Sociology, 40*(3), 343–73.

Chaudhuri, M. (2005). Betwixt The State and Everyday Life: Identity Formation among Bengali Migrants in a Delhi Slum. In M. Thapan (ed), *Transnational Migration and the Politics of Identity*. SAGE Publications.

Chaudhury, S. & Leonesio, M. (1997). Life-Cycle Aspects of Poverty among Older Women. *Social Security Bulletin*, 60(2), 17–36.

Cheng, T. (1989). Urbanization and Minor Psychiatric Morbidity. *Social Psychiatry and Psychiatric Epidemiology*, 24, 309–16.

Chesler, P. (1972). *Women and Madness*. New York: Double Day.

Chew, P. (1978). How to Handle Hysterical Factory Workers. *Occupational Health and Safety*, 47(2), 50–53.

Chiu, L., Ganesan, S., Clark, N., & Morrow, M. (2005). Spirituality and Treatment Choices by South and East Asian Women with Serious Mental Illness. *Transcultural Psychiatry*, 42(4), 630–56.

Chodorow, N. (1978). *The Reproduction of Mothering*. London: University of California Press.

Choi, P., & Nicolson, P. (1994). *Female Sexualities: Psychology, Biology and Social Context*. Hemel Hempstead: Harvester Wheatsheaf.

Chossudovsky, M. (1994). *The Globalisation of Poverty: Impacts of IMF and World Bank Reforms*. Penang, MY: Zed Books.

Christakis, N., Ware, N., & Kleinman, A. (2001). Illness Behavior in the Health Transition in the Developing World. In D. Matcha (Ed.), *Readings in Medical Sociology* (pp. 143–59). Boston: Allyn and Bacon.

Clarke, A., Shim, J., Mamo, L., Fosket, J., & Fishman, F. (2003). Biomedicalization: Technoscientific Transformations of Health, Illness, and U.S. Biomedicine. *American Sociological Review*, 68, 161–94.

Cohen, L. (1998). *No Aging in India: Alzheimer's, The Bad Family, and Other Modern Things*. Berkeley: University of California Press.

Coker, E. (2004). Travelling Pains: Embodied Metaphors of Suffering among Southern Sudanese Refugees in Cairo. *Culture, Medicine and Psychiatry*, 28, 15–39.

Connell, R. (1987). *Gender and Power*. Cambridge: Polity Press.

Corney, R. (1990). A Survey of Professional Help Sought by Patients for Psychosocial Problems. *British Journal of General Practice*, 40, 365–68.

Craft, N. (1997). Women's Health is a Global Issue. *British Medical Journal*, 315, 1154–57.

Crapanzano, V & Garrison, V. (1977). Introduction, In *Case Studies in Spirit Possession*. New York: John Wiley.

Crossley, N. (1998). R. D. Laing and the British Anti-psychiatry: A Socio-historical Analysis. *Social Science and Medicine*, 47(7), 877–89.

Da Matta, R. (1984). On Carnaval, Informality and Magic: A Point of View from Brazil. In E. Bruner (Ed.), *Text, Play and Story: The Construction and Reconstruction of Self and Society* (pp. 230–46). Washington D.C.: American Ethnological Society.

Das Gupta, M., & Chen, L. (1996). Introduction. In M. Das Gupta, L. Chen, & T. Krishnan (Eds), *Health, Poverty and Development in India* (pp. 1–24). Delhi: Oxford University Press.

Das, R., & Das, V. (2005). *The Interface between Mental Health and Reproductive Health of Women among the Urban Poor in Delhi*. Trivandrum: Achutha Menon Centre for Health Science Studies, Sree Chitra Tirunal Institute for Medical Sciences and Technology.

Das, V. (1995). *Critical Events: An Anthropological Perspective on Contemporary India*. Delhi: Oxford University Press.

———. (1997). Language and the Body: Transactions in the Construction of Pain. In A. Kleinman, V. Das, & M. Lock (Eds), *Social Suffering* (pp. 67–91). New Delhi: Oxford.

Das, V., & Das, R. (2007). How the Body Speaks: Illness and Lifeworld among the Urban Poor. In J. Biehl, B. Good, & A. Kleinman (Eds), *Subjectivity: Ethnographic Investigations* (pp. 66–97). Berkeley: University of California Press.

Davar, B. (1995). Mental Illness in Indian Women. *Economic and Political Weekly*, 30(45), 2879–86.

———. (1999). *Mental Health of Indian Women: A Feminist Agenda*. New Delhi: SAGE Publications.

———. (2000). Writing Phenomenology of Mental Illness: Extending the Universe of Ordinary Discourse. In A. Raghuramaraju (Ed.), *Existence, Experience and Ethics* (pp. 51–82). New Delhi: D.K. Printworld.

———. (2001). Gender and Mental Health: Inter-Disciplinary Perspectives. In B. Davar (Ed.), *Mental Health from a Gender Perspective*. New Delhi: SAGE Publications.

Davar, B. V. (2008). From Mental Illness to Disability: Choices for Women Users/Survivors of Psychiatry in Self and Identity Constructions. *Indian Journal of Gender Studies*, 261–90.

Davar, B., & Lokohare, M. (2009). Recovering from Psychosocial Traumas: The Place of Dargahs in Maharashtra. *Economic and Political Weekly*, 44(16), 60–67.

De Beauvoir, S. (1984). *The Second Sex (trans J. Cape, 1953)*. Harmondsworth: Penguin.

Desai, Sonalde, Dubey, A, Joshi, B.L, Sen, M, Shariff, A. & Reeve Vanneman. 2010. *Human Development in India: Challenges for a Society in Transition*. New Delhi: Oxford University Press, p. 234.

Deckard, B. (1979). *The Women's Movement: Political, Socioeconomic, and Psychological*. New York: Harper and Row.

Dennerstein, L., Astbury, J., & Morse, C. (1993). *Psychosocial and Mental Health Aspects of Women's Health*. Geneva: WHO.

Deshmukh-Ranadive, J. (2002). *Space for Power-Women's Work and Family Strategies in South and South-East Asia*. Delhi: Rainbow Publishers.

———. (2008). Introduction. In *Democracy in the Family: Insights from India* (pp. 1–24). New Delhi: SAGE Publications.

Deshpande, A. (2002). Asset Versus Autonomy? The Changing Face of the Gender-Caste Overlap in India. *Feminist Economics, 8*(2), 19–35.

Desjarlais, R., Eisenberg, L., Good, B., & Kleinman, A. (1995). *World Mental Health: Problems and Priorities in Low-income countries.* Oxford: Oxford University Press.

Dhanda, A. (2000). *Legal Order and Mental Disorder.* New Delhi: SAGE Publications.

Dhanraj, D., Batliwala, S., & Misra, G. (2002, October 3–6). A South Asian Perspective on Future Challenges for the Global Women's Movement. *Paper Presented at the Ninth AWID (Association for Women's Rights in Development).* Guadalajara, Mexico.

Donaldson, E. (2002). The Corpus of the Madwoman: Toward a Feminist Disability Studies Theory of Embodiment and Mental Illness. *NWSA Journal, 14*(3), 99–119.

Douglas, M. (2004). Traditional Culture- Let's Hear No More about it. In V. Rao, & M. Walton (Eds), *Culture and Public Action* (pp. 85–109). Stanford: Stanford University Press.

———. (1970). *Natural Symbols.* New York: Vintage.

Doyal, L. (1995). *What Makes Women Sick: Gender and the Political Economy of Health.* London: MacMillan.

D'Souza, V. (2012). Sociocultural Marginality: A Theory of Urban Slums and Poverty in India. In A. Dasgupta (Ed.), *On the Margins: Tribes, Castes and Other Social Categories* (Vol. 4, pp. 32–45). New Delhi: SAGE Publications.

Dube, L. (1986). Seed and Earth. In L. Dube (Ed.), *Visibility and Power: Essays on Women in Society and Development* (pp. 22–53). Delhi: Oxford University Press.

———. (1996). Caste and Women. In *Caste: Its Twentieth Century Avatar* (pp. 1–27). New Delhi: Viking.

———. (1997). *Women and Kinship: Comparitive Perspective on Gender in South and South-East Asia.* Tokyo: United Nations University Press.

———. (2001). *Anthropological Intersections in Gender: Intersecting Fields.* New Delhi: Thousand Oaks: SAGE Publications.

Dube, L., & Dube, S. (1986). Women in India: Hinduism, and the Category of Politics. *Paper Presented at the pre-Congress symposium on Women, Religion and Politics, IPSA Research Committee on Sex Roles and Politics and ISA Research Committee on Women in Society.* New Delhi: Eleventh World Congress of Sociology.

Durant, W., & Durant, A. (1967). *The Story of Civilization: Volume 10- The Age of Rousseau.* New York: Simon and Schuster.

Durkheim, E. (1897 [1952]). *Suicide.* London: Routledge & Kegan Paul.

———. (1964 [1893]). *The Division of Labour in Society.* London: Macmillan.

Dutta, M., Kapilshrami, M., & Tiwari, V. (2004). Knowledge, Awareness and Extent of Male Participation in Key Areas of Reproductive and Child Health in an Urban Slum of Delhi. *Health and Population Perspectives and Issues, 27,* 49–66.

Ecks, S., & Basu, S. (2009). The Unlicensed Lives of Antidepressants in India: Generic Drugs, Unqualified Practitioners, and Floating Prescriptions. *Transcultural Psychiatry, 46*(1), 86–106.

Ehrenreich, B., & English, D. (1974). *Complaints and Disorders: The Sexual Politics of Sickness (Glass mountain Pamphlet No.2)*. London: Compendium.

El-Islam, M. (1980). Symptom Onset and Involution of Delusions. *The International Journal of Social Psychiatry, 15*, 157–60.

Eshun, S., & Gurung, A. (2009). *Introduction to Culture and Psychopathology: Culture and Mental Health*. Malden, M.A.: Wiley-Blackwell.

Eskell-Blockland, L. (2009). Listening to Oral Traditions in a Re-searching for Praxis in a Non-Western Context. *Journal of Health Management, 11*(2), 355–73.

Evans-Pritchard, E. (1931). Sorcery and Native Opinion Source: Africa. *Journal of the International African Institute, 4*(1), 22–55.

Fabrega, H. (1972). Medical Anthropology. *Bienn. Review of Anthropology, 1971*, 167–229.

———. (2009). *History of Mental Illness in India: A Cultural Psychiatry Retrospective*. Delhi: Motilal Banarsidass Publishers.

Faris, R., & Dunham, W. (1939). *Mental Disorders In Urban Areas*. Chicago: Chicago University Press.

Ferlander, S. (2007). The Importance of Different Forms of Social Capital for Health. *Acta Sociologica, 50*(2), 115–28.

Few, A., Stephens, D., & Rouse-Arnett, M. (2003). Sister-to-Sister Talk: Transcending Boundaries and Challenges in Qualitative Research with Black Women. *Family Relations, 52*(3), 205–15.

Figlio, K. (1987). The Lost Subject of Medical Sociology. In G. Scambler (Ed.), *Sociological Theory and Medical Sociology* (pp. 77–107). London: Tavistock Publications.

First, M., & Zimmerman, M. (2006). Including Laboratory Tests in DSM-V Diagnostic Criteria. *American Journal of Psychiatry, 163*, 2041–42.

Firth, R. (1967). Ritual and Drama in Malay Spirit Mediumship. *Comparitive Studies in Society and History, 9*(2), 190–207.

Folkman, S., & Lazarus, R. (1986). Stress Processes and Depressive Symptomatology. *Journal of Abnormal Psychology, 95*, 105–13.

Fontana, A., & Frey, J. (2000). The Interview: From Structured Text to Negotiated Text. In N. Denzin, & Y. Lincoln (Eds), *Handbook of Qualitative Research*. New Delhi: SAGE Publications.

Foucault, M. (1967). *Madness and Civilization*. London: Tavistock.

———. (1972). *The Archaeology of Knowledge*. London: Tavistock.

Foucault, M. (1979/1990). *The History of Sexuality, Vol. 1: An Introduction*. Harmondsworth: Penguin.

———. (1995 [1975]). *Discipline and Punish*. New York: Vintage Books.

Fromm, E. (2002 [1956]). *The Sane Society*. London and New York: Routledge Classics.

Frost, L., & Hoggett, P. (2008). Human Agency and Social Suffering. *Critical Social Policy, 28*(4), 438–60.

Gandhi, N. (2008). Women Adjusting for Survival: Women Workers, New Economic Policies and Adjustments within the Family and Households. In J. Deshmukh-Ranadive (Ed.), *Democracy in the Family. Insights from India* (pp. 25–54). New Delhi: SAGE Publications.

Ganesh, K. (1998). Gender and Kinship Studies: Indian Material and Context. In C. Risseeuw, & K. Ganesh (Eds), *Negotiation and Social Space: A Gendered Analysis of Changing Kin and Security Networks in South Asia* (pp. 113–33). New Delhi: SAGE Publications.

Gannon, L. (1998). The Impact of Mental and Sexual Politics on Women's Health. *Feminism and Psychology, 8*(3), 285–302.

George, L., Ellison, C., & Larson, D. (2002). Explaining the Relationships between Religious Involvement and Health. *Psychological Inquiry, 13*, 190–200.

Geschiere, P. (1997). *The Modernity of Witchcraft: Politics and the Occult in Postcolonial Africa*. Charlottesville: University of Virginia Press.

———. (1998). Globalization and the Power of Indeterminate Meaning: Witchcraft and Spirit Cults in Africa and East Asia. *Development and Change, 29*(4), 811–37.

Ginsberg, F., & Rapp, R. (1991). The Politics of Reproduction. *Annual Review of Anthropology, 20*(1), 311–43.

Goel, S. L & Goel, A. (2008). *Women Health Education*. New Delhi: Deep and Deep Publications.

Goffman, E. (1959). *The Presentation of Self in Everyday Life*. New York: Anchor.

———. (1961). *Asylums: Essays on the Social Situation of Asylum Patients and Other Inmates*. Garden City, NJ: Anchor Books.

———. (1968). *Stigma: Notes on the Management of Spoiled Identity, Reprinted 1990*. London: Penguin.

Goldner, V., Penn, P., Sheinberg, M., & Walker, G. (1990). Love and Violence: Gender Paradoxes in Volatile Attachments. *Family Process, 26*(4), 343–63.

Gone, J. P. (2008). Introduction: Mental Health Discourse as Western Cultural Proselytization. *Ethos, 36*(3), 310–15.

Good, B., & Good, M. (1986). The Cultural Context of Diagnosis and Therapy: A View From Medical Anthropology. In M. Miranda, & H. Kitano (Eds), *Medical Health Research and Practice in Minority Communities: Development of Culturally Sensitive Training Programs* (pp. 1–28). Washington D.C.: DHHS Publication.

Government of India. (1982). *National Mental Health Programme for India*. New Delhi: Ministry of Health and Family Welfare.

Grover, S. (2011). *Marriage, Love, Caste & Kinship Support: Lived Experiences of the Urban Poor in India*. New Delhi: Social Science Press.

Gupta, I., & Mitra, A. (2004). Economic Growth, Health and Poverty: An Exploratory Study for India. *Development Policy Review, 22*(2), 193–206.

Gupta, R. (1983). *Planning and Development of Towns.* New Delhi: Oxford and IBH Publishing Company.

Gurung, R. (2006). *Health Psychology: A Cultural Approach.* San Francisco: Wadsworth Publishing.

Gururaj G., Varghese M., Benegal V., Rao G.N., Pathak K., Singh L.K.,... & NMHS collaborators group. National Mental Health Survey of India, 2015–16: Prevalence, Patterns and Outcomes. Bengaluru, National Institute of Mental Health and Neuro Sciences, NIMHANS Publication No. 129, 2016.

Halford, W. K., Price, J., Kelly, A. B., Bouma, R., & Young, M. D. (2001). Helping Female Partners of Men Abusing Alcohol: A Comparison of Three Treatments. *Addiction, 96,* 1497–1508.

Hamilton, J.A. (1994). Feminist Theory and Health Psychology: Tools for Egalitarian, Women's Centered Approach to Women's Health (pp. 56–66). New Delhi: SAGE.

Haw, C. (2000). Psychological Perspectives on Women's Vulnerability to Mental Illness. In D. Kohen (Ed.), *Women and Mental Health* (pp. 65–105). London: Routledge.

Heninger, G. R. (1999). Psychiatric Research in the 21st Century: Opportunities and Limitations. *Molecular Psychiatry, 4,* 429–36.

Hollingshead, A., & Redlich, F. (1958). *Social Class and Mental Illness.* New York: Wiley.

Holmshaw, J., & Hillier, S. (2000). Gender and Culture: A Sociological Perspective to Mental Health Problems in Women. In D. Kohen (Ed.), *Women and Mental Health* (pp. 39–64). London: Routledge.

Honneth, A. (1995). *The Struggle for Recognition: The Moral Grammar of Social Conflicts*(trans. Joel Andersen). Cambridge: Polity Press.

Horowitz, A. (1977). The Pathways into Psychiatric Treatment: Some Differences between Men and Women. *Journal of Health and Social Behaviour, 18,* 169–78.

ICD-10. (1992). International Classification of Diseases. Classification of Mental and Behavioural Disorders. 10th revision. Geneva: World Health Organization.

International Institute for Population Sciences (IIPS) and ORC Macro (2000). National Family Health Survey (NFHS-2): 1998–99 (India). Mumbai: IIPS.

Jacobs, M., Munro, P., & Adams, N. (1995). Palimpsest: (Re)reading Women's Lives. *Qualitative Inquiry, 1*(3), 327–45.

Jagori & UN Women. (2011). *Safe Cities Free of Violence against Women and Girls Initiative: Report of the Baseline Survey 2010.* New Delhi.

Jain, S., & Jadhav, S. (2009). Pills that Swallow Policy: Clinical Ethnography of a Community Mental Health Program in Northern India. *Transcultural Psychiatry, 46*(1), 60–85.

Jaisinki, J., Asdigian, N., & Kantor, G. (1997). Ethnic Adaptations to Occupational Strain: Work-Related Stress, Drinking and Wife Assault among Anglo and Hispanic Husbands. *Journal of Interpersonal Violence, 12*(6), 814–31.

Jenkins, J., & Valiente, M. (1994). Bodily Transactions of the Passion: El Calor among Salvadorian Women Refugees. In T. Csordas (Ed.), *Embodiments and Experince*. Cambridge: Cambridge University.

Johansson, E., Hamberg, K., Westman, G., & Lindgren, G. (1999). The Meanings of Pain: An Exploration of Women's Description of Symptoms. *Social Science and Medicine, 48*, 1791–1802.

John, M. (1999). Gender, Development and Women's Movement. In R. S. Rajan (Ed.), *Signposts: Gender Issues In Post-Independence India*. New Delhi: Kali for Women.

Johnson, S., & Buszewicz, M. (1996). Women's Mental Illness. In K. Abel, M. Buszewicz, S. Davison (Eds), *Planning Community Mental Health Services for women: A Multiprofessional Handbook* (pp. 6–19). London: Routledge.

Jordanova, L. (1989). *Sexual Visions: Images of Gender in Science and Medicine between the Eighteenth and Twentieth Centuries*. London: Harvester Wheatsheaf.

Joshi, P., Singh, M., Guha-Sapir, D., & Marx, M. (2009). Social Contours of Mental Illness in a Peri-Urban Resettlement Delhi. *The Eastern Anthropologist, 62*(3), 345–59.

Judge, K., & Patterson, I. (2001). State of India's Health. *Treasury Working Paper 01/29*. Wellington.

Kakar, S. (1982). *Shamans, Mystics and Doctors*. New Delhi: Oxford University Press.

———. (1995). *The Colours Of Violence*. New Delhi: Penguin.

Kakar, S., & Kakar, K. (2007). *The Indians: Portrait of a People*. New Delhi: Penguin Books.

Kandel, B., Davies, M., & Raveis, V. (1985). The Stressfulness of Daily Social Roles for Women: Marital, Occupational and Household Roles. *Journal of Health and Social Behaviour, 26*(1), 64–78.

Kannabiran, K. (2005). *The Violence of Normal Times: Essays on Women's Lived Realities*. New Delhi: Women Unlimited.

Kantor, P., & Nair, P. (2003). Risks and Responses among the Urban Poor. *Indian Journal of International Development, 15*, 957–67.

Kapadia, K. (1995). *Siva and Her Sisters: Gender, Caste and Class in Rural South India*. Oxford: Westview Press.

Karlekar, M. (1988). Strategies for Family Survival. *Women's Studies Quarterly, 16*(3/4; Fall-Winter), 91–99.

———. Breaking the Silence. In M. Khullar, & I. Taehakyyo (Eds), *Writing the Women's Movement* (pp. 300–24). New Delhi: Zubaan.

Kawachi, I., & Kennedy, B. (2002). *The Health of Nations: Why Inequality is Harmful to your Health*. New York: NY Press.

Kellet, P., & Tipple, G. (2000). The Home as Workplace: A Study of Income-Generating Activities within the Domestic Setting. *Environment and Urbanization*, 12(1), 203–14.

Khlat, M., Sermet, C., & Le Pape, A. (2000). Women's Health in Relation with their Family and Work Roles: France in the Early 1990s. *Social Science and Medicine*, 50, 1807–25.

Kielman, K. (2002, July 18–19). Gender, Well-being and Quality of Life. *Paper Presented at Gender, Health and Politics Workshop in South Asia, 2002, sponsored by the South Asia Institute and the Department of Tropical Hygiene and Public Health*. Heidelberg: University of Heidelberg.

Kiev, A. (1972). *Transcultural Psychiatry*. New York: Free Press.

Kirmayer, L., & Minas, I. (2000). The Future of Cultural Psychiatry: An International Perspective. *Canadian Journal of Psychiatry*, 45(5), 438–46.

Kishwar, M. (1998). Learning to Take People Seriously. In M. Thapan (Ed.), *Anthropological Journeys* (pp. 293–311). Hyderabad: Orient Longman.

Kishwar-e-Narmada. (1990). Madness and Power: Realities and Myth, The Indian Women. Himachal Pradesh: ASK.

Kleinman, A. (1974). The Cognitive Structure of Traditional Medical Systems. *Ethnomedicine*, 3, 27–49.

———. (1975). Explanatory Models in Healthcare Relationships. *Health of the Family (National Council for International Health Symposium)* (pp. 159–72). Washington, DC: NCIH.

———. (1980). *Patients and Healers in the Context of Culture*. Berkeley: University of California Press.

———. (1987). Anthropology and Psychiatry: The Role of Culture in Cross-Cultural Research on Illness. *British Journal of Psychiatry*, 151(4), 447–54.

———. (1997). 'Everything That Really Matters': Social Suffering, Subjectivity, and the Remaking of Human Experience in a Disordering World. *The Harvard Theological Review*, 90(3), 315–35.

Kleinman, A., & Benson, P. (2006). Anthropology in the Clinic: The Problem of Cultural Competency and How to Fix It. *PLoS Med*, 3(10), e294. doi:10.1371/journal.pmed.0030294

Kleinman, A., Eisenberg, L., & Good, B. (2006). Culture, Illness and Care: Clinical Lessons From Anthropologic and Cross-Cultural Research. *The Journal of Lifelong Learning in Psychiatry*, 6(1), 140–49.

Kleinman, S., & Copp, M. (1993). *Emotions and Fieldwork*. Newbury Park, CA: SAGE Publications.

Kohen, D. (2000). Introduction. In D. Kohen (Ed.), *Women and Mental Health* (pp. 1–16). London: Routledge.

Kumar, A. (2005). District Mental Health Programme in India: A Case Study. *Journal of Health and Development*, 1(1), 24–35.

Lahelma, E., Arber, S., Kivela, K., & Roos, E. (2001). Marriage, Motherhood and Work among British and Finnish Women: Multiple Health Burden or Multiple Buffer? *Social Science and Medicine, 54*, 727–40.

Leeson, J. & Gray, J. (1978). *Women and Medicine*. London: Tavistock Publications.

Leff, J. (1981). *Psychiatry around the Globe: A Transcultural View*. New York: Marcel Dekker.

Leighton, A. (1959). *My Name is Legion: Foundations for a Theory of Man in Relation to Culture*. New York: Basic Books.

Leon, W., & Gilson, L. (2001). International Perspectives on Health Inequalities and Policy. *British Medical Journal, 322*, 591–94.

Lewis, J. (1971). *Ecstatic Religion: An Anthropological Study of Spirit Possession and Shamanism*. Harmonds-worth, England: Penguin.

Lewis, O. (1965). *Village Life in Northern India: Studies in a Delhi Village*. New York: Random House.

Lim, L. (1978). *Women Workers in Multinational Corporations: The Case of the Electronics Industry in Malaysia and Singapore*. Ann Arbor: Michigan Occasional Papers in Women's Studies, No. 9.

Lister, R. (2004). A Politics of Recognition and Respect: Involving People with Experience of Poverty in Decision-making that Affects their Lives. In J. Anderson, & B. Sim (Eds), *The Politics of Inclusion and Empowerment*. Hampshire: Palgrave Macmillan.

Litman, T. (1974). The Family as a Basic Unit in Health and Medical Care. *Social Science and Medicine, 8*(9–10), 495–519.

Lopez, I. (1993). Agency and Constraint: Sterilization and Reproductive Freedom Among Puerto Rican Women in New York City. *Urban Anthropology and Studies of Cultural Systems and World Economic Development, 22*(3/4), 299–323.

Lovell, T. (2007). Introduction. In N. Fraser, & P. Bourdieu (Eds), *(Mis)recognition, Social Inequality and Social Justice*. London: Routledge.

Low, S. (1994). Embodied Metaphors: Nerves as Lived Experience. In T. Csordas (Ed.), *Embodiment and Experience: The Existential Ground of Culture and Self* (pp. 139–162). Ohio: Case Western Reserve University.

Lu, F., Linn, R., & Mezzich, J. (1995). Issues in the Assessment and Diagnosis of Culturally Diverse Individuals. In J. Oldham, & M. Riba (Eds), *Review of Psychiatry* (pp. 477–510). Washington D.C: American Psychiatry Press.

Ludmir, A., & Lewis, G. (2005). Is there a Gender Difference on the Association between Informal Work and Common Mental Disorders? *Social Psychiatry and Psychiatric Epidemiology, 40*(8), 622–27.

Lundberg, U., & Frankenhauser, M. (1999). Stress and Workload of Men and Women in High-ranking Positions. *Journal of Occupational Health Psychology, 4*, 131–41.

Lund F., & Srinivas S. (2000). *Learning from Experience: A Gendered Approach to Social Protection for Workers in the Informal Economy*. ILO: Geneva.

MacAndrew, C., & Edgerton, R. (1969). *Drunken Comportment*. Chicago: Aldine.

Madan, T. (1965). *Family and Kinship: A Study of the Pandits of Rural Kashmir*. New York: Asia Publishing House.

Madhiwalla, N., & Jesani, A. (1997). Morbidity among Women in Mumbai City: Impact of Work and Environment. *Economic and Political Weekly*, 32(43), WS38–WS44.

Magar, V. (2000). Reconceptualizing Domestic Violence in Delhi's Slums. Multidimensional Factors and Empowerment Approaches. *PhD dissertation*. Chapel Hill: University of North Carolina.

MaKinen, I., & Ferlander, S. (2009). Social Capital, Gender and Self-rated health: Evidence from the Moscow Health Survey 2004. *Social Science and Medicine*, 69, 1323–32.

Malson, H. (1998). *The Thin Woman: Feminism, Post-structuralism and the Social Psychology of Anorexia Nervosa*. London: Routledge.

Malson, H., & Swann, C. (2003). Re-producing 'Woman's Body': Reflections on the (dis) place (ments) of 'Reproduction' for (post) Modern Women. *Journal of Gender Studies*, 12(3), 191–201.

Marsella, A. (1993). Counselling and Psychotherapy with Japan American: Cross-Cultural Consideration. *American Journal of Orthopsychiatry*, 63(2), 200–08.

———. (1995). Urbanization, Mental Health and Psychosocial Well-being: Some Historical Perspectives and Considerations. In T. Harpham, & I. Blue (Eds), *Urbanization and Mental Health in Developing Countries* (pp. 17–38). Aldershot: Avebury.

Marshall, H., & Woollett, A. (2000). Fit to Reproduce? The Regulative Role of Pregnancy Texts. *Feminism and Psychology*, 10(3), 351–66.

Massey, D. (1996). The Age of Extremes: Concentrated Affluence and Poverty in the Twenty-first century. Demography. *Demography*, 33, 395–412.

Maton, K. (2012 [2008]). Habitus. In M. Grenfell (Ed.), *Pierre Bourdieu. Key Concepts* (pp. 49–66). Jaipur: Rawat Publications.

Matthews, S., & Powers, C. (2000). Socioeconomic Gradients in Psychological Distress: A Focus on Women, Social Roles and Work-home Characteristics. *Social and Economic Patterning of Health among Women* (pp. 331–56). Tunis: Committee for International Cooperation in National Research in Demography, United National Population Fund.

McGuire, M. (2010). A Blind Eye to the Politics of the Body Politic? Bourdieu and Medical Anthropology. *Culturepedia*, 1, 73–85.

Mead, G. H. (1934). *Mind, Self and Society: From the Standpoint of a Social Behaviourist*. (C. Morris, Ed.) Chicago: Chicago University Press.

Mechanic, D. (1972). Social Psychological Factors Affecting the Presentation of Bodily Complaints. *New England Journal of Medicine*, 286, 1132–39.

Mehotra, N. (1993). A Study of Women's Organisations and Women's Activism in Delhi. *Unpublished Ph.D. Thesis*. University of Delhi.

Mehrotra, N. (1997). Grassroots Women Activism: A Case Study from Delhi. *Indian Anthropologist, 27*(2), 19–38.

———. (2002). Perceiving Feminism: Some Local Responses. *Sociological Bulletin, 51*(1), 57–79.

———. (2004). Women, Disability, and Social Support in Rural Haryana. *Economic and Political Weekly, XXXIX*(52), 5640–44.

———. (2006). Negotiating Gender and Disability in Rural Haryana. *Sociological Bulletin, 55*(3), 406–26.

———. (2011). Disability Rights Movements in India: Politics and Practice. *Economic and Political Weekly, XLVI*(6), 65–72.

Mehrotra, N., & Vaidya, S. (2008). Exploring Constructs Of Intellectual Disability And Personhood In Haryana And Delhi. *Indian Journal of Gender Studies, 15*(2), 317–40.

Menon, U., & Shweder, R. (1998). The Return of the White Man's Burden: The Encounter Between the Moral Discourse of Anthropology and the Domestic Lives of Hindu Women. In R. Shweder (Ed.), *Welcome to Middle Age! (And Other Cultural Fictions)* (pp. 139–89). Chicago: University of Chicago Press.

Menon-Sen, K., & Bhan, G. (2008). *Swept off the Map: Surviving Eviction and Resettlement in Delhi*. New Delhi: Yoda Press.

Mies, M. (1983). Towards a Methodology for Feminist Research. In G. Bowles, & D. Klein (Eds), *Theories of Women's Studies* (pp. 117–39). London: Routledge and Kegan Paul.

Miles, A. (1987). *Women and Mental Illness: The Social Context of Female Neurosis*. Brighton: Wheatsheaf Books.

Mills, C. (1959). *The Sociological Imagination*. Oxford: Oxford University Press.

Minkowitz, T. (2011). Recognizing Forced and Coerced Psychiatric Interventions against Women, Men and Children as a Harmful Cultural Practice. *Submission for Joint CEDAW-CRC General Recommendation/General Comment on Harmful Practices*.

Mirza, Arshad & Singh, N. (2017). Mental Health Policy in India: Seven Sets of Questions and Some Answers (4 September 2017). Available at SSRN: https://ssrn.com/abstract=3033286, accessed on April 6, 2018.

Mohanty, C. T. (1991). Under Western Eyes: Feminist Scholarships and Colonial Discourses. In C. Mohanty, & et al. (Eds), *Third World Women and Politics of Feminism* (pp. 51–81). Bloomington: Indiana University Press.

Mohindra, K. (2009). *Women's Health and Poverty Alleviation in India*. New Delhi: Academic Foundation.

Moore, H. (1988). *Feminism and Anthropology*. Cambridge: Polity Press.

———. (2003). *A Passion for Difference*. Cambridge: Polity Press.

Moos R. H., Finney J. W., Cronkite R. C. (1990). *Alcoholism Treatment: Context, Process, and Outcome*. New York: Oxford University Press.

Myerhoff, B., & Ruby, J. (1982). Introduction. In J. Ruby (Ed.), *A Crack in the Mirror* (pp. 1–39). Philadelphia: Philadelphia University Press.

Nabokov, I. (2000). Deadly Power: A Funeral to Counter Sorcery in South India. *American Ethnologist, 27*(1), 147–68.

Nandi, D., Das, N., Chaudhari, A., Bannerjee, G., Datta, P., Ghosh, A., & et al. (1980). Mental Morbidity and Urban life: An Epidemiological Study. *Indian Journal of Psychiatry, 22*, 324–30.

Nandy, A. (1980). Woman versus Womanliness in India: An Essay in Cultural and Political Psychology. In A. Nandy (Ed.), *At the Edge of Psychology: Essays in Politics and Culture* (pp. 32–46). Delhi: Oxford University Press.

Naples, N. (2003). *Feminism and Method: Ethnography, Discourse Analysis, and Activist Research*. New York: Routledge.

Nasser, M. (1997). *Culture, Weight and Consciousness*. London: Routledge.

Nathanson, C. (1980). Social Roles and Health Status among Women: The Significance. *Social Science and Medicine, 14*(A), 463–71.

National Crime Records Bureau. (2016). Crime in India. Ministry of Home Affairs.

Nayar, M. & Mehrotra, N. (2017). Invisible People, Invisible Violence: Lives of Women with Intellectual and Psychosocial Disabilities, in Kalpana Kannabiran and Asha Hans (Eds) *India Social Development Report 2016: Disability Rights Perspectives*. New Delhi: Oxford University Press.

Nazroo, J., Edwards, A., & Brown, G. (1998). Gender Differences in the Prevalence of Depression: Artefact, Alternative Disorders, Biology or Roles? *Sociology of Health and Illness, 3*, 312–30.

Newmann, J. (1984). Sex Differences in Symptoms of Depression: Clinical Disorder or Normal Distress? *Journal of Health and Social Behaviour, 25*, 136–59.

Nguyen, V., & Peschard, K. (2003). Anthropology, Inequality and Disease: A Review. *Annual Review Anthropology, 32*, 447–74.

Nichter, M. (1981). Idioms of Distress: Alternatives in the Expression of Psychosocial Distress: A Case Study from South India. *Culture, Medicine and Psychiatry, 5*(4), 379–408.

———. (1989). *Anthropology and International Health. South Asian Case Studies*. London: Kluwer Academic Publishers.

Nichter, M. (2002). Social Relations of Therapy Management. In M. Nichter, & M. Lock (Eds), *New Horizons in Medical Anthropology* (pp. 81–110). London: Routledge Press.

———. (2008). Coming to Our Senses: Appreciating the Sensorial in Medical Anthropology. *Transcultural Psychiatry, 45*, 163–97.

Nichter, M., & Thompson, J. (2006). For My Wellness, Not Just My Illness: North Americans' Use of Dietary Supplements. *Culture, Medicine and Psychiatry, 30*, 175–222.

Nichter, M., & Vuckovic, N. (1994). Agenda for an Anthropology of Pharmaceutical Practice. *Social Science and Medicine, 39* (11), 1509–25.
Oakley, A. (1972). *Sex, Gender and Society*. London: Maurice Temple Smith Ltd.
———. (1981). Interviewing Women: A Contradiction in Terms. In H. Roberts (Ed.), *Doing Feminist Research* (pp. 30–61). London: Routledge & Kegan.
———. (1984). *The Captured Womb: A History of the Medical Care of Pregnant Women*. Oxford: Basil Blackwell.
Obeysekere, G. (1985). Depression, Buddhism and the Work of Culture in Sri Lanka. In A. Kleinman, & B. Good (Eds), *Culture and Depression* (pp. 134–52). Berkeley: University of California Press.
———. (1990). Culturally Constituted Defenses and the Theory of Collective Motivation in Personality and the Cultural Construction of Society. In D. Jordan, & M. Swartz (Eds), *Papers in Honour of Melford E. Spiro* (pp. 80–97). Tuscaloosa and London: University of Alabama Press.
Ong, A. (1987). *Spirits of Resistance and Capitalist Discipline: Factory Women in Malaysia*. Albany: State University of New York Press.
Osella, C., & Osella, F. (1998). Friendship and Flirting: Micro-Politics in Kerala, South India. *The Journal of the Royal Anthropological Institute, 4*(2), 189–206.
Osella, F., & Osella, C. (2000). *Social Mobility in Kerala: Modernity and Identity in Conflict*. London: Pluto Press.
Palriwala, R. & Risseeuw, C. (Eds). (1996). Introduction, in Palriwala & Risseeuw (Eds), *Shifting Circles of Support: Contextualizing Kinship and Gender in South Asia and Sub-Saharan Africa*. New Delhi: SAGE Publications.
Paltiel, F. L. (1993). Mental Health of Women in the Americas. In E. Gomez (Ed.), *Gender, Women and Health in the Americas* (p. Scientific Publication; 541). Washington D.C.: PAHO.
Pande, M. (2003). *Stepping Out. Life and Sexuality in Rural India*. New Delhi: Penguin.
Panini, M. (1995). The Social Logic of Economic Liberalization. *Sociological Bulletin, 44*(1), 33–62.
Pargament, K., Echemendia, R., Johnson, S., Cook, P., Macgath, C., & Myers, C. (1987). The Conservative Church: Psychosocial Advantages and Disadvantages. *American Journal of Communitiy Psychology, 15*, 269–86.
Parker, S., Fernandes, J., & Weiss, M. (2003). Contextualizing Mental Health: Gendered Experiences in a Mumbai Slum. *Anthropology and Medicine, 10*(3), 291–308.
Parson, C., & Wekely, F. (1991). Idioms of Distress Somatic Responses of Distress in Every Day Life. *Culture, Medicine and Psychiatry, 15*, 111–13.
Parsons, T. (1951). *The Social System*. London: Routledge.
Patel, V. (2001). Cultural Factors and International Epidemiology. *British Medical Bulletin, 57*(1), 33–45.

Patel, V. (2003). Efficacy and Cost-effectiveness of Drug and Psychological Treatments for CMDs in General Healthcare in Goa, India: A Randomized, Controlled Trial. *Lancet, 361*(9351), 33–39.

Patel, V., Araya, R., Chatterjee, S., Chisholm, D., Cohen, A., De Silva, M., van Ommeren, M. (2007, 4 September). Treatment and Prevention of Mental Disorders in Low-income and Middle-income Countries. doi:10.1016/S0140-6736(07)61240-9

Patel, V., Araya, R., Lima, M., Ludermir, A., & Todd, C. (1999). Women, Poverty and Common Mental Disorders in Four Restructuring Societies. *Social Science and Medicine, 49*(11), 1461–71.

Patel, V., Kirkwood, B., Pednekar, B., Pereira, S., Barros, P., Fernandes, J., . . . Mabey, D. (2006). Gender Disadvantage and Reproductive Health Risk Factors for Common Mental Disorders in Women: A Community Survey in India. *Archives of General Psychiatry, 63*, 404–13.

Patel, V., Kirkwooyd, B., Pednekar, S., Weiss, H., & Mabey, D. (2006). Risk Factors for Common Mental Disorders in Women: Population-based Longitudinal Study. *British Journal of Psychiatry, 189*, 547–55.

Patel, V., Rodrigues, M., & Desouza, N. (2002). Gender, Poverty, and Postnatal Depression: A Study of Mothers in Goa, India. *American Journal of Psychiatry, 159*(1), 43–47.

Patel, V., Weobong, B., Weiss, H.A., Anand, A., Bhat, B. Katti, B., Kirkwood, B. & Fairburn, C.G. (2017). The Healthy Activity Program (HAP), a Lay counselor delivered brief psychological treatment for severe depression, in primary care in India: a randomised controlled trial, *Lancet* 2017; 389: 176–85.

Pathare, S. (2005). Less than 1 per cent of our Health Budget is Spent on Mental Health. *Infochange Agenda, 2*, 29–30.

Pattanaik, D. (2006). *Myth = Mithya: A Handbook of Hindu Mythology*. New Delhi Penguin.

Paykel, E. (1991). Depression in Women. *British Journal of Psychiatry, 158*(Supplement 10), 22–29.

Pearlin, L. I. (1989). The Sociological Study of Stress. *Journal of Health and Social Behaviour, 30*(3), 241–56.

Pelto, P., & Pelto, G. (1970). *The Anthropological Research: The Structure of Inquiry, Second edition*. London: Cambridge University Press.

Phoenix, A., & Woollett, A. (1991). Motherhood: Social Construction, Politics and Psychology. In A. Phoenix, A. Woollett, & E. Lloyd (Eds), *Motherhood: Meanings, Practices and Ideologies* (pp. 13–27). London: SAGE Publications.

Phoon, W. (1982). Outbreaks of Mass Hysteria at Workplaces in Singapore: Some Patterns and Modes of Presentation. In M. Colligan, Penne-baker, & L. Murphy (Eds), *Mass Psychogenic Illness: A Social Psychological Analysis* (pp. 21–31). Hillsdale, NJ: Lawrence Eelbaum Associates.

Porter, R. (1987). *Mind Forg'd Manacles*. Harmondsworth: Penguin.
Premrajan, K., Danabalan, M., Chandrasekar, R., & Srinivasa, D. (1993). Prevalence of Psychiatric Morbidity in an Urban Community of Pondicherry. *Indian Journal of Psychiatry, 35*, 99–102.
Putnam, R. (1995). Bowling Alone: America's Decline in Social Capital. *Journal of Democracy, 6*, 65–78.
Quinn, N. (1977). Anthropological Studies on Women's Status. *Annual Review of Anthropology, 6*, 181–225.
Ram, K. (2001). The Female Body of Possession: A Feminist Perspective on Rural Tamil Women's Experiences. In B. Davar (Ed.), *Mental Health from a Gender Perspective* (pp. 181–216). New Delhi: SAGE Publications.
Reiter, R. (1975). *Towards an Anthropology of Women*. New York: Monthly Review Press.
Reay, D. (2004). Gendering Bourdieu's Concepts of Capitals? Emotional Capital, Women and Social Class, *The Sociological Review, 52* (2), 57–74.
Riley, D. (1988). *Am I that Name? Feminism and the Category of 'Women' in History*. Basingstroke: Macmillan.
Risman, B. (1998). *Gender Vertigo: American Families in Transition*. New Haven, CT: Yale University Press.
Rivers, W. (1924). *Medicine, Magic and Religion*. London and New York: Routledge Classics.
Robins, E., & Guze, S. (1970). Establishment of Diagnostic Validity in Psychiatric Illness: Its Application to Schizophrenia. *American Journal of Psychiatry, 126*(7), 983–87.
Robinson, R. (2008). Betwixt Kin and Community. *Asian Population Studies, 4*(2), 177–94.
Rodman, M. (1992). Empowering Place: Multilocality and Multivocality. *American Anthropologist, 94*(3), 640–56.
Rodrigues M, Patel V, Jaswal S, de Souza N. Listening to Mothers: Qualitative Studies on Motherhood and Depression from Goa, India. *Social Science & Medicine*, 2003; 57: 1797–1806.
Romberg, R. (2003). *Witchcraft and Welfare: Spiritual Capital and the Business of Magic in Modern Puerto Rico*. Austin: University of Texas Press.
Rosaldo, M. (1980). The Use and Abuse of Anthropology: Reflections on Feminism and Cross Cultural Understanding. *Signs: Journal of Women in Culture and Society, 5*, 389–417.
Rose, R. (1998). *Getting Things Done with Social Capital: New Russia Barometer VII, Studies in Public Policy, No. 303*. Glasgow: University of Strathcyde.
Rosenthal, T., & Siegal, B. (1959). Magic and Witchcraft: An Interpretation from Dissonance Theory. *Southwestern Journal of Anthropology, 15*(2), 143–67.
Ross, C. E., & Van Willigen, M. (1997). Education and the Subjective Quality of Life, *Journal of Health and Social Behavior*, 38, 275–97.

Russo, N., & Green, B. (1993). Women and Mental Health. In F. Denmark, & M. Paludi (Eds), *Psychology of Women: A Handbook of Issues and Theories*. Westport, CN: Greenwood.

Sadock, B. J., & Sadock, V. A. (2003). *Kaplan and Sadock's Synopsis of Psychiatry: Behavioral Sciences, Clinical Psychiatry*. Baltimore: Williams and Wilkins.

Sam, D., & Moreira, V. (2002). The Mutual Embeddedness of Culture and Mental Illness. In W. Lonner, D. Dineel, S. Hayes, & D. Sattler (Eds), *Online Readings in Psychology and Culture*. Bellingham, Washington, USA: Centre for Cross-Cultural Research, Western Washington University.

Samuelson, H., & Steffen, V. (2004). The Relevance of Foucault and Bourdieu for Medical Anthropology: Exploring New Sites. *Anthropology and Medicine, 11*(1), 3–10.

Sandhya. (1994). *Widowhood: A Socio-Psychiatric Study*. New Delhi: Mohit Publications.

Saracen, B., & Batbui, C. (1997). Poverty and Mental Illness. *Canadian Journal of Psychiatry, 42*, 285–90.

Sarin, M. (1989). *Himachali Women: A Situational Analysis*. Jagjit Nagar: SUTKA.

Savyasaachi. (1998). Unlearning Fieldwork: The Flight of the Arctic Tern. In M. Thapan (Ed.), *Anthropological Journeys* (pp. 83–112). Hyderabad: Orient Longman.

Sayers, J. (1982). *Biological Politics: Feminist and Anti-Feminist Perspectives*. London: Tavistock.

Scheff, T. (1966). *Being Mentally Ill: A Sociological Theory*. London: Weidenfield, Nicolson.

Scheier, M., & Carver, C. (1987). Dispositional Optimism and Physical Well-being: The Influence of Generalized Outcome Expectancies on Health. *Journal of Personality, 55*, 169–210.

Schell, L. (1997). Culture as a Stressor: A Revised Model of Biocultural Interaction. *American Journal of Physical Anthropology, 102*, 67–77.

Scheper-Hughes, N. (1992). *Death without Weeping: The Violence of Everyday Life in Brazil*. Berkeley: University of California Press.

Schwab, & Schwab. (1978). *Sociocultural Roots of Mental Illness: An Epidemiologic Survey*. New York: Plenum Medical B.

Scull, A. (1993). *The Most Solitary of Afflictions*. New York: Yale University Press.

Seaman, M.V. (1997) 'Psychopathology in Women and Men: Focus on Female Hormones', *American Journal of Psychiatry, 154*(12): 1641–7.

Searle-Chatterjee, M. (1981). *Reversible Sex Roles: The Special Case of the Benares Sweepers*. Oxford: Pergamom Press.

Sebstad, J., & Cohen, M. (2001). *Microfinance, Risk Management, and Poverty*. Washington D.C: World Bank.

Seligman, R. (2005). 'Distress, Dissociation, and Embodied Experience: Reconsidering the Pathways to Mediumship and Mental Health'. *Ethos, 31*(1), 71–99.

Selye, H. (1974). *Stress without Distress.* New York: Lippencot.

Sen, B., Nandi, D., Mukherjee, S., Mishra, D., Bannerjee, G., & Sarkar, S. (1984). Psychiatric Morbidity in an Urban Slum-dwelling Community. *Indian Journal of Psychiatry, 26,* 185–93.

Sethi, B., Gupta, S., & Rajkumar. (1967). Three Hundred Urban Families: A Psychiatric Study. *Indian Journal of Psychiatry, 9,* 280–302.

Shramshakti: Report of the National Commission on Self-employed Women and Women in the Unorganized Sector. 1988. Delhi: Government of India.

Shackle, E. (1985). Psychiatric Diagnosis as an Ethical Problem. *Journal of Medical Ethics, 11*(3), 132–34.

Shah, A. (2001). Gender Issues in Mental Health: A Clinical Psychology Perspective. In B. Davar (Ed.), *Mental Health from a Gender Perspective* (pp. 61–81). New Delhi: SAGE Publications.

Shakespeare, T. (1996). Disability, Identity and Difference. In C. Barnes, & G. Mercer (Eds), *Exploring the Divide* (pp. 92–113). Leeds: The Disability Press.

Sharma, M. (2010). Symbols of Empowerment: Possession, Ritual and Healers in Himachal Himalaya (North India). *Journal of Asian and African Studies, 45*(2), 196–208.

Shatrughana, V. (1999). Foreword. In B. Davar (Ed.), *Mental Health of Indian Women: A Feminist Agenda* (pp. 11–17). New Delhi: SAGE Publications.

Shirali, K. A., & Kanwar, S. (1987). Mental Illness and Hill Women: A Demographic Study. *Journal of Personality and Clinical Studies, 3*(2), 103–08.

Showalter, E. (1985). *The New Feminist Criticism: Essays on Women, Literature, and Theory.* New York: Pantheon.

———. (1987). *The Female Malady: Women, Madness and the English Culture.* London: Virago.

Simmel, G. (1969 [reprint of 1905 essay]). The Metropolis and Mental Life. In *Classic Essays on the Culture of Cities* (pp. 47–60). New York: Appleton.

———. (1984). *Georg Simmel: On Women, Sexuality and Love* (trans., intro.) G. Oakes. New Haven: Yale University Press.

Skeggs, B. (2004). Exchange, Value and Affect: Bourdieu and 'the Self', *The Sociological Review 52* (s2), 75–95.

Smith, D. & David, S. (1975). *Women Look at Psychiatry: I'm not Mad, I'm Angry.* Vancouver: Press Gang.

Smith, D. (1978). 'K is mentally ill': The Anatomy of a Factual Account. *Sociology, 12,* 23–53.

———. (1979). A Sociology for Women. In J. Sherman, & E. Beck (Eds), *The Prism of Sex Essays in the Sociology of Knowledge: Proceedings of a Symposium* (pp. 135–87). Madison: University of Wisconsin Press.

———. (1987). *The Everyday World as Problematic: A Feminist Sociology.* Toronto: University of Toronto Press.

———. (1990). *Texts, Facts and Femininity: Exploring the Relations of Ruling.* Routledge: USA and Canada.

Smith, J. (1983). Feminist Analyses of Gender: A Mystique. In M. Lowe, & R. Hubbard (Eds), *Women's Nature: Rationalization of Inequality*. New York: Pergamon.

Spilka, B., Shaver, P., & Kirkpatrick, L. (1985). A General Attribution Theory for the Psychology of Religion. *Journal for the Scientific Study of Religion*, 24, 1–20.

Sreekanth, Y. (2009). Bullying: An Element Accentuating Social Segregation. *International Journal of Primary, Elementary and Early Years Education*, 37(3), 233–45.

Srinivasa, M. R. (1992). Mental Health. In *State of India's Health* (pp. 400–14). New Delhi: Voluntary Health Association of India.

Sriram. (1991). 'Research on Marital Violence: Some Trends, Implications and Emerging Issues' in Unit for Family Studies', TISS (eds) *Research on Families with Problems in India*, Vol. II, 483–95. Mumbai: TISS Publications.

Srivastava, V. (2002). Some Thoughts on the Anthropology of Mental Health and Illness with Special Reference to India. *Anthropologist* (Special Issue No. 1), 149–61.

Stafford, M., & Marmot, M. (2003). Neighbourhood Deprivation and Health: Does it Affect us all Equally? *International Journal of Epidemiology*, 32(3), 357–66.

Stimson, G. (1974). Obeying Doctor's Orders. *Social Science and Medicine*, 8(2), 97–104.

Stone, W. (2001). *Measuring Social Capital*. Melbourne: Australian Institute of Family Studies.

Sujatha, V. (2003). *Health by the People: Sociology of Medical Lore*. Jaipur: Rawat Publications.

Szasz, T. (1961). The Uses of Naming and the Origin of the Myth of Mental Illness. *American Psychologist*, 16, 59–65.

Szasz, T. (1970). The Myth of Mental Illness. *American Psychologist*, 15, 113–18.

Tantam, D. (1991). The Anti-psychiatry Movement. In G. Berrios, & H. Freeman (Eds), *150 Years of British Psychiatry* (pp. 333–50). London: Gaskell.

Taylor, C. (1992). The Politics of Recognition. In *Multi-Culturalism and 'The Politics of Recognition'*. Princeton, N.J: Princeton University Press.

Teoh, J.-I., Soewondo, S., & Sidharta, M. (1975). Epidemic Hysteria in Malaysian Schools: An Illustrative Episode. *Psychiatry*, 38(3), 258–68.

Thapan, M. (1995). Gender, Body and Everyday Life. *Social Scientist*, 23(7/9), 32–58.

———. (2006). Habitus, Performance and Women's Experience: Understanding Embodiment and Identity in Everyday Life. In R. Lardinois, & M. Thapan (Eds), *Reading Pierre Bourdieu* (pp. 199–228). New Delhi: Routledge.

———. (2009). *Living the Body: Embodiment, Womanhood and Identity in Contemporary India*. New Delhi: SAGE Publications.

The International Council on Women's Health Issues. (1992, August). *Copenhagen Conference Statement: Fifth International Congress on Women's Health Issues*. Copenhagen, Denmark.

Tipple, A., Kellet, P., & Masters, G. (1996). *Mixed Uses in Residential Areas: A Pilot Study Final Report*. Centre for Architectural Research and Development Overseas. Tyne: University of Newscastle.

Tonnies, F. (1887 [1967]). *Gemeinschaft und Gesellschaft (Community and Society)*. (C. Loomis, Trans.) New York: Harper Torchbooks.

Trivedi, J., Sareen, H., & Dhyani, M. (2008). Rapid Urbanization: Its Impact on Mental Health: A South Asian Perspective. *Indian Journal of Psychiatry, 50*, 161–65.

Turner, V. (1979). Frame, Flow and Reflection: Ritual and Drama as Public Liminality. *Japanese Journal of Religious Studies, 6*(4), 465–99.

Uberoi, H., Shirali, K., & Sadgopal, M. (1995). *Dance of Madness*. Shimla: Kishwar.

UNESCO. (2002). *Universal Declaration on Cultural Diversity*. Retrieved November 29, 2006, from www.unesco.orgconfgen/press_rel/021101_clt_diversity.shtml

United Nations Population Division. (2002). *World Population Prospects: The 2000 Revision*. New York: United Nations.

UNDP. (1995). *Human Development Report 1995*. New York: OUP.

Ussher, J. (1991). *Women's Madness: Misogyny or Mental Illness*. Hemel Hempstead: Harvester Wheatsheaf.

———. (2006). *Managing the Monstrous Feminine: Regulating the Reproductive*. London: Routledge.

Vaidya, S. (2011). Mothering as Ideology and Practice: The Experiences of Mothers of Children with Autism Spectrum Disorder. In M. Walks, & N. McPherson (Eds), *An Anthropology of Mothering* (pp. 226–39). Ontario: Demeter Press.

Valentine, C. (1973). Alternative Views of Poverty and Poor, Present and Future. In J. Feagin (Ed.), *The Urban Scene* (pp. 166–74). Random House, Inc.

Vatuk, S. 1969. A Structural Analysis of the Hindi Kinship Terminology, *Contributions to Indian Sociology, 3*(1): 94–115.

Verghese, A., Beig, A., Senseman, L., Rao, S., & Benjamin, V. (1973). A Social and Psychiatric Study of a Representative Group of Families in Vellore Town. *Indian Journal of Medical Research, 61*, 608–19.

Vindhya, U. (2001). Mental Healthcare: A Review of Gender Differences. *International Journal of Diabetes in Developing Countries, 21*, 86–96.

Vishwanath, K., & Mehrotra, S. (2007). 'Shall We Go Out?' Women's Safety in Public Spaces in Delhi. *Economic and Political Weekly, 42*(17), 1542–48.

Wagstaff, A. (2001). Poverty and Health. *CMH Working Paper Series (Paper No. WG15)*. Cambridge and Geneva.

Walby, S. (1989). Theorizing Patriarchy. *Sociology, 23*, 213–34.

———. (2000). Analyzing Social Inequality in the Twenty-first Century: Globalization and Modernity Restructure Inequality. *Contemporary Sociology, 29*, 814–18.

Walkerdine, S. (1988). *The Mastery of Reason: Cognitive Development and the Production of Rationality*. London: Routledge.
Walks, M. (2011). Introduction: Identifying an Anthropology of Mothering. In M. Walks, N. McPherson (Eds), *An Anthropology of Mothering* (pp. 1–27). Ontario: Demeter Press.
Walsh, M. (1977). *Doctors Wanted: No Women Need Apply*. Haven, CT: Yale University Press.
Ward, M. (1996). *A World Full Of Women*. Boston: Allyn and Bacon.
Ware, N., & Kleinman, A. (1992). Culture and Somatic Experience: The Social Course of Illness in Neurasthenia and Chronic Fatigue Syndrome. *Psychosomatic Medicine, 54*, 546–60.
Waxler, N. (1974). Culture and Mental Illness: A Social Labelling Perspective. *Journal of Nervous and Mental Diseases, 159*(6), 379–95.
White, K. (2002). *An Introduction to the Sociology of Health and Illness*. London, California and New Delhi: SAGE Publications.
———. (2009). *An Introduction to the Sociology of Health and Illness, Second edition*. London: SAGE Publications.
WHO. (1978). Risk Approach for MCH Care. *WHO Publication No.39*.
Wilkinson, R. (1996). *Unhealthy Societies: The Afflictions of Inequality*. London, UK: Routledge.
Williams, L. (2002). Trying on Gender, Gender Regimes and the Process of Becoming Women. *Gender and Society, 16*(1), 29–52.
Wirth, L. (1938). Urbanism as a Way of Life. *American Journal of Sociology, 44*, 3–24.
———. (1964). *Urbanism as a Way of Life*. Chicago: Chicago University Press.
Wolf, M. (1992). *A Thrice-Told Tale: Feminism, Postmodernism, and Ethnographic Responsibility*. California: Stanford University Press.
World Bank. (1990). *World Development Report: Poverty*. New York: Oxford University Press.
World Bank. (2001). *World Development Report 2000/2001: Attacking Poverty*. Oxford and New York: Oxford University Press.
World Health Organization. (2017). *Depression and Other Common Mental Disorders: Global Health Estimates*. Geneva: WHO.
World Health Organization (Department of Mental Health and Substance Abuse) (2008). *Gender Disparities in Mental Health*. Geneva: WHO.
World Health Organization. (2001). *Mental Health: New Understanding, New Hope*. Geneva: World Health Organization.
———. (2000). *World Health Report 2000*. Geneva: WHO.
———. (1998). *The World Health Report: Executive Summary*. Geneva: World Health Organization.
World's Women 2015: Trends and Statistics, 2015, United Nations, Accessed on 18 March 2018 from https://unstats.un.org/unsd/gender/downloads.html

Worthington, E. J., Kurusu, A., McCullough, E. M., & Sandage, J. S. (1996). Empirical Research on Religion and Psychotherapeutic Processes and Outcomes: A 10-year review and research prospects. *Psychological Bulletin, 119*, 448–87.

Yoshima, M. (2002). Battered Women's Coping Strategies and Psychological Distress: Differences by Immigration Status. *American Journal of Community Psychology, 30*(3), 429–50.

Zimmerman, M. (1980). *Foundations of Medical Anthropology: Anatomy, Physiology, Biochemistry, Pathology in Cultural Context*. Philadelphia: Saunders.

———. (1987). The Women's Health Movement: A Critique of Medical Enterprise and the Position of Women. In H. B. B., & M. Ferree (Eds), *Analyzing Gender: A Handbook of Social Science Research* (pp. 442–72). New Delhi: SAGE Publications.

Index

abnormality, 1
aspirations, 203–06

Bengali-speaking Muslims, 70
body and mind, 199–203
Bourdieu's
    conceptualization of social suffering, 219
    notion
    organization, space, 35

childhood years, 191–92
common mental disorders (CMDs), 218

depressive disorders, 1
distress, 45–49
    liminal state, 127–29
District Mental Health Programme (DMHP), 57–59, 64
doctors with degrees, 122–27
doxa, 217

ethnographic research strategy, 62

feminist approaches, 62

Gender and Poverty Report, 50
gender regime, 36, 144–46

breaking barriers
    breadwinners vs homemakers, 149–55
    obedient body, 146–49
globalization, 37
    affects, 38

habitus, 35
health and healing, 116–19
    continuum of healers, 119–20
    private doctor, 122
    workers, 82–84
household and distress, 155–57
    marital
        bond formation, 157–59
        violence, 159–60
    mothering, process, 162–73
        financial constraints, 173–85
        relationships outside marriage, 160–162
household income, 78

identity, 206–13
illness experiences, 95
    suffering woman, 96–99
        distress, 105–09
        future concerns, 104–05
        negative life events, 104–05
        stressful daily routine, 99–101

Index

illness
  disability, 8–10
  India
    anthropology, 18–21
informal social capital, 110
informal sources, 115
initial interactions, 190–91
intimate relations, 196–98

liberalization, privatization and globalization (LPG), 5

macro-level changes, 215
madness
  connotations, 86–87
  human and social realm
    shock theory, 92
    unfavourable social position, 92–95
  supernatural realm, 87–91
marriage and separation, 192–94
mental disorders, 5–7
  India, 7–8
mental health
  India
    anthropology, 18–21
mental illness
  anthropological
    India, 17
  policies, 54–57
  theoretical approach, 10
    sociological perspectives, 16–17
multi-disciplinary approach, 62

oppressive social conditions
  medicalization, 219

paid work, 114
psychosocial distress, 215, 221
  narrative, 216

reciprocal relationships, 80–82
reflexive ethnography, 62

self-employed men, 77
self-reporting questionnaire (SRQ), 72
Shramshakti Report, 50
sister-to-sister talk, 112
slum rehabilitation schemes
  Jahangirpuri, 64–69
social
  capital, 110
  drift, 41
  isolation, 41
  space, 34, 45–49
  suffering, 185–88, 220
  trends and epidemiological issues
    studies, 4
starting work, 194–96
stress and coping, 220
structural adjustment programmes (SAPs), 37, 52
structural changes
  Jahangirpuri, 131
    crime, 140–44
    crime against women, 134–36
    educational facilities, 136–40
    present, 132–33
suffering
  social origins, 218

unequal gender roles, 3
unlearning
  practice and discourse, 72
urbanization, 37
  mental health, 39
    early studies, 42
    historical perspective, 40
    later studies, 43
    slum in India, 43–45

women, 45–49
women and psychosocial distress
  biological model, 31–33
  diathesis-stress model, 31

feminist perspectives from India, 25–28
historical developments, 21–24
  Dorothy Smith model, 25
  Phyllis Chesler analysis, 24
perspectives, 28–31

women
  households and distress, 52–54

Jahangirpuri
  communication, 73
  number of children, 79
  occupation details, 76
  work and distress, 49–52
women's health, 2
women's reproductive biology, 3
World Bank Report, 50

ABOUT THE AUTHOR

Mahima Nayar is a scholar with fifteen years' experience in practice, research and academics. She has worked in the area of recovering and rehabilitating women and children from vulnerable situations, women facing domestic violence and survivors of sexual assault (women and children), persons with psychosocial disabilities and their families. She has also taught at the Tata Institute of Social Sciences, Mumbai in areas related to disability, children and families.